WRITER: **JONATHAN HICKMAN**

PENCILER: **STEVE EPTING**

INKERS: **RICK MAGYAR** WITH **STEVE EPTING**

COLORIST: **FRANK D'ARMATA**

LETTERER: **VC'S JOE CARAMAGNA**

COVER ART: **JOCK**

ASSISTANT EDITOR: **JAKE THOMAS**

EDITORS: **TOM BREVOORT** WITH **LAUREN SANKOVITCH**

COLLECTION EDITOR: **JENNIFER GRÜNWALD**
ASSISTANT EDITORS: **ALEX STARBUCK & NELSON RIBEIRO**
EDITOR, SPECIAL PROJECTS: **MARK D. BEAZLEY**
SENIOR EDITOR, SPECIAL PROJECTS: **JEFF YOUNGQUIST**
SVP OF PRINT & DIGITAL PUBLISHING SALES: **DAVID GABRIEL**
BOOK DESIGN: **JEFF POWELL**

EDITOR IN CHIEF: **AXEL ALONSO**
CHIEF CREATIVE OFFICER: **JOE QUESADA**
PUBLISHER: **DAN BUCKLEY**
EXECUTIVE PRODUCER: **ALAN FINE**

NEW AVENGERS VOL. 1: EVERYTHING DIES. Contains material originally published in magazine form as NEW AVENGERS #1-6. First printing 2013. ISBN# 978-0-7851-6836-2. Published by MARVEL WORLDWIDE, INC., a subsidiary of MARVEL ENTERTAINMENT, LLC. OFFICE OF PUBLICATION: 135 West 50th Street, New York, NY 10020. Copyright © 2013 Marvel Characters, Inc. All rights reserved. All characters featured in this issue and the distinctive names and likenesses thereof, and all related indicia are trademarks of Marvel Characters, Inc. No similarity between any of the names, characters, persons, and/or institutions in this magazine with those of any living or dead person or institution is intended, and any such similarity which may exist is purely coincidental. **Printed in the U.S.A.** ALAN FINE, EVP - Office of the President, Marvel Worldwide, Inc. and EVP & CMO Marvel Characters B.V.; DAN BUCKLEY, Publisher & President - Print, Animation & Digital Divisions; JOE QUESADA, Chief Creative Officer; TOM BREVOORT, SVP of Publishing; DAVID BOGART, SVP of Operations & Procurement, Publishing; C.B. CEBULSKI, SVP of Creator & Content Development; DAVID GABRIEL, SVP of Print & Digital Publishing Sales; JIM O'KEEFE, VP of Operations & Logistics; DAN CARR, Executive Director of Publishing Technology; SUSAN CRESPI, Editorial Operations Manager; ALEX MORALES, Publishing Operations Manager; STAN LEE, Chairman Emeritus. For information regarding advertising in Marvel Comics or on Marvel.com, please contact Niza Disla, Director of Marvel Partnerships, at ndisla@marvel.com. For Marvel subscription inquiries, please call 800-217-9158. **Manufactured between 5/6/2013 and 6/17/2013 by R.R. DONNELLEY, INC., SALEM, VA, USA.**

10 9 8 7 6 5 4 3 2 1

PREVIOUSLY IN NEW AVENGERS

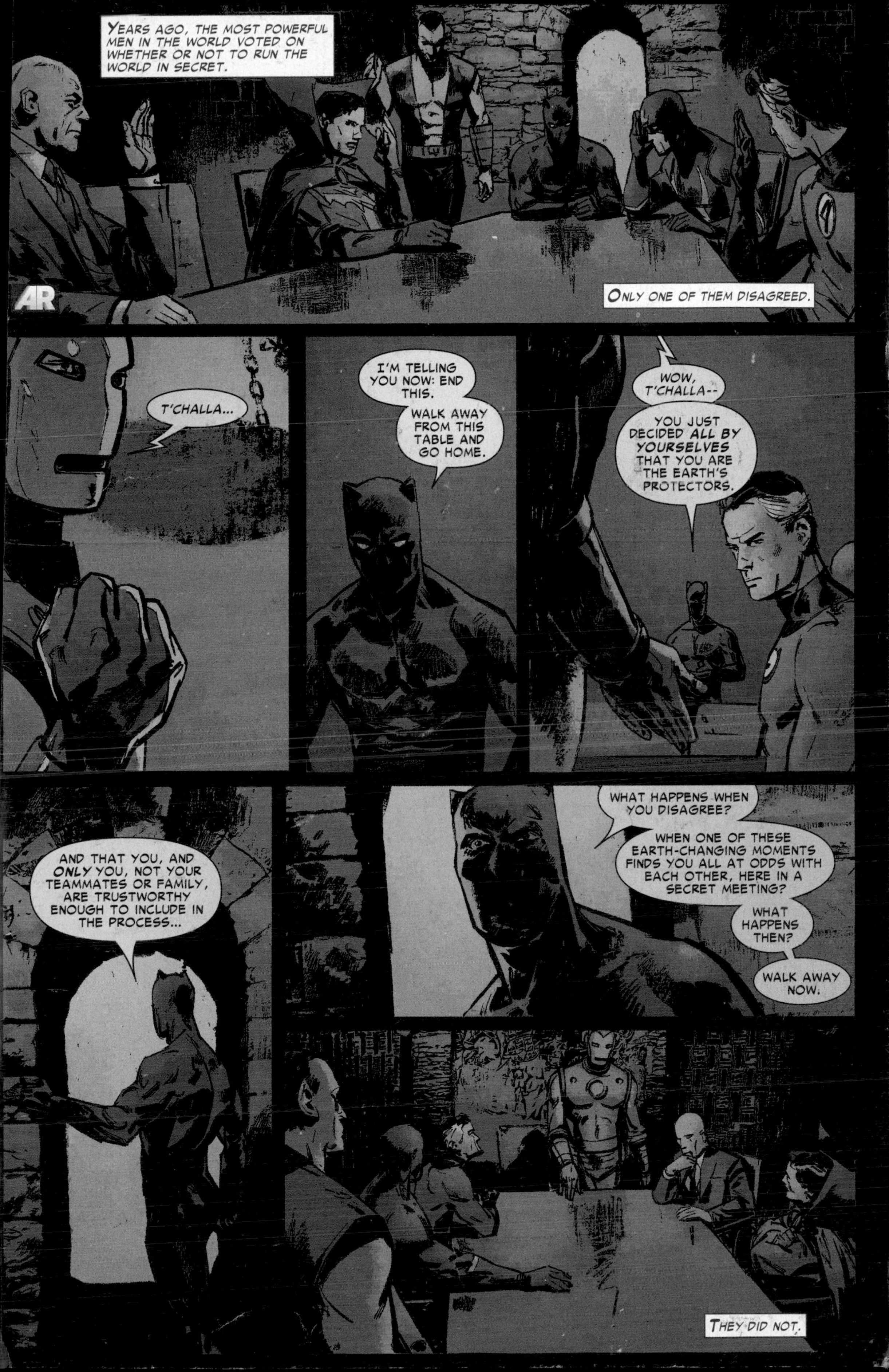

YEARS AGO, THE MOST POWERFUL MEN IN THE WORLD VOTED ON WHETHER OR NOT TO RUN THE WORLD IN SECRET.
ONLY ONE OF THEM DISAGREED.
T'CHALLA...
I'M TELLING YOU NOW: END THIS.
WALK AWAY FROM THIS TABLE AND GO HOME.
WOW, T'CHALLA--
YOU JUST DECIDED ALL BY YOURSELVES THAT YOU ARE THE EARTH'S PROTECTORS.
AND THAT YOU, AND ONLY YOU, NOT YOUR TEAMMATES OR FAMILY, ARE TRUSTWORTHY ENOUGH TO INCLUDE IN THE PROCESS...
WHAT HAPPENS WHEN YOU DISAGREE?
WHEN ONE OF THESE EARTH-CHANGING MOMENTS FINDS YOU ALL AT ODDS WITH EACH OTHER, HERE IN A SECRET MEETING?
WHAT HAPPENS THEN?
WALK AWAY NOW.
THEY DID NOT.

MEMENTO MORI

AR

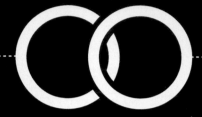

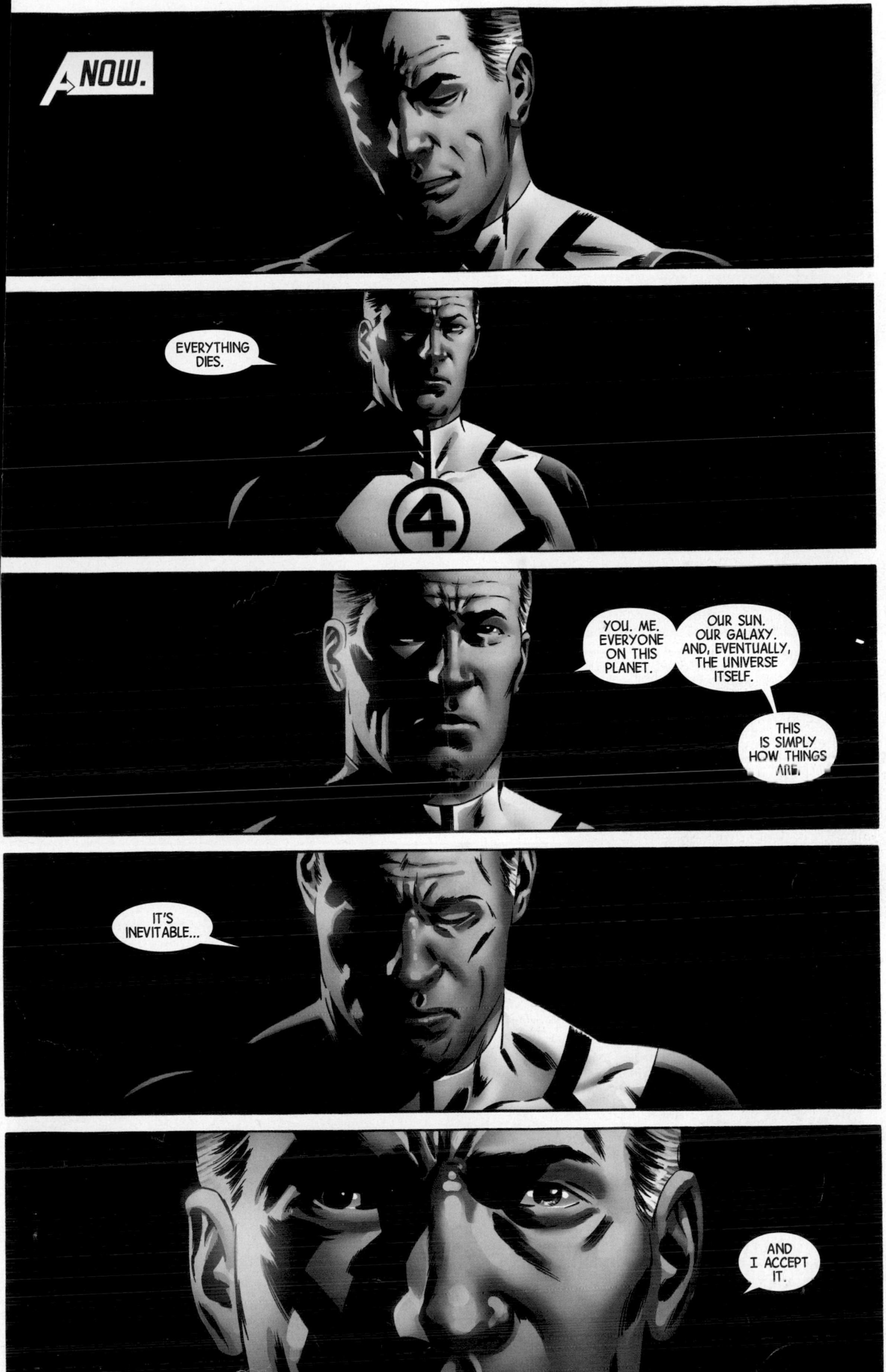
NOW.
EVERYTHING DIES.
YOU. ME. EVERYONE ON THIS PLANET.
OUR SUN. OUR GALAXY. AND, EVENTUALLY, THE UNIVERSE ITSELF.
THIS IS SIMPLY HOW THINGS ARE.
IT'S INEVITABLE...
AND I ACCEPT IT.

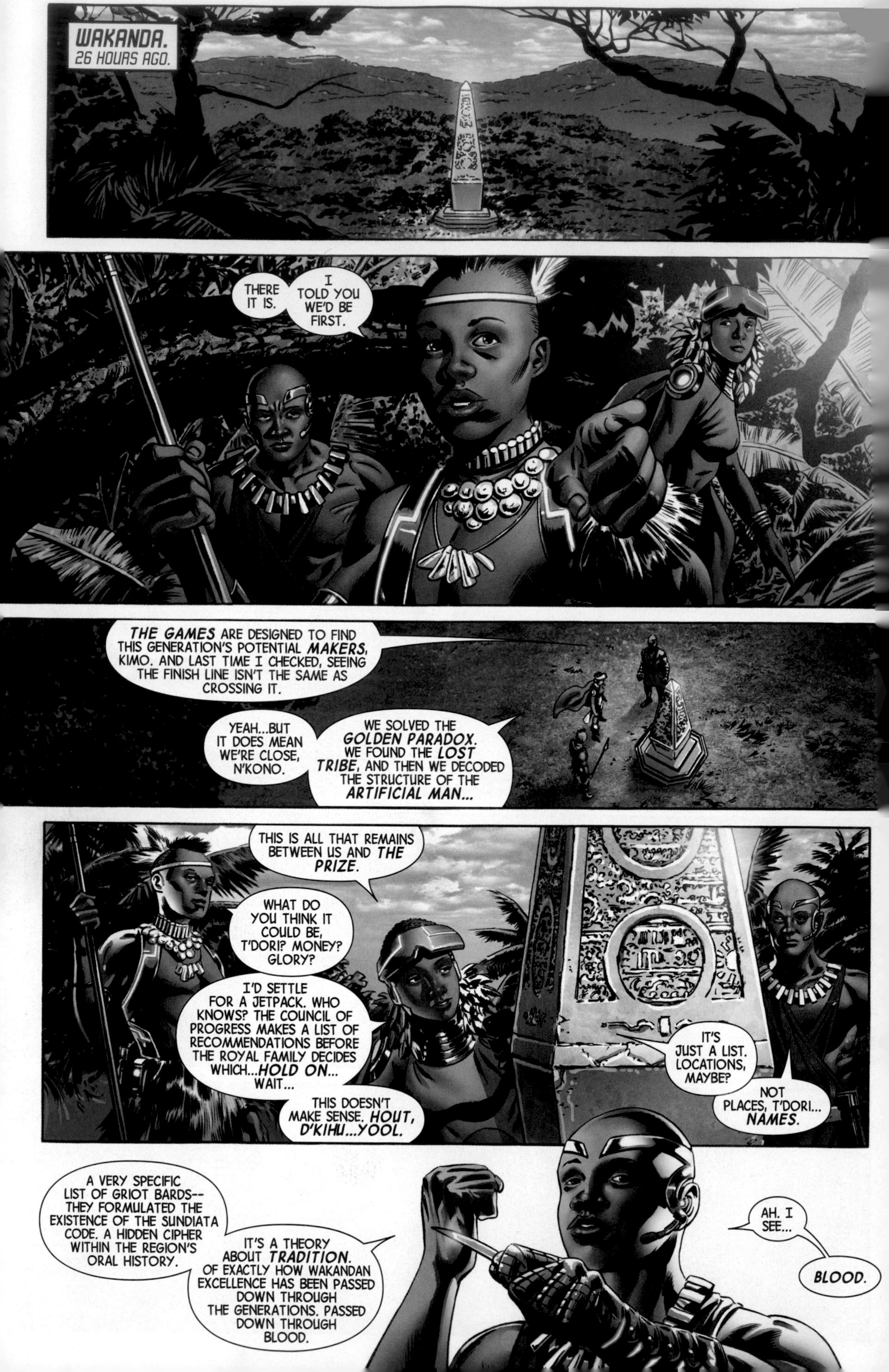
WAKANDA. 26 HOURS AGO.
THERE IT IS.
I TOLD YOU WE'D BE FIRST.
THE GAMES ARE DESIGNED TO FIND THIS GENERATION'S POTENTIAL MAKERS, KIMO. AND LAST TIME I CHECKED, SEEING THE FINISH LINE ISN'T THE SAME AS CROSSING IT.
YEAH...BUT IT DOES MEAN WE'RE CLOSE, N'KONO.
WE SOLVED THE GOLDEN PARADOX. WE FOUND THE LOST TRIBE, AND THEN WE DECODED THE STRUCTURE OF THE ARTIFICIAL MAN...
THIS IS ALL THAT REMAINS BETWEEN US AND THE PRIZE.
WHAT DO YOU THINK IT COULD BE, T'DORI? MONEY? GLORY?
I'D SETTLE FOR A JETPACK. WHO KNOWS? THE COUNCIL OF PROGRESS MAKES A LIST OF RECOMMENDATIONS BEFORE THE ROYAL FAMILY DECIDES WHICH...HOLD ON... WAIT...
THIS DOESN'T MAKE SENSE. HOUT, D'KIHU...YOOL.
IT'S JUST A LIST. LOCATIONS, MAYBE?
NOT PLACES, T'DORI... NAMES.
A VERY SPECIFIC LIST OF GRIOT BARDS-- THEY FORMULATED THE EXISTENCE OF THE SUNDIATA CODE. A HIDDEN CIPHER WITHIN THE REGION'S ORAL HISTORY.
IT'S A THEORY ABOUT TRADITION. OF EXACTLY HOW WAKANDAN EXCELLENCE HAS BEEN PASSED DOWN THROUGH THE GENERATIONS. PASSED DOWN THROUGH BLOOD.
AH. I SEE...
BLOOD.

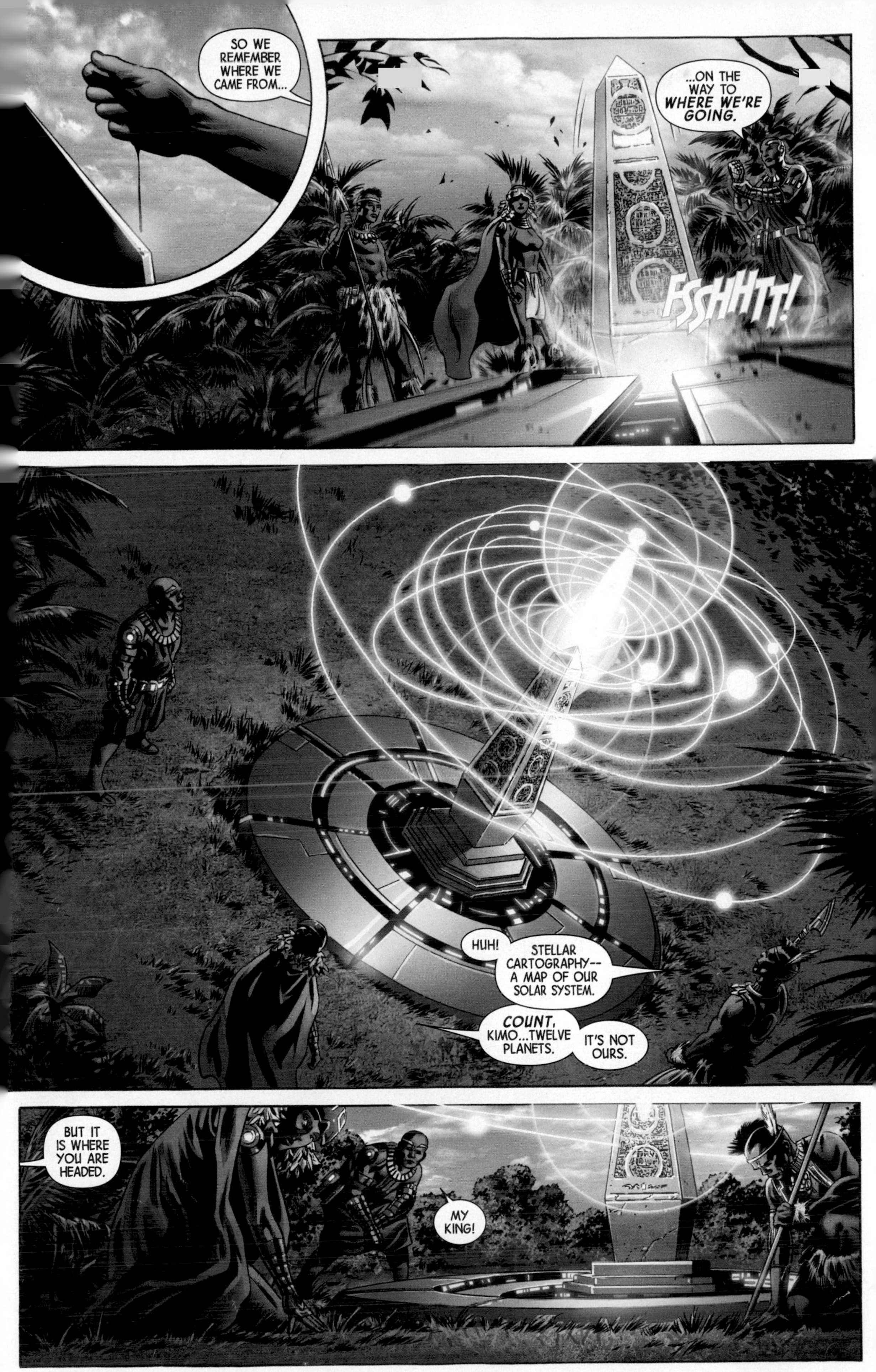
SO WE REMEMBER WHERE WE CAME FROM...
...ON THE WAY TO WHERE WE'RE GOING.
FSSHHTT!
HUH!
STELLAR CARTOGRAPHY-- A MAP OF OUR SOLAR SYSTEM.
COUNT, KIMO...TWELVE PLANETS.
IT'S NOT OURS.
BUT IT IS WHERE YOU ARE HEADED.
MY KING!

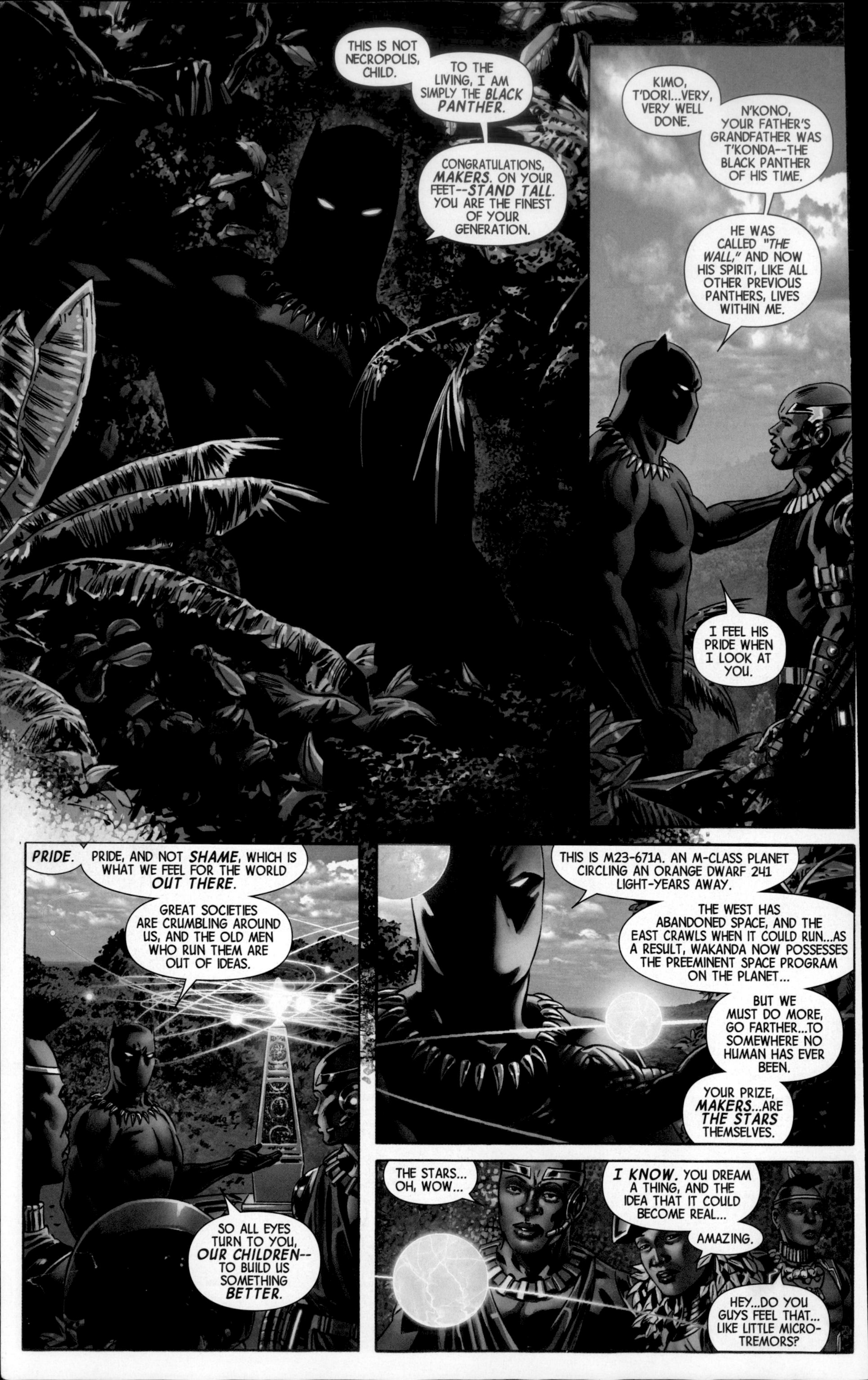

THIS IS NOT NECROPOLIS, CHILD.
TO THE LIVING, I AM SIMPLY THE BLACK PANTHER.
CONGRATULATIONS, MAKERS. ON YOUR FEET--STAND TALL. YOU ARE THE FINEST OF YOUR GENERATION.
KIMO, T'DORI...VERY, VERY WELL DONE.
N'KONO, YOUR FATHER'S GRANDFATHER WAS T'KONDA--THE BLACK PANTHER OF HIS TIME.
HE WAS CALLED "THE WALL," AND NOW HIS SPIRIT, LIKE ALL OTHER PREVIOUS PANTHERS, LIVES WITHIN ME.
I FEEL HIS PRIDE WHEN I LOOK AT YOU.
PRIDE.
PRIDE, AND NOT SHAME, WHICH IS WHAT WE FEEL FOR THE WORLD OUT THERE.
GREAT SOCIETIES ARE CRUMBLING AROUND US, AND THE OLD MEN WHO RUN THEM ARE OUT OF IDEAS.
SO ALL EYES TURN TO YOU, OUR CHILDREN--TO BUILD US SOMETHING BETTER.
THIS IS M23-671A. AN M-CLASS PLANET CIRCLING AN ORANGE DWARF 241 LIGHT-YEARS AWAY.
THE WEST HAS ABANDONED SPACE, AND THE EAST CRAWLS WHEN IT COULD RUN...AS A RESULT, WAKANDA NOW POSSESSES THE PREEMINENT SPACE PROGRAM ON THE PLANET...
BUT WE MUST DO MORE, GO FARTHER...TO SOMEWHERE NO HUMAN HAS EVER BEEN.
YOUR PRIZE, MAKERS...ARE THE STARS THEMSELVES.
THE STARS... OH, WOW...
I KNOW. YOU DREAM A THING, AND THE IDEA THAT IT COULD BECOME REAL...
AMAZING.
HEY...DO YOU GUYS FEEL THAT... LIKE LITTLE MICRO-TREMORS?

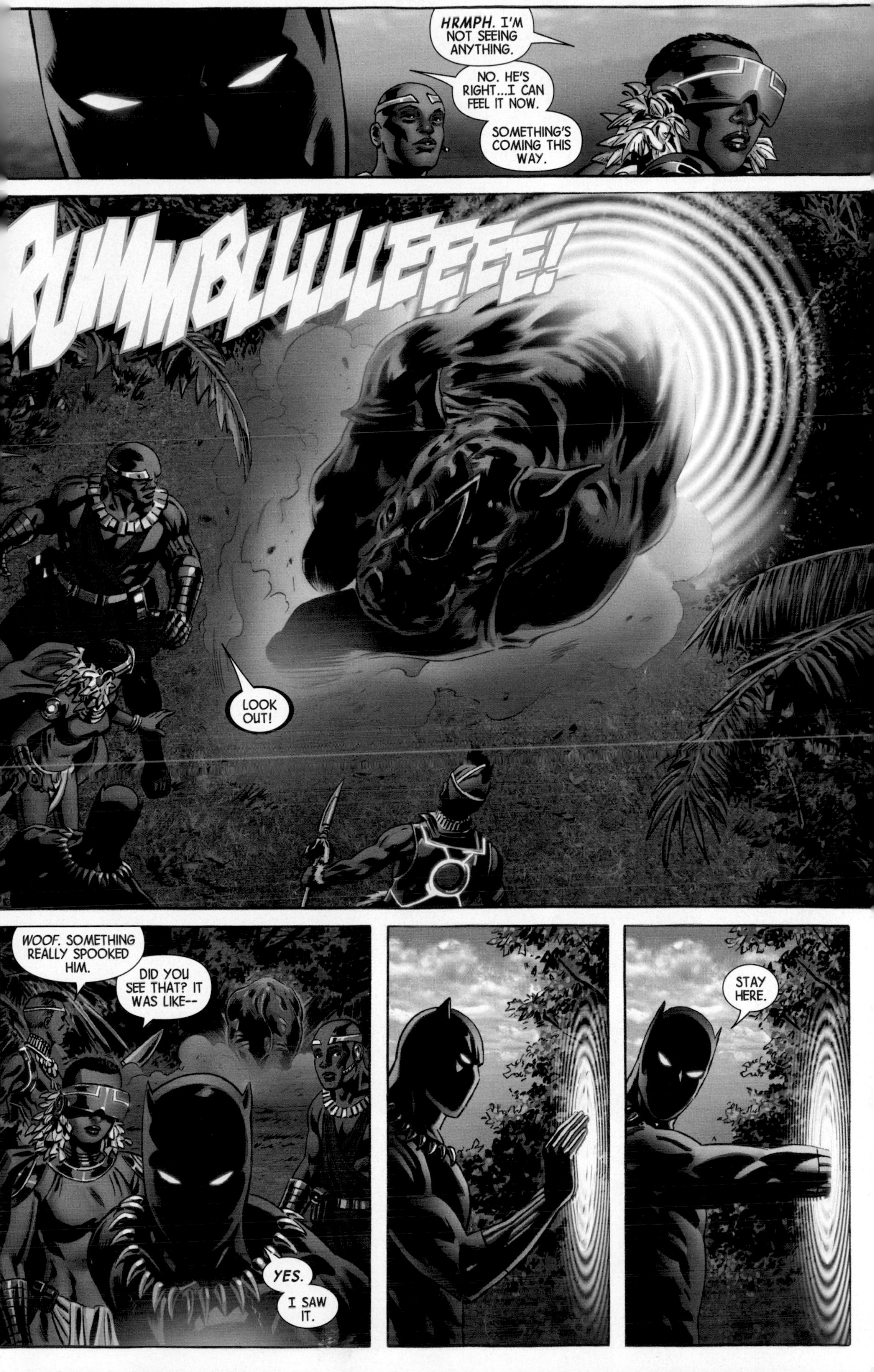
HRMPH. I'M NOT SEEING ANYTHING.
NO. HE'S RIGHT...I CAN FEEL IT NOW.
SOMETHING'S COMING THIS WAY.
RUMMBLLLLLEEEEE!
LOOK OUT!
WOOF. SOMETHING REALLY SPOOKED HIM.
DID YOU SEE THAT? IT WAS LIKE--
YES.
I SAW IT.
STAY HERE.

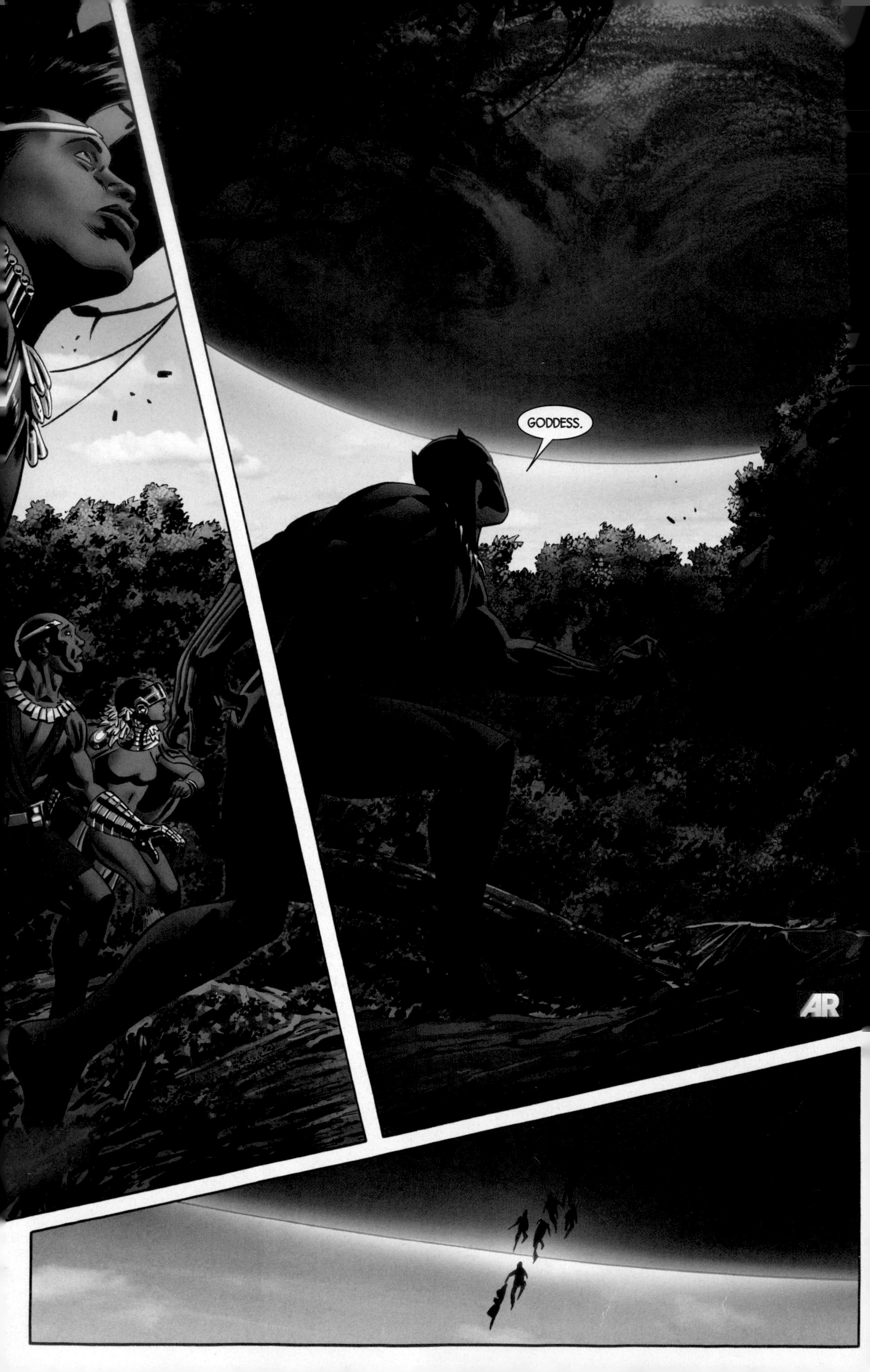
GODDESS.

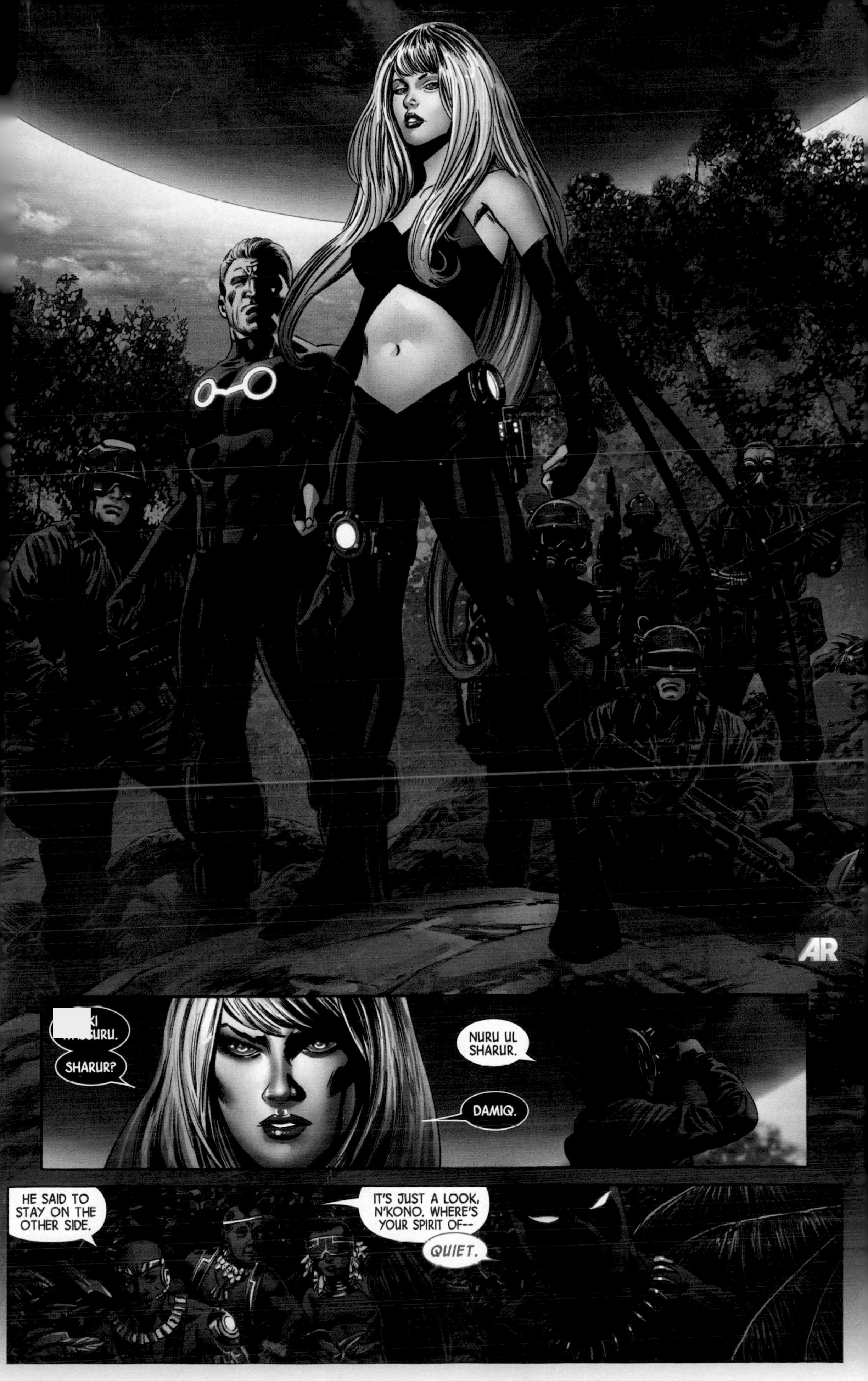
SHARUR?
NURU UL SHARUR.
DAMIQ.
HE SAID TO STAY ON THE OTHER SIDE.
IT'S JUST A LOOK, N'KONO. WHERE'S YOUR SPIRIT OF--
QUIET.

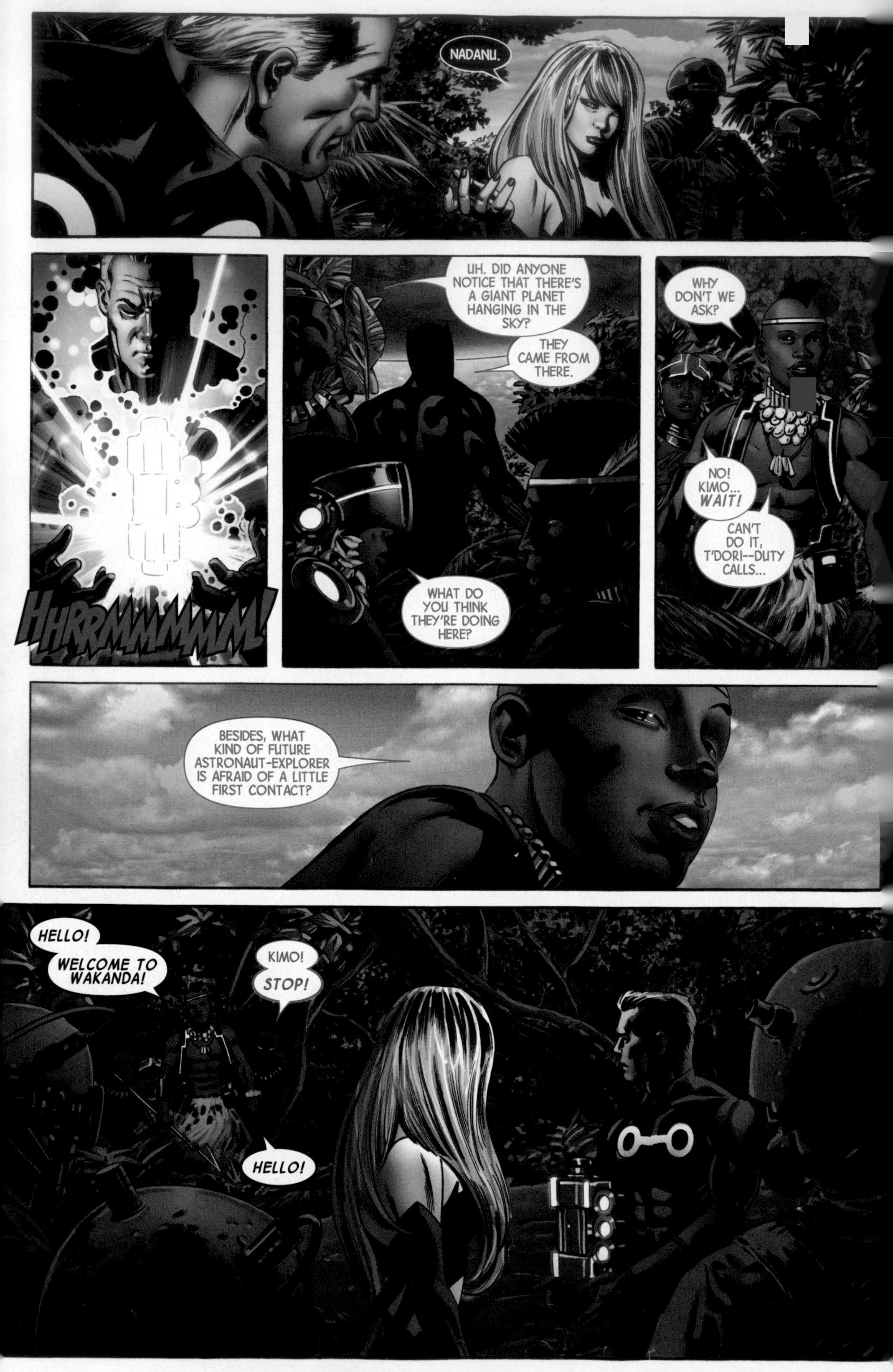
NADANU.
HHRRMMMMMM!
UH. DID ANYONE NOTICE THAT THERE'S A GIANT PLANET HANGING IN THE SKY?
THEY CAME FROM THERE.
WHAT DO YOU THINK THEY'RE DOING HERE?
WHY DON'T WE ASK?
NO! KIMO... WAIT!
CAN'T DO IT, T'DORI--DUTY CALLS...
BESIDES, WHAT KIND OF FUTURE ASTRONAUT-EXPLORER IS AFRAID OF A LITTLE FIRST CONTACT?
HELLO!
WELCOME TO WAKANDA!
KIMO!
STOP!
HELLO!

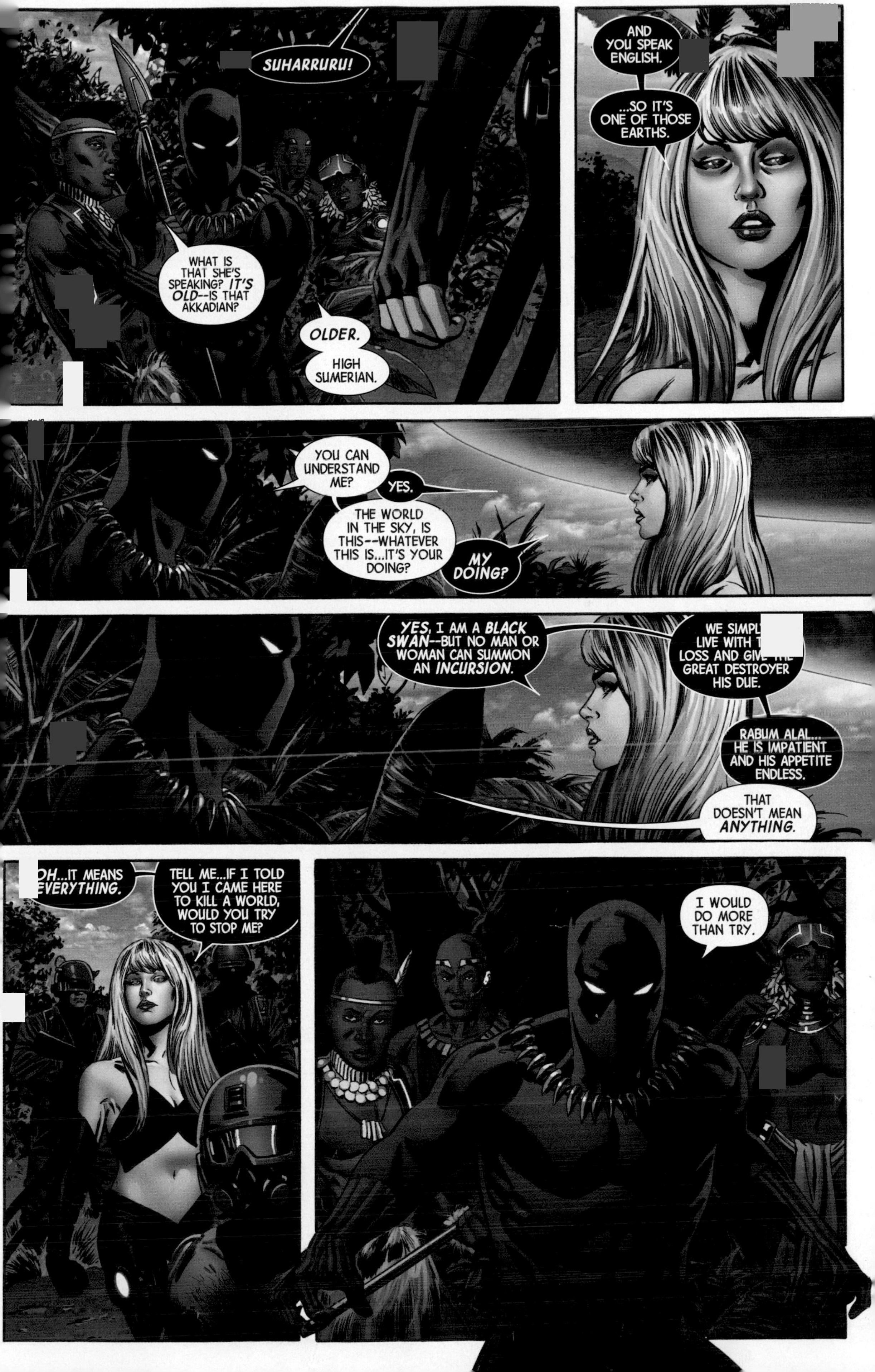
SUHARRURU!
WHAT IS THAT SHE'S SPEAKING? IT'S OLD--IS THAT AKKADIAN?
OLDER.
HIGH SUMERIAN.
AND YOU SPEAK ENGLISH.
...SO IT'S ONE OF THOSE EARTHS.
YOU CAN UNDERSTAND ME?
YES.
THE WORLD IN THE SKY, IS THIS--WHATEVER THIS IS...IT'S YOUR DOING?
MY DOING?
YES, I AM A BLACK SWAN--BUT NO MAN OR WOMAN CAN SUMMON AN INCURSION.
WE SIMPLY LIVE WITH T LOSS AND GIVE THE GREAT DESTROYER HIS DUE.
RABUM ALAL... HE IS IMPATIENT AND HIS APPETITE ENDLESS.
THAT DOESN'T MEAN ANYTHING.
OH...IT MEANS EVERYTHING.
TELL ME...IF I TOLD YOU I CAME HERE TO KILL A WORLD, WOULD YOU TRY TO STOP ME?
I WOULD DO MORE THAN TRY.

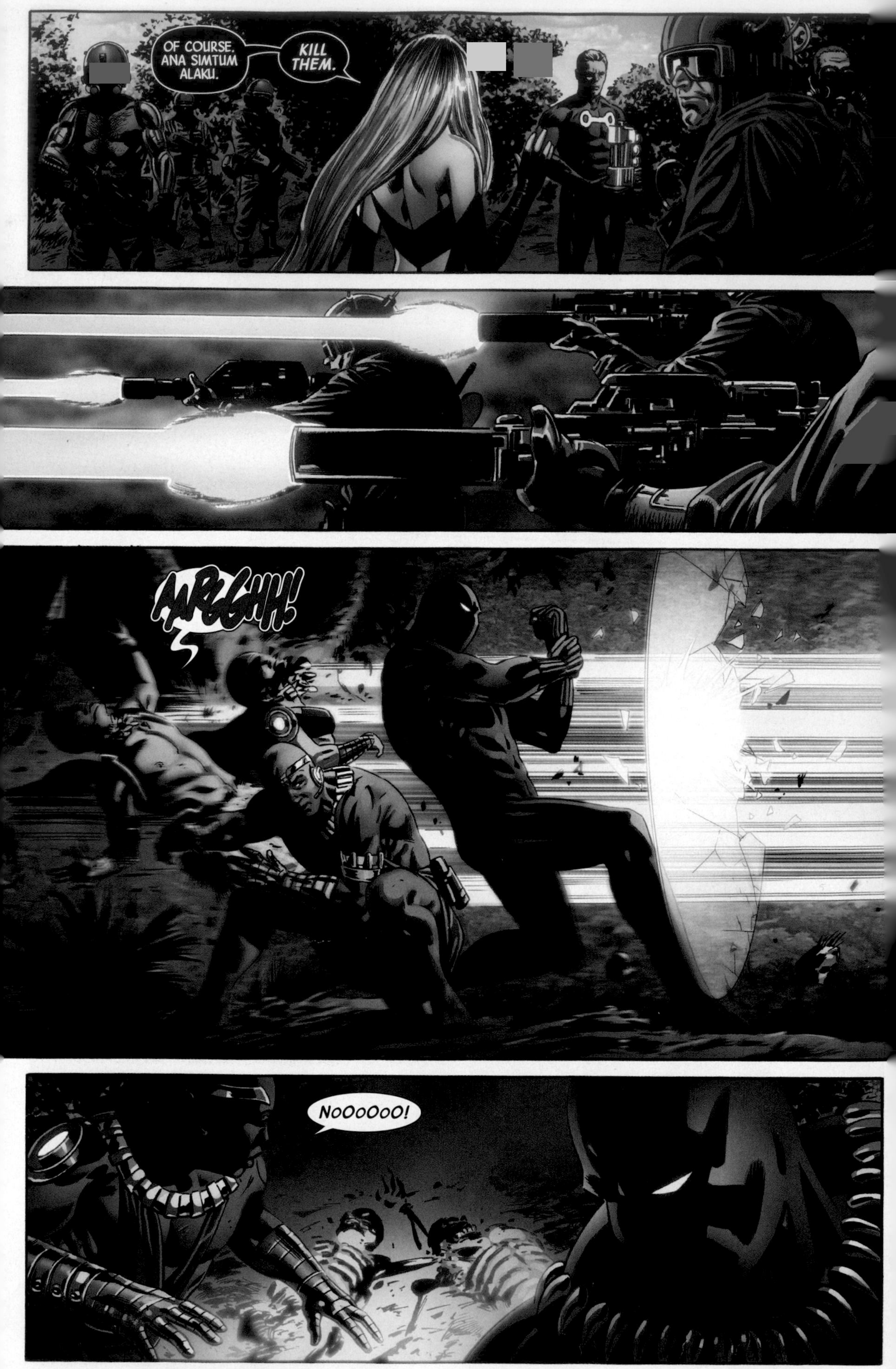
OF COURSE. ANA SIMTUM ALAKU.
KILL THEM.
AARGGHH!
NoOoOoO!

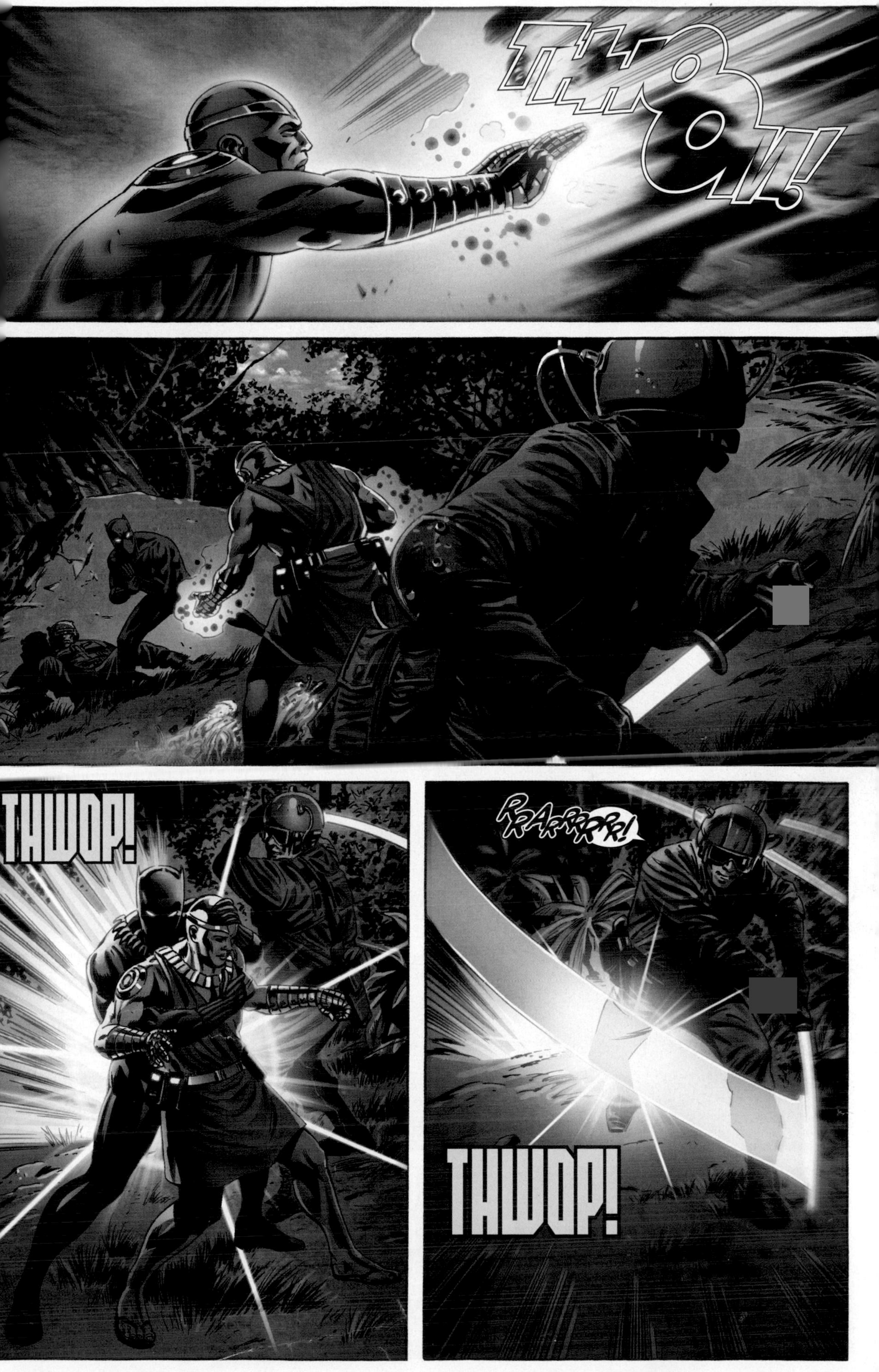
THOOM!
THWOP!
RRARRRRRR!
THWOP!

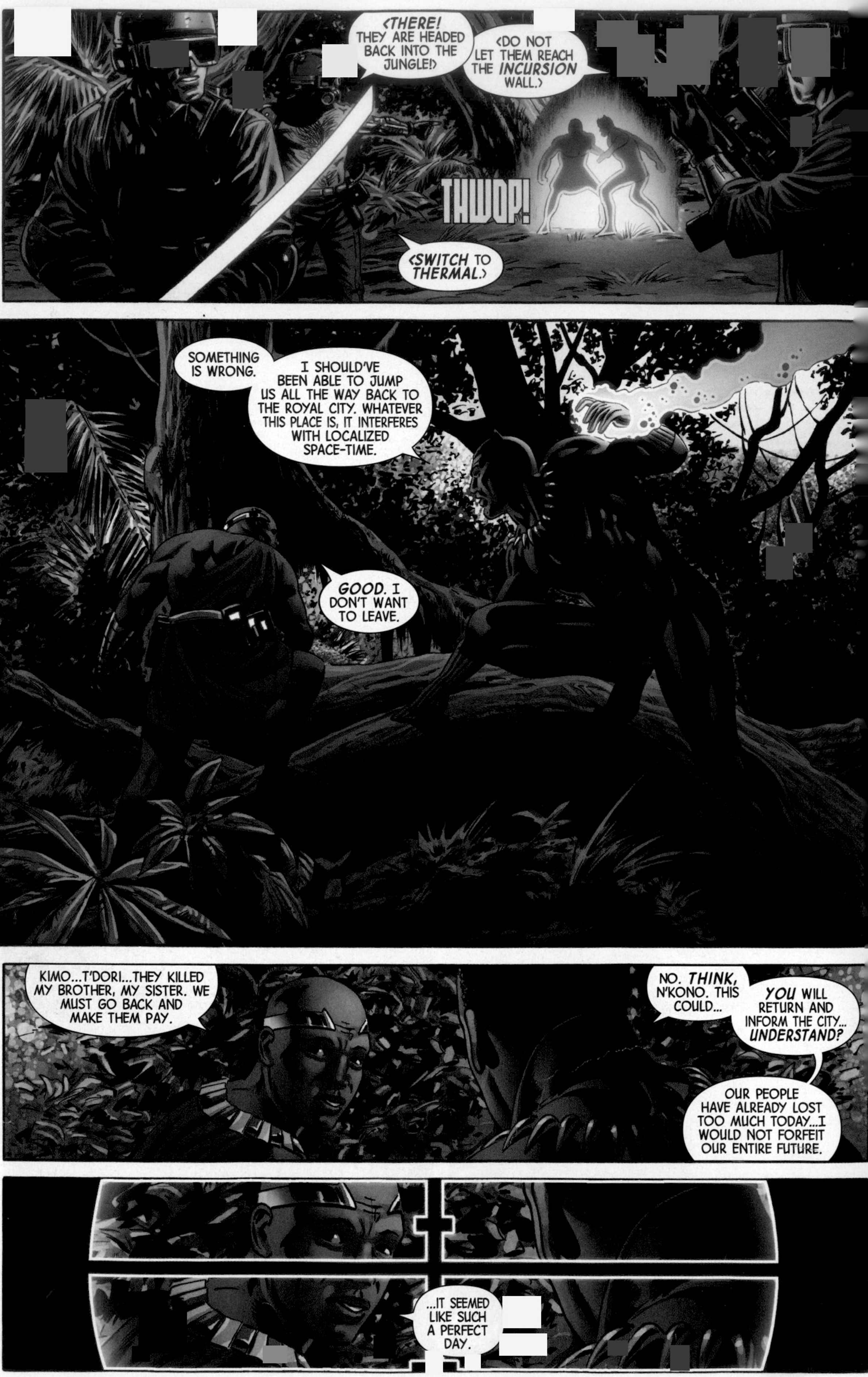

‹THERE! THEY ARE HEADED BACK INTO THE JUNGLE!›
‹DO NOT LET THEM REACH THE INCURSION WALL.›
THWOP!
‹SWITCH TO THERMAL.›
SOMETHING IS WRONG.
I SHOULD'VE BEEN ABLE TO JUMP US ALL THE WAY BACK TO THE ROYAL CITY. WHATEVER THIS PLACE IS, IT INTERFERES WITH LOCALIZED SPACE-TIME.
GOOD. I DON'T WANT TO LEAVE.
KIMO...T'DORI...THEY KILLED MY BROTHER, MY SISTER. WE MUST GO BACK AND MAKE THEM PAY.
NO. THINK, N'KONO. THIS COULD...
YOU WILL RETURN AND INFORM THE CITY... UNDERSTAND?
OUR PEOPLE HAVE ALREADY LOST TOO MUCH TODAY...I WOULD NOT FORFEIT OUR ENTIRE FUTURE.
...IT SEEMED LIKE SUCH A PERFECT DAY.

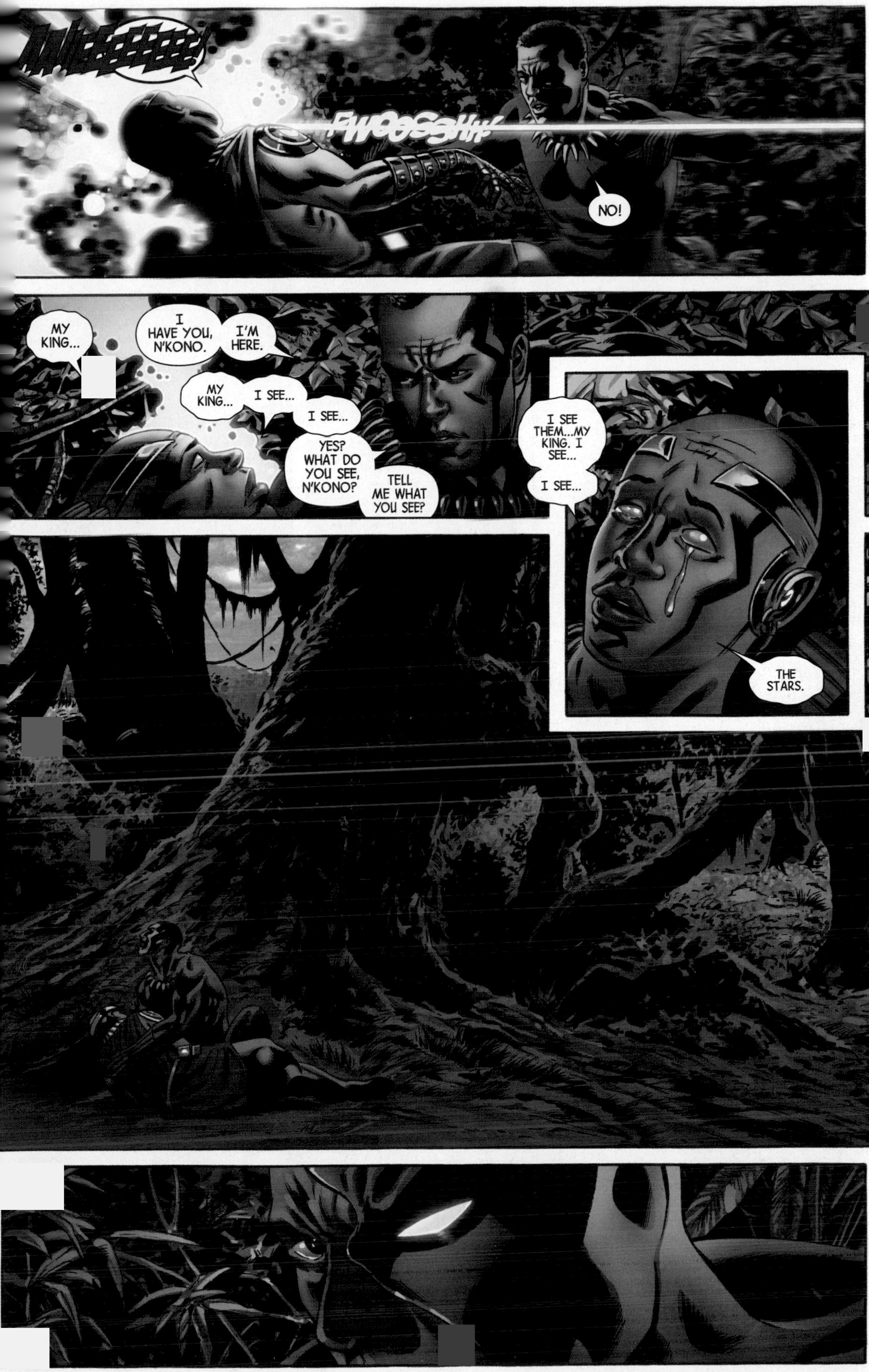
FWOOSSHH
NO!
MY KING...
I HAVE YOU, N'KONO.
I'M HERE.
MY KING...
I SEE...
I SEE...
YES? WHAT DO YOU SEE, N'KONO?
TELL ME WHAT YOU SEE?
I SEE THEM...MY KING. I SEE...
I SEE...
THE STARS.

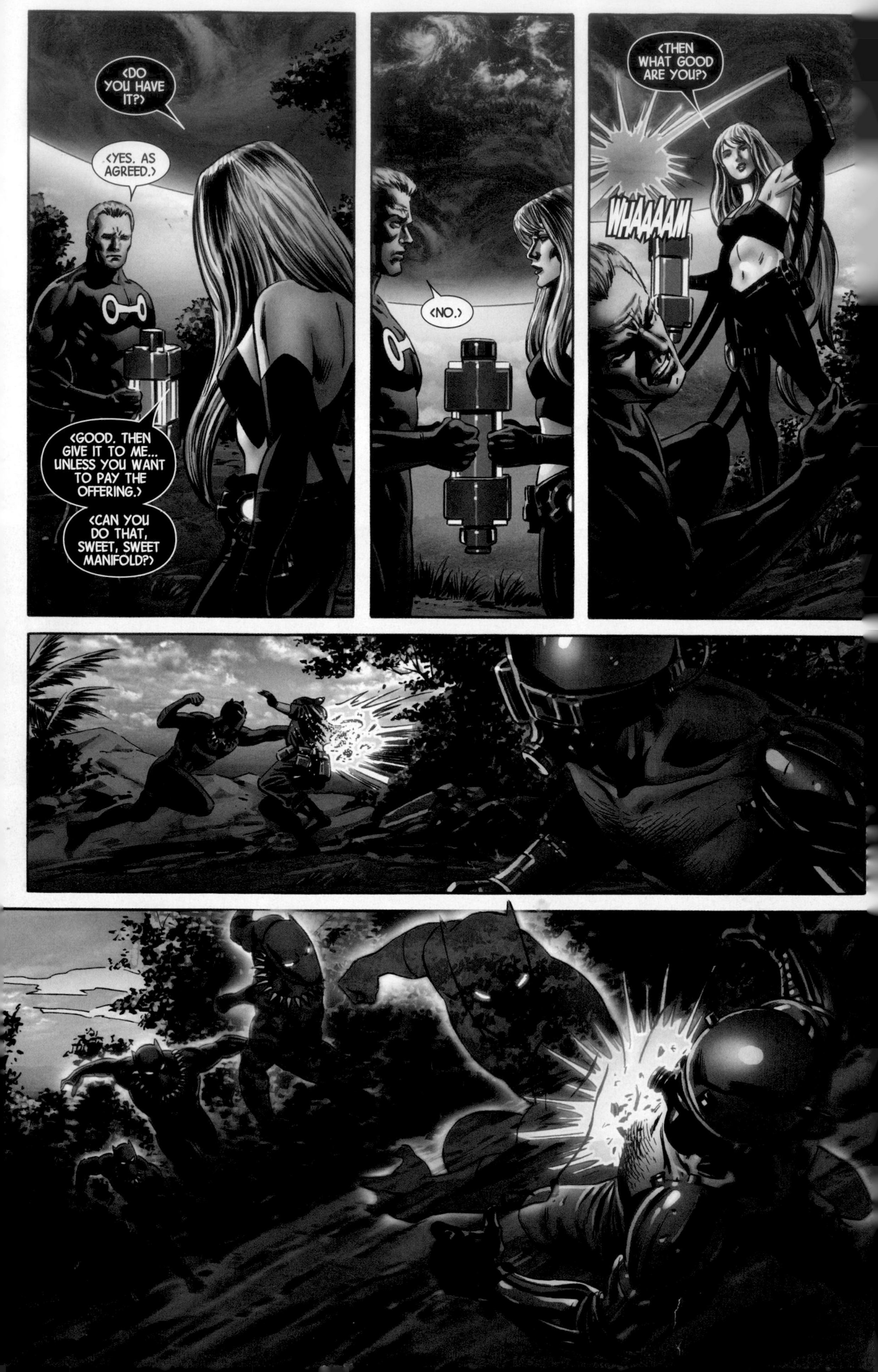

<DO YOU HAVE IT?>
<YES. AS AGREED.>
<GOOD. THEN GIVE IT TO ME... UNLESS YOU WANT TO PAY THE OFFERING.>
<CAN YOU DO THAT, SWEET, SWEET MANIFOLD?>
<NO.>
<THEN WHAT GOOD ARE YOU?>
WHAAAAM

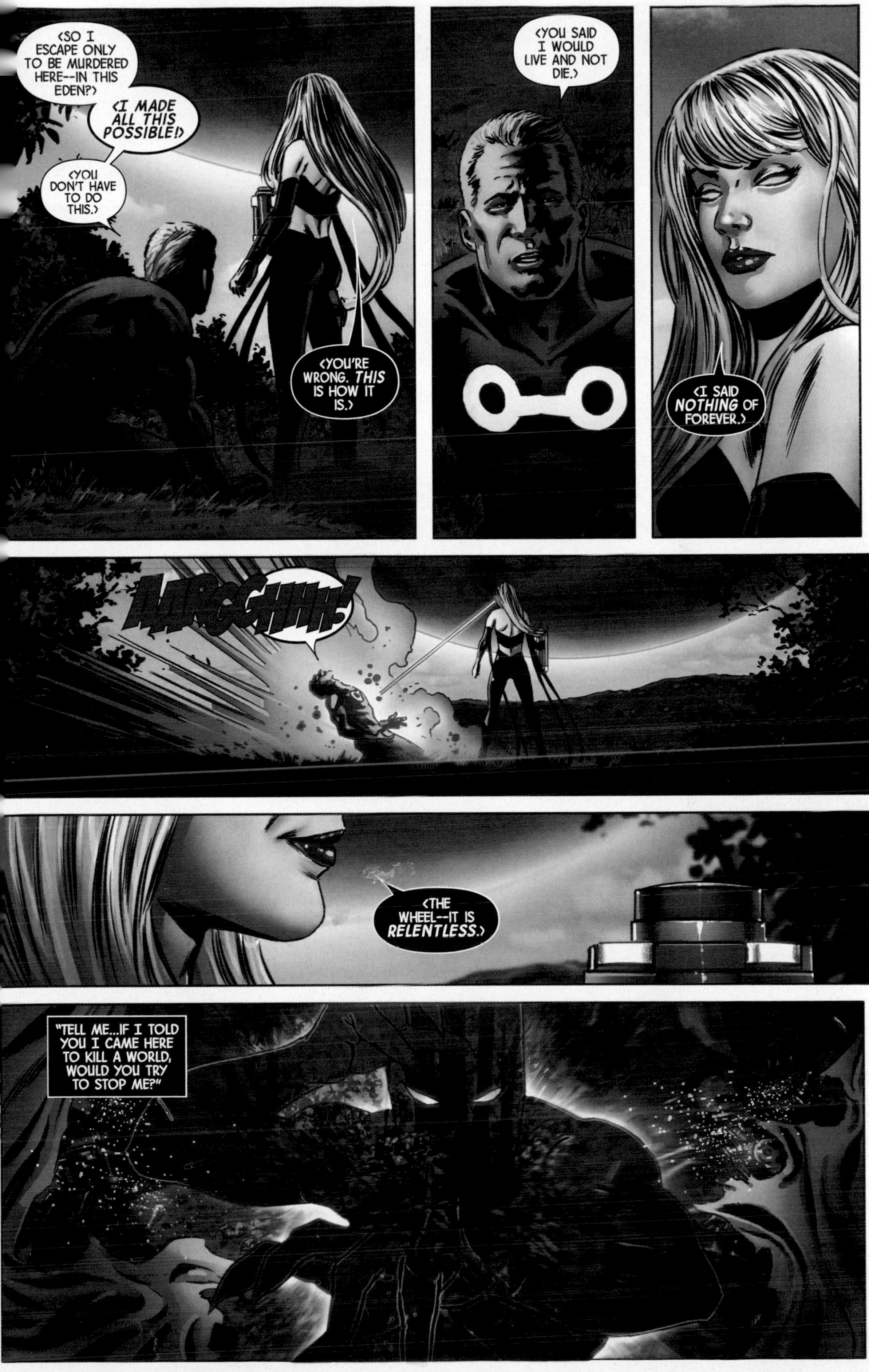

<SO I ESCAPE ONLY TO BE MURDERED HERE--IN THIS EDEN?>
<I MADE ALL THIS POSSIBLE!>
<YOU DON'T HAVE TO DO THIS.>
<YOU'RE WRONG. THIS IS HOW IT IS.>
<YOU SAID I WOULD LIVE AND NOT DIE.>
<I SAID NOTHING OF FOREVER.>
AARGGHHH!
<THE WHEEL--IT IS RELENTLESS.>
"TELL ME...IF I TOLD YOU I CAME HERE TO KILL A WORLD, WOULD YOU TRY TO STOP ME?"

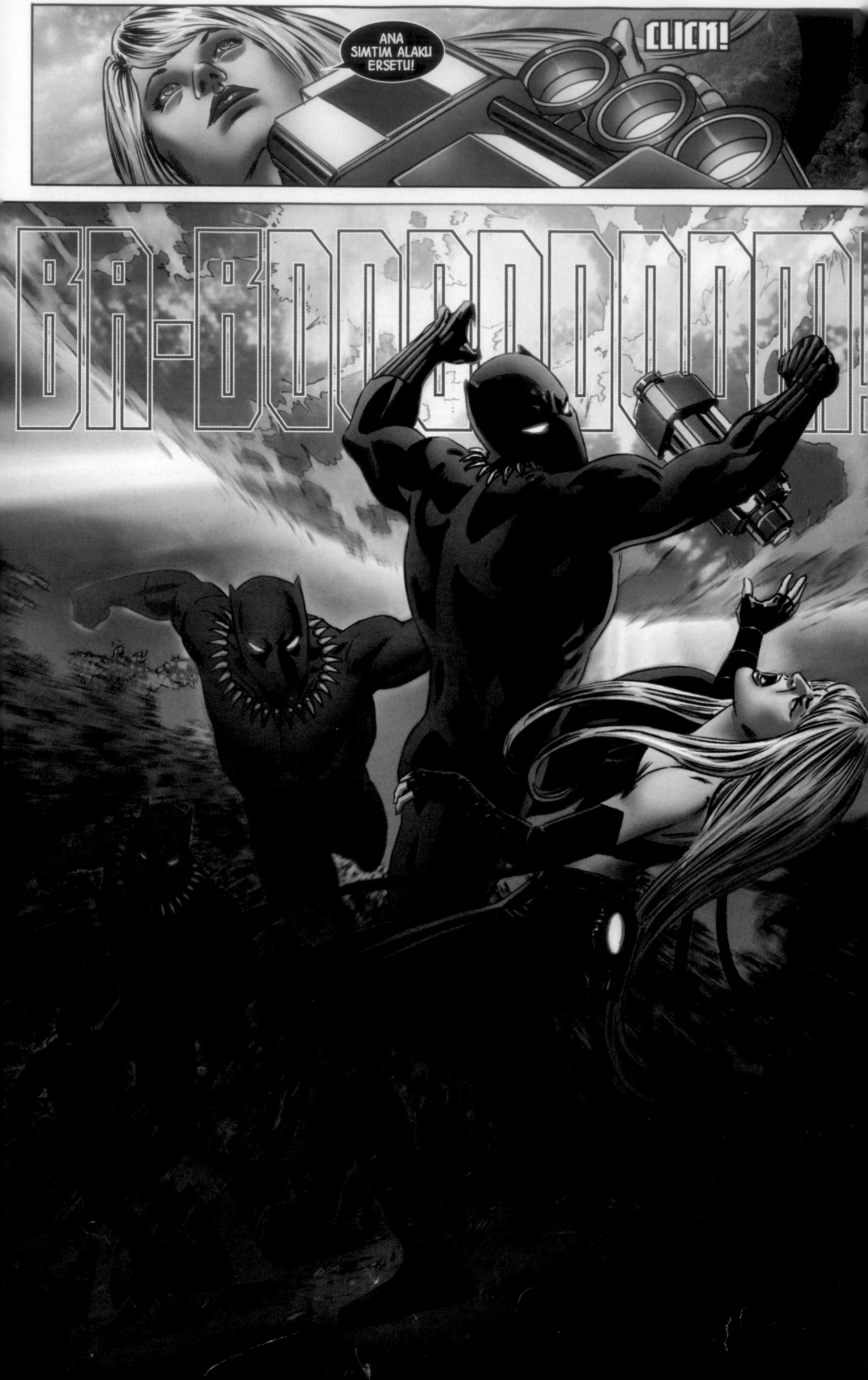
ANA SIMTIM ALAKU ERSETU!
CLICK!
BA-BOOOOOOM!

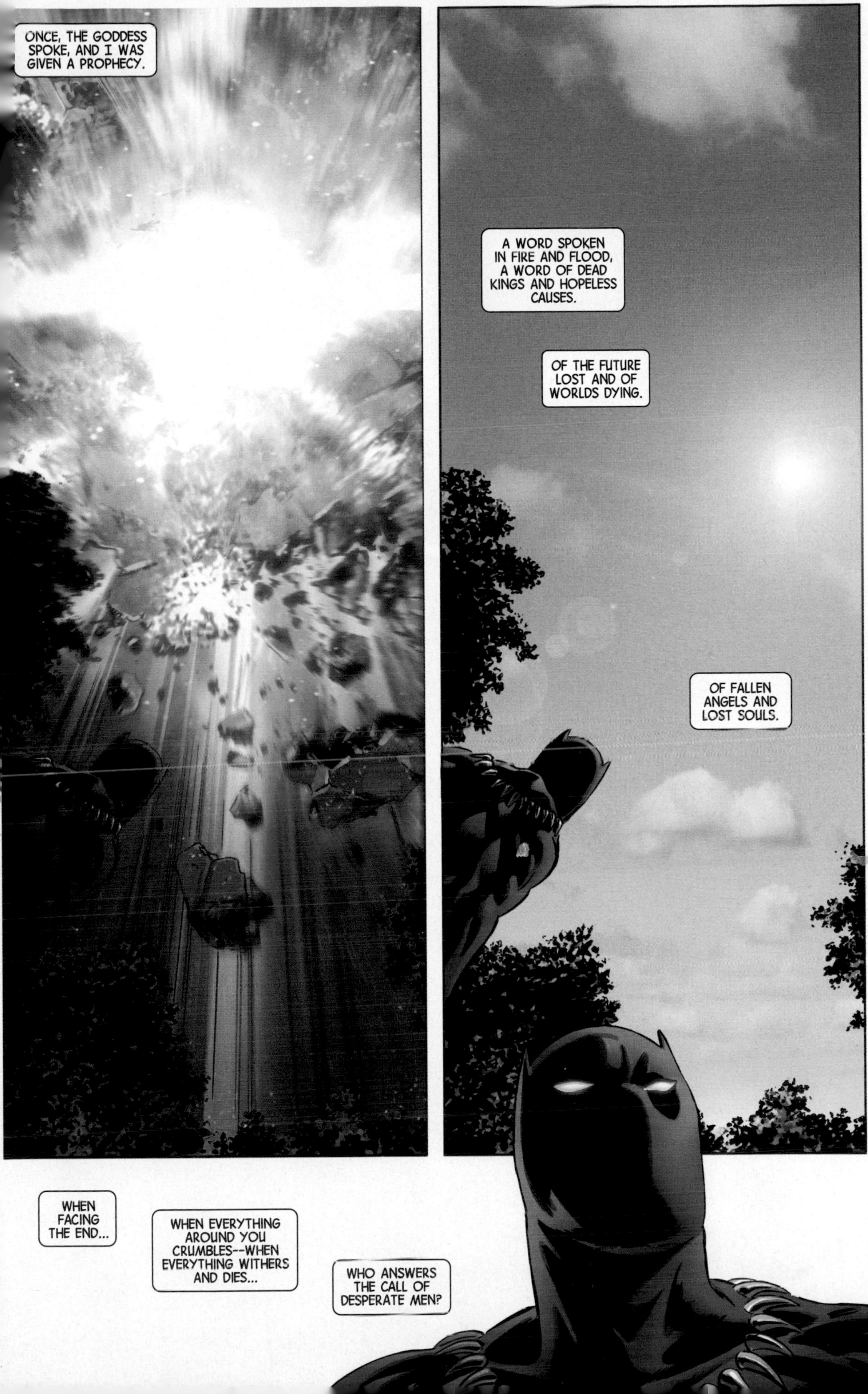
ONCE, THE GODDESS SPOKE, AND I WAS GIVEN A PROPHECY.
A WORD SPOKEN IN FIRE AND FLOOD, A WORD OF DEAD KINGS AND HOPELESS CAUSES.
OF THE FUTURE LOST AND OF WORLDS DYING.
OF FALLEN ANGELS AND LOST SOULS.
WHEN FACING THE END...
WHEN EVERYTHING AROUND YOU CRUMBLES--WHEN EVERYTHING WITHERS AND DIES...
WHO ANSWERS THE CALL OF DESPERATE MEN?

NEW AVENGERS:

ILLUM

INATI

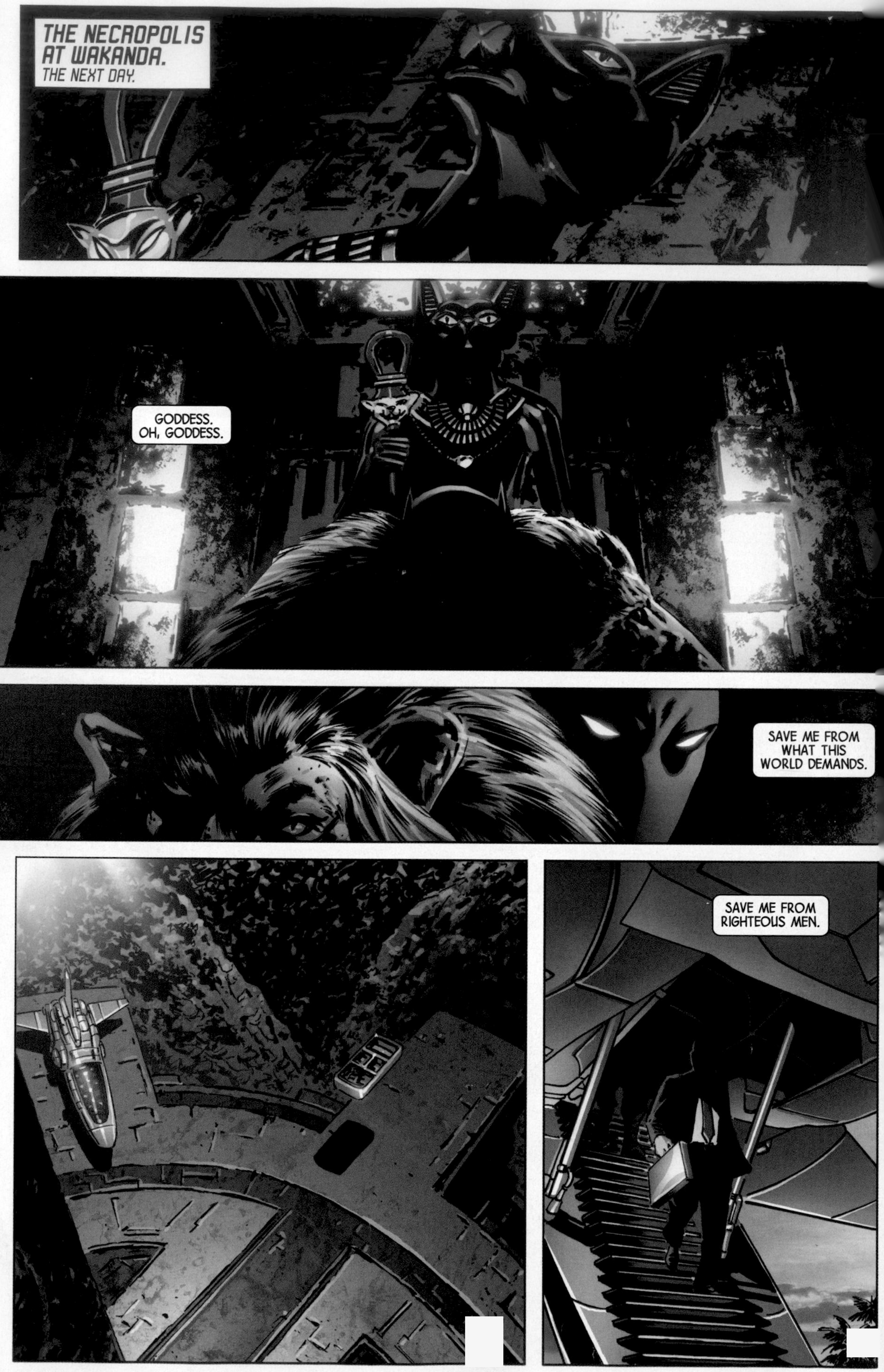
THE NECROPOLIS AT WAKANDA.
THE NEXT DAY.
GODDESS. OH, GODDESS.
SAVE ME FROM WHAT THIS WORLD DEMANDS.
SAVE ME FROM RIGHTEOUS MEN.

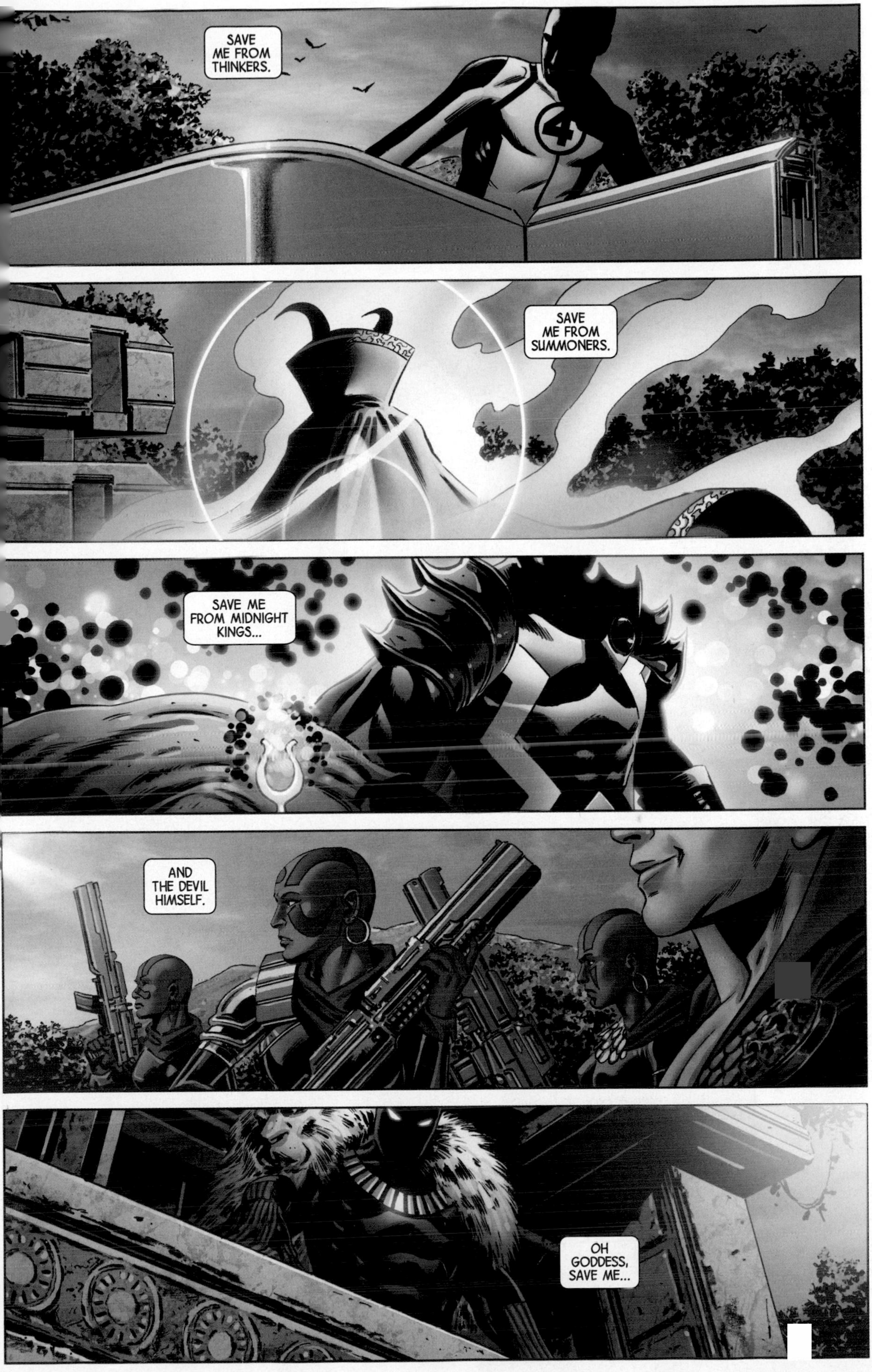
SAVE ME FROM THINKERS.
SAVE ME FROM SUMMONERS.
SAVE ME FROM MIDNIGHT KINGS...
AND THE DEVIL HIMSELF.
OH GODDESS, SAVE ME...

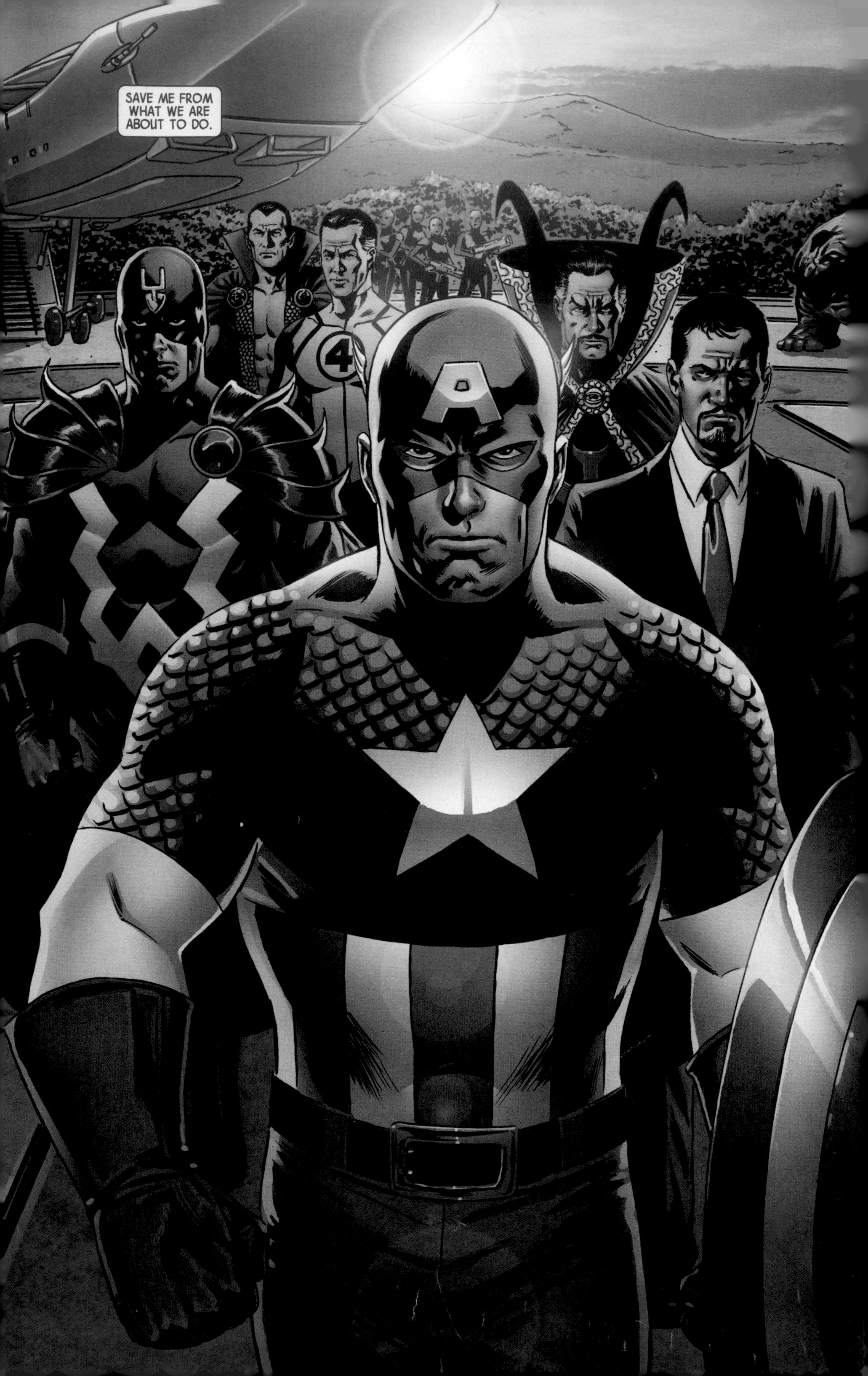
SAVE ME FROM WHAT WE ARE ABOUT TO DO.

"IN SECRET,
THEY RULE"

THE ILLUMINATI

- HOLDERS OF THE INFINITY GEMS -

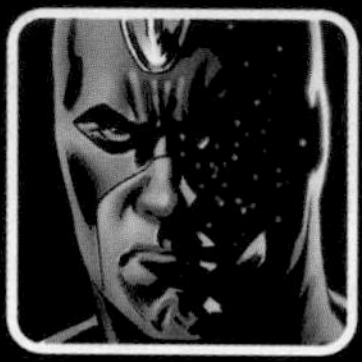

BLACK BOLT
Celestial Messiah

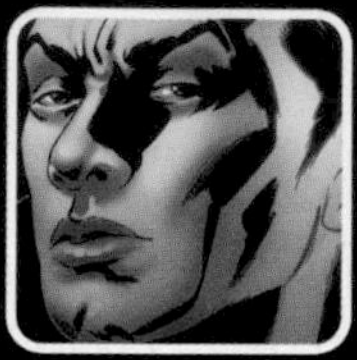

NAMOR
Imperius Rex
(THE POWER GEM)

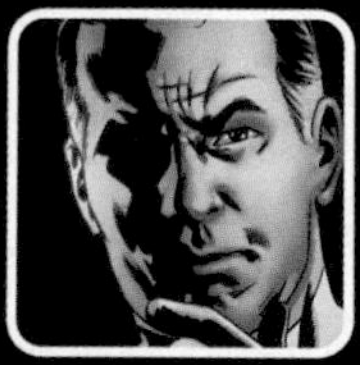

REED RICHARDS
Universal Builder
(THE REALITY GEM)

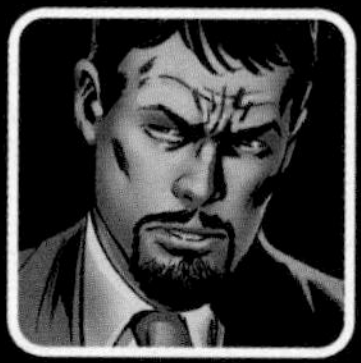

IRON MAN
Master of Machines
(THE SPACE GEM)

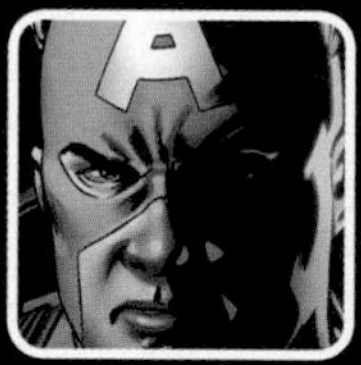

CAPTAIN AMERICA
Hero of Legend
(THE TIME GEM)

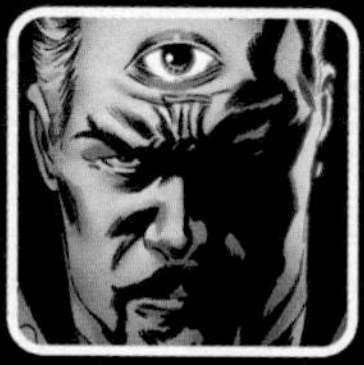

DOCTOR STRANGE
Sorcerer Supreme
(THE SOUL GEM)

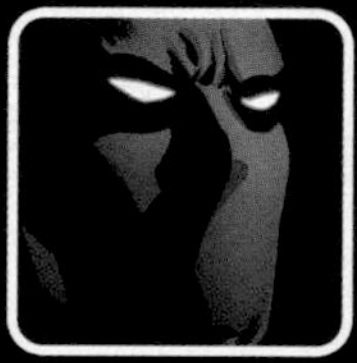

BLACK PANTHER
King of the Dead

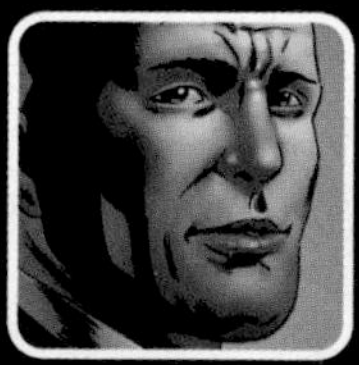

PROFESSOR XAVIER
Deceased
(THE MIND GEM)

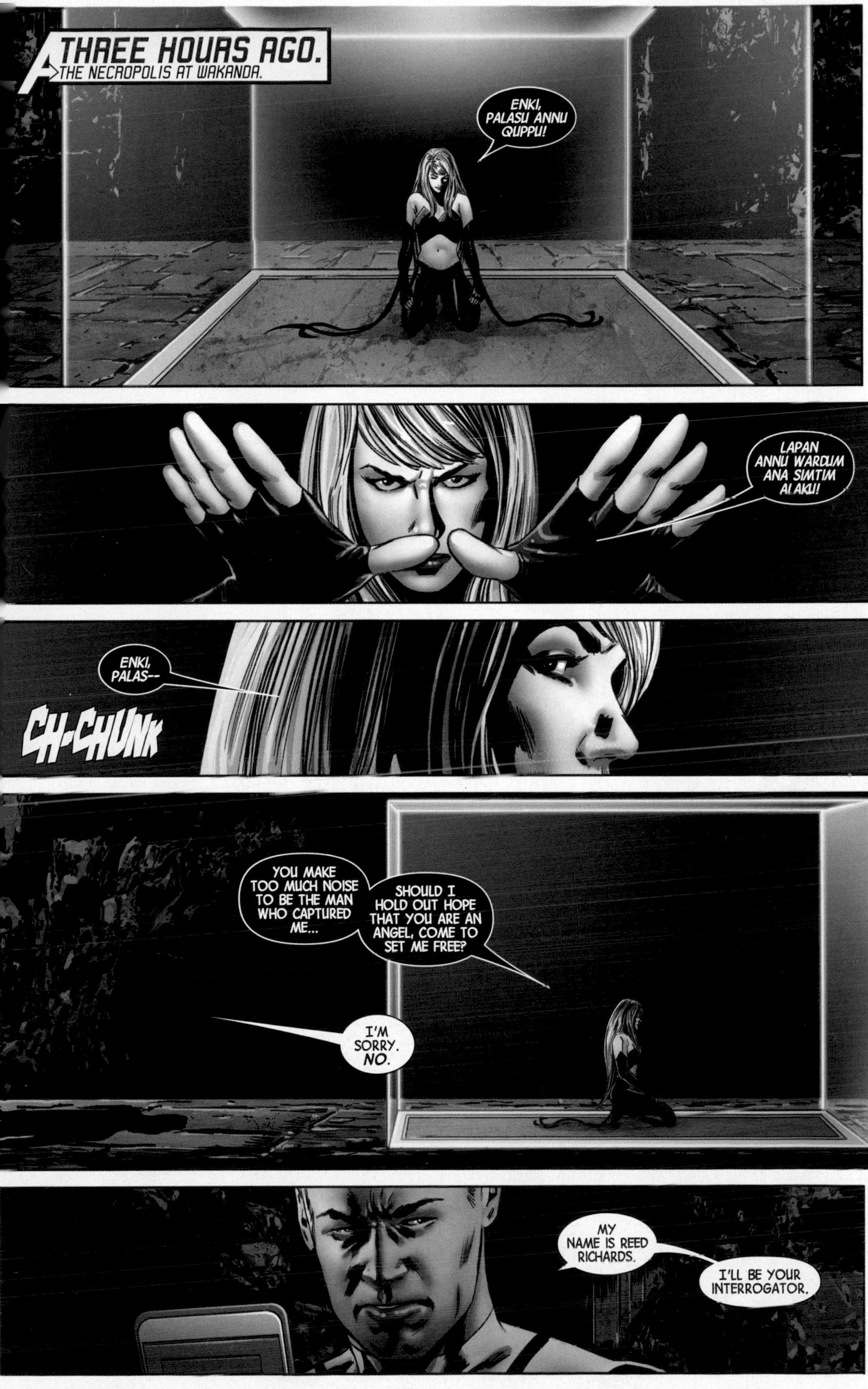
THREE HOURS AGO.
THE NECROPOLIS AT WAKANDA.
ENKI, PALASU ANNU QUPPU!
LAPAN ANNU WARDUM ANA SIMTIM ALAKU!
ENKI, PALAS--
CH-CHUNK
YOU MAKE TOO MUCH NOISE TO BE THE MAN WHO CAPTURED ME...
SHOULD I HOLD OUT HOPE THAT YOU ARE AN ANGEL, COME TO SET ME FREE?
I'M SORRY. NO.
MY NAME IS REED RICHARDS.
I'LL BE YOUR INTERROGATOR.

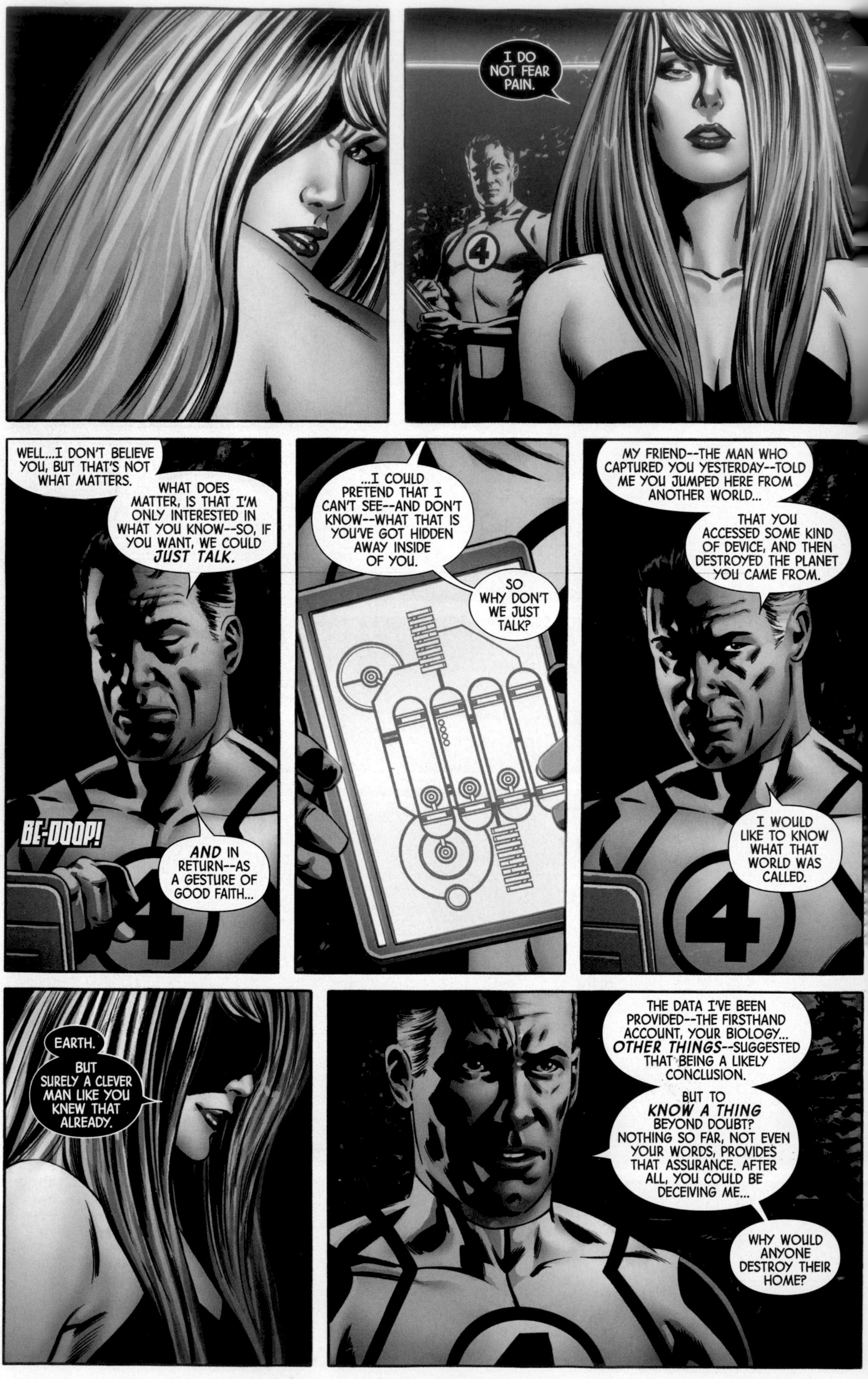
I DO NOT FEAR PAIN.
WELL...I DON'T BELIEVE YOU, BUT THAT'S NOT WHAT MATTERS.
WHAT DOES MATTER, IS THAT I'M ONLY INTERESTED IN WHAT YOU KNOW--SO, IF YOU WANT, WE COULD JUST TALK.
BE-DOOP!
AND IN RETURN--AS A GESTURE OF GOOD FAITH...
...I COULD PRETEND THAT I CAN'T SEE--AND DON'T KNOW--WHAT THAT IS YOU'VE GOT HIDDEN AWAY INSIDE OF YOU.
SO WHY DON'T WE JUST TALK?
MY FRIEND--THE MAN WHO CAPTURED YOU YESTERDAY--TOLD ME YOU JUMPED HERE FROM ANOTHER WORLD...
THAT YOU ACCESSED SOME KIND OF DEVICE, AND THEN DESTROYED THE PLANET YOU CAME FROM.
I WOULD LIKE TO KNOW WHAT THAT WORLD WAS CALLED.
EARTH.
BUT SURELY A CLEVER MAN LIKE YOU KNEW THAT ALREADY.
THE DATA I'VE BEEN PROVIDED--THE FIRSTHAND ACCOUNT, YOUR BIOLOGY... OTHER THINGS--SUGGESTED THAT BEING A LIKELY CONCLUSION.
BUT TO KNOW A THING BEYOND DOUBT? NOTHING SO FAR, NOT EVEN YOUR WORDS, PROVIDES THAT ASSURANCE. AFTER ALL, YOU COULD BE DECEIVING ME...
WHY WOULD ANYONE DESTROY THEIR HOME?

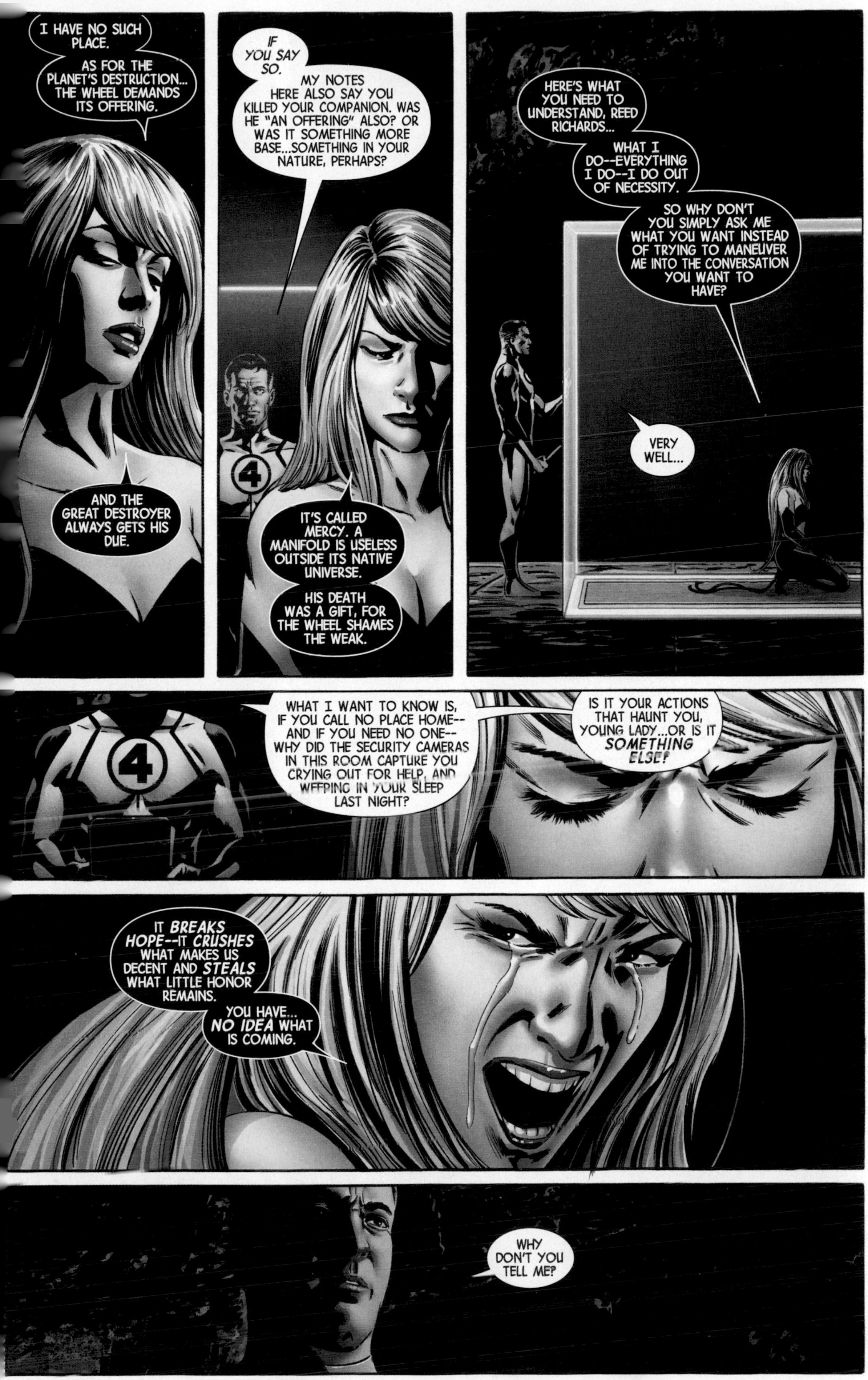
I HAVE NO SUCH PLACE.
AS FOR THE PLANET'S DESTRUCTION... THE WHEEL DEMANDS ITS OFFERING.
AND THE GREAT DESTROYER ALWAYS GETS HIS DUE.
IF YOU SAY SO.
MY NOTES HERE ALSO SAY YOU KILLED YOUR COMPANION. WAS HE "AN OFFERING" ALSO? OR WAS IT SOMETHING MORE BASE...SOMETHING IN YOUR NATURE, PERHAPS?
IT'S CALLED MERCY. A MANIFOLD IS USELESS OUTSIDE ITS NATIVE UNIVERSE.
HIS DEATH WAS A GIFT, FOR THE WHEEL SHAMES THE WEAK.
HERE'S WHAT YOU NEED TO UNDERSTAND, REED RICHARDS...
WHAT I DO--EVERYTHING I DO--I DO OUT OF NECESSITY.
SO WHY DON'T YOU SIMPLY ASK ME WHAT YOU WANT INSTEAD OF TRYING TO MANEUVER ME INTO THE CONVERSATION YOU WANT TO HAVE?
VERY WELL...
WHAT I WANT TO KNOW IS, IF YOU CALL NO PLACE HOME--AND IF YOU NEED NO ONE--WHY DID THE SECURITY CAMERAS IN THIS ROOM CAPTURE YOU CRYING OUT FOR HELP, AND WEEPING IN YOUR SLEEP LAST NIGHT?
IS IT YOUR ACTIONS THAT HAUNT YOU, YOUNG LADY...OR IS IT SOMETHING ELSE?
IT BREAKS HOPE--IT CRUSHES WHAT MAKES US DECENT AND STEALS WHAT LITTLE HONOR REMAINS.
YOU HAVE... NO IDEA WHAT IS COMING.
WHY DON'T YOU TELL ME?

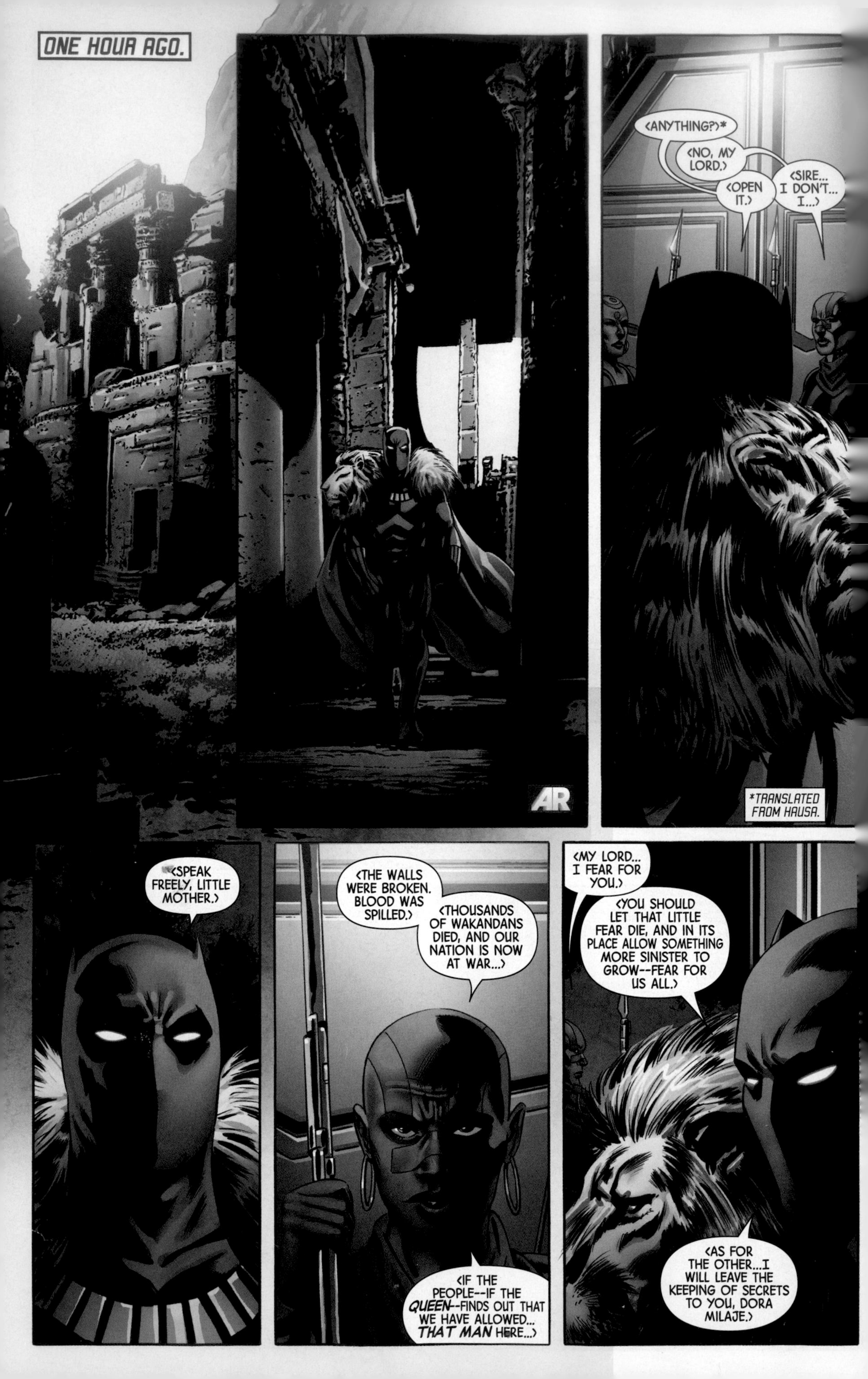
ONE HOUR AGO.
AR
<ANYTHING?>*
<NO, MY LORD.>
<OPEN IT.>
<SIRE... I DON'T... I...>
*TRANSLATED FROM HAUSA.
<SPEAK FREELY, LITTLE MOTHER.>
<THE WALLS WERE BROKEN. BLOOD WAS SPILLED.>
<THOUSANDS OF WAKANDANS DIED, AND OUR NATION IS NOW AT WAR...>
<IF THE PEOPLE--IF THE QUEEN--FINDS OUT THAT WE HAVE ALLOWED... THAT MAN HERE...>
<MY LORD... I FEAR FOR YOU.>
<YOU SHOULD LET THAT LITTLE FEAR DIE, AND IN ITS PLACE ALLOW SOMETHING MORE SINISTER TO GROW--FEAR FOR US ALL.>
<AS FOR THE OTHER...I WILL LEAVE THE KEEPING OF SECRETS TO YOU, DORA MILAJE.>

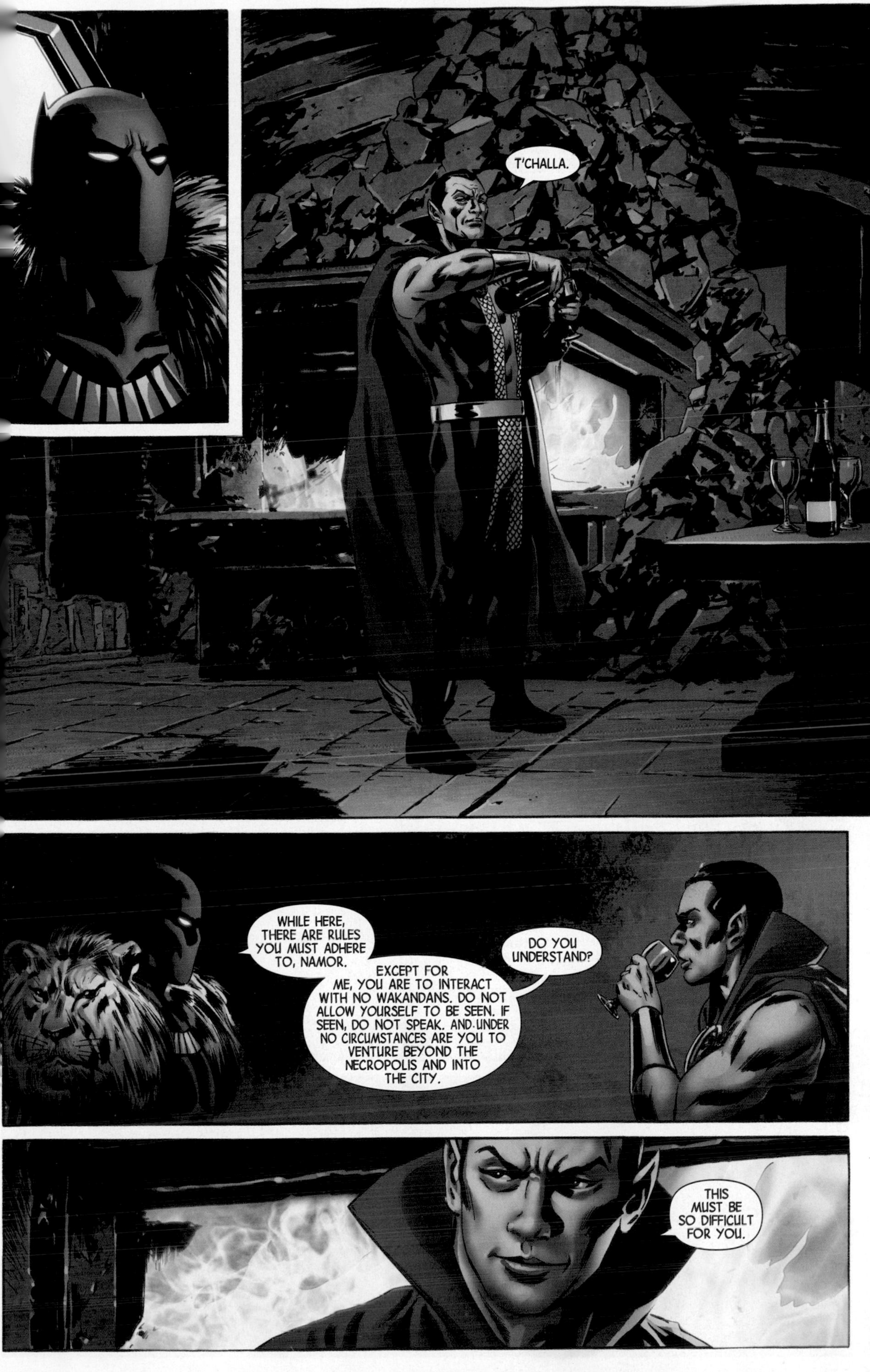
T'CHALLA.
WHILE HERE, THERE ARE RULES YOU MUST ADHERE TO, NAMOR.
EXCEPT FOR ME, YOU ARE TO INTERACT WITH NO WAKANDANS. DO NOT ALLOW YOURSELF TO BE SEEN. IF SEEN, DO NOT SPEAK. AND UNDER NO CIRCUMSTANCES ARE YOU TO VENTURE BEYOND THE NECROPOLIS AND INTO THE CITY.
DO YOU UNDERSTAND?
THIS MUST BE SO DIFFICULT FOR YOU.

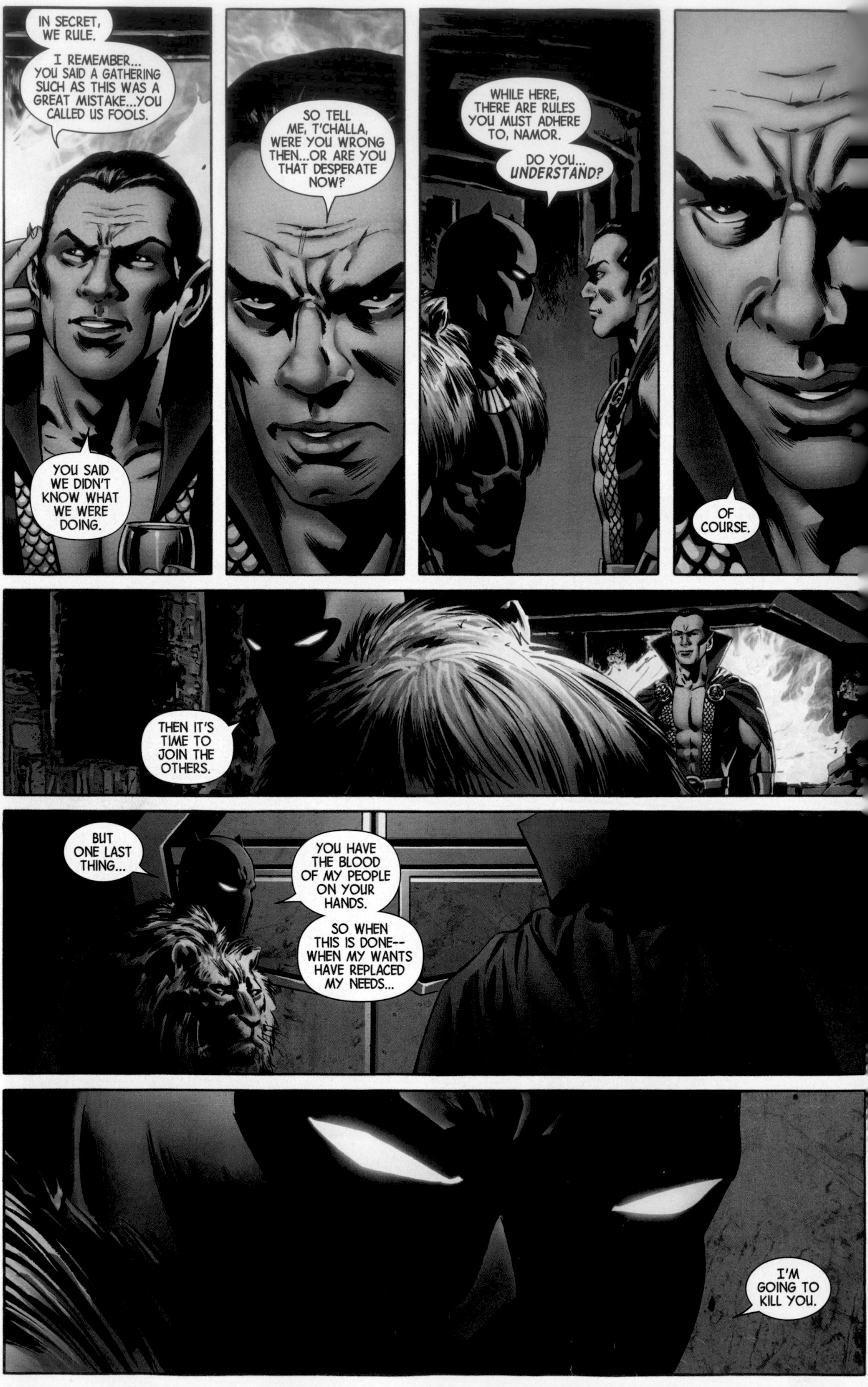
IN SECRET, WE RULE.
I REMEMBER... YOU SAID A GATHERING SUCH AS THIS WAS A GREAT MISTAKE...YOU CALLED US FOOLS.
YOU SAID WE DIDN'T KNOW WHAT WE WERE DOING.
SO TELL ME, T'CHALLA, WERE YOU WRONG THEN...OR ARE YOU THAT DESPERATE NOW?
WHILE HERE, THERE ARE RULES YOU MUST ADHERE TO, NAMOR.
DO YOU... UNDERSTAND?
OF COURSE.
THEN IT'S TIME TO JOIN THE OTHERS.
BUT ONE LAST THING...
YOU HAVE THE BLOOD OF MY PEOPLE ON YOUR HANDS.
SO WHEN THIS IS DONE-- WHEN MY WANTS HAVE REPLACED MY NEEDS...
I'M GOING TO KILL YOU.

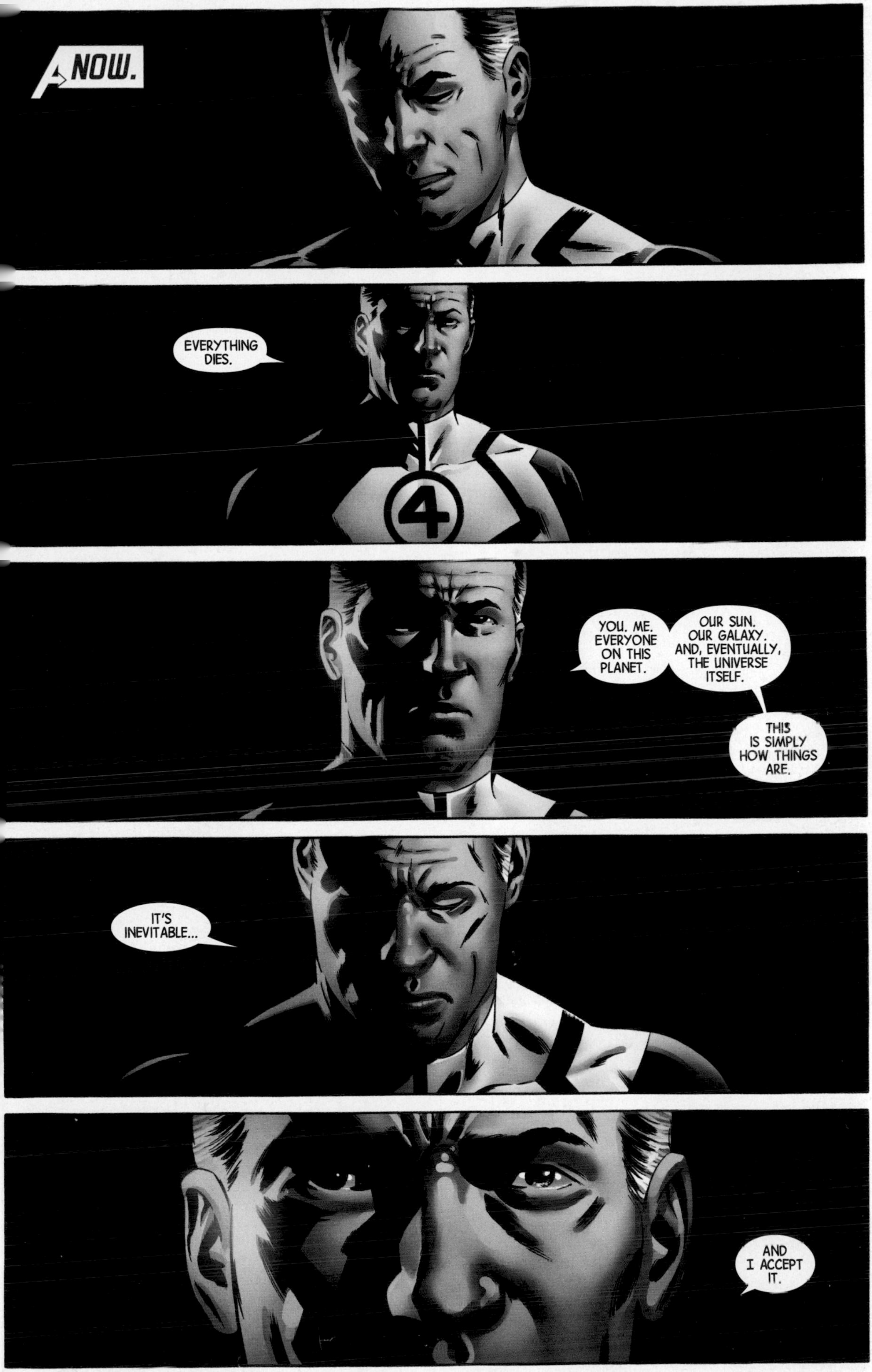
NOW.
EVERYTHING DIES.
YOU. ME. EVERYONE ON THIS PLANET.
OUR SUN. OUR GALAXY. AND, EVENTUALLY, THE UNIVERSE ITSELF.
THIS IS SIMPLY HOW THINGS ARE.
IT'S INEVITABLE...
AND I ACCEPT IT.

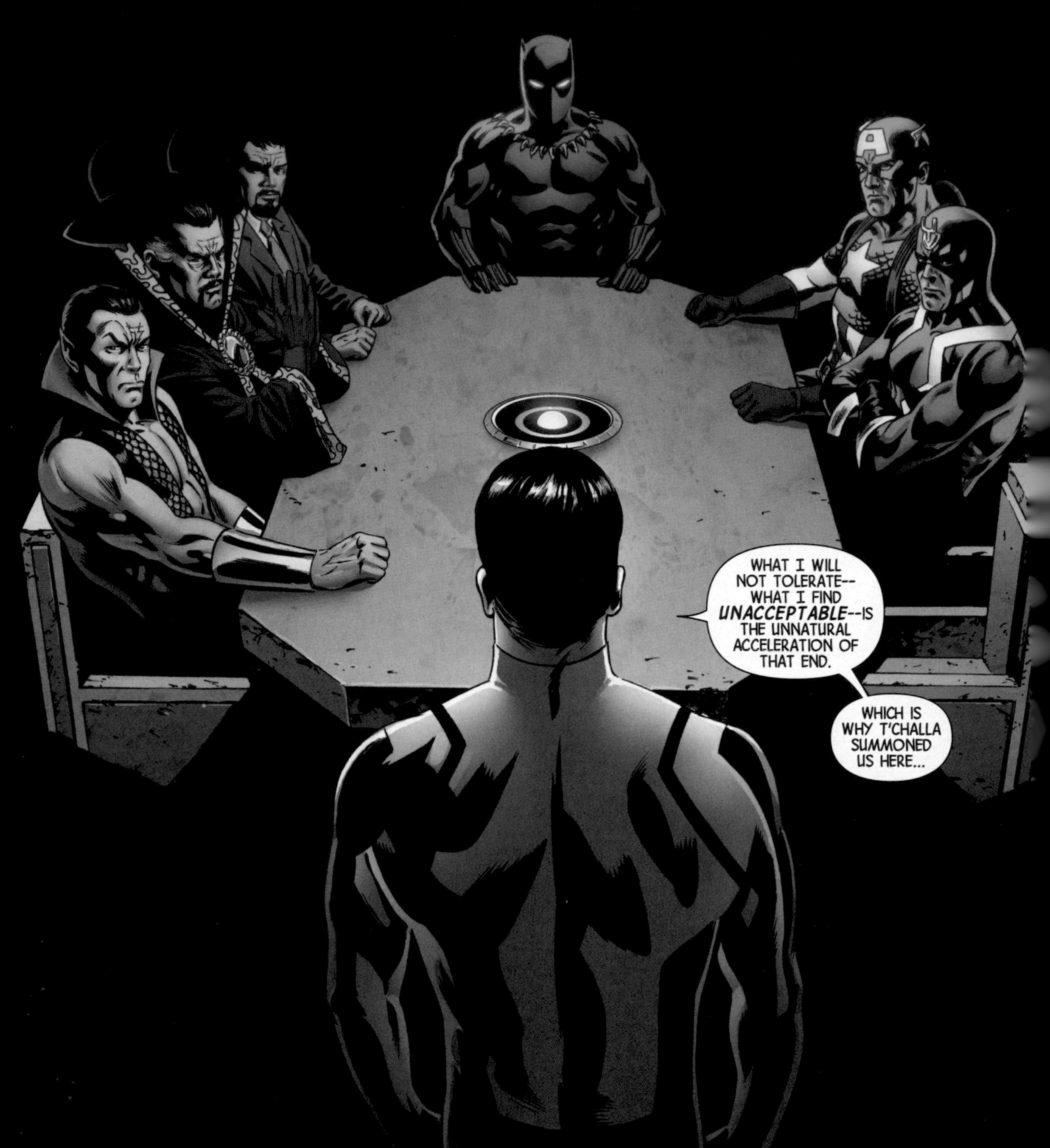
WHAT I WILL NOT TOLERATE-- WHAT I FIND UNACCEPTABLE--IS THE UNNATURAL ACCELERATION OF THAT END.
WHICH IS WHY T'CHALLA SUMMONED US HERE...

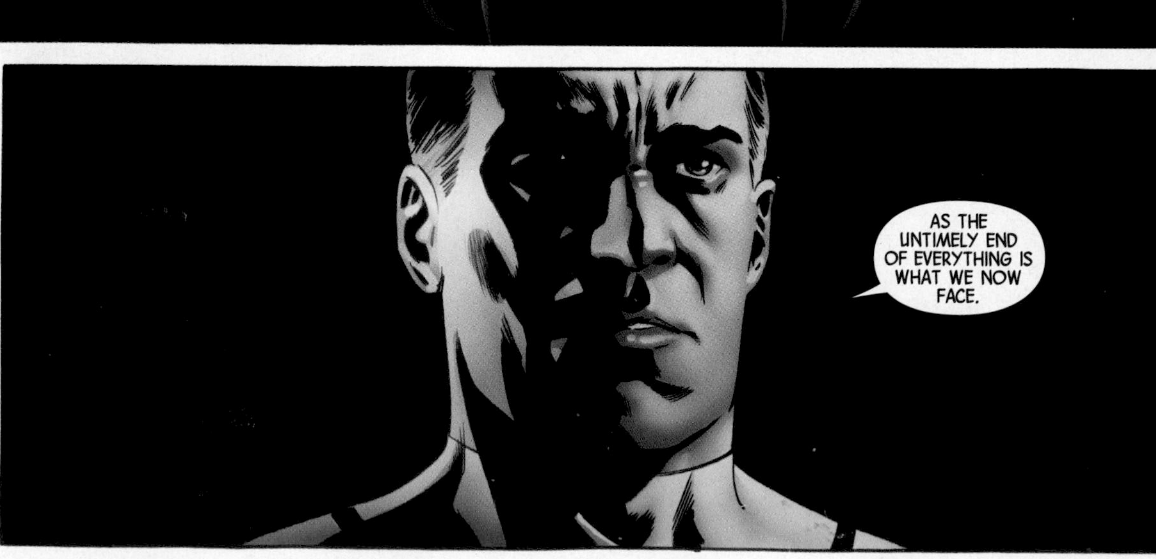
AS THE UNTIMELY END OF EVERYTHING IS WHAT WE NOW FACE.

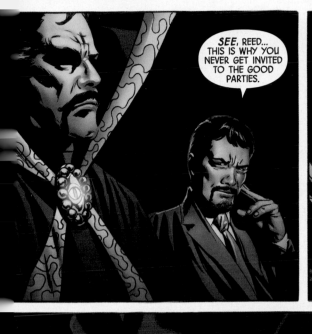

SEE, REED... THIS IS WHY YOU NEVER GET INVITED TO THE GOOD PARTIES.

MANY, MANY TIMES HAVE WE FACED THE WORLD'S END.

AND EACH TIME YOU REFUSED TO ANSWER OUR CALL--YOU REFUSED TO JOIN US...

WHAT MAKES THIS SO DIFFERENT, T'CHALLA?

THE FUTURE OF MY PEOPLE DIED IN MY ARMS YESTERDAY, STEPHEN.

WHAT FOLLOWED...*IT DWARFED THAT.*

THEN WHAT--

NO. BEFORE WE GET TO WHAT BROUGHT US HERE...

THERE ARE PRECAUTIONS THAT NEED TO BE TAKEN.

WE HAVE BEEN INFILTRATED BEFORE. *PLAYED FOR FOOLS.*

IF MATTERS ARE THIS GRAVE, I WOULD KNOW IF ONE OF YOU IS NOT WHO YOU SAY YOU ARE...

PROVE YOURSELVES.

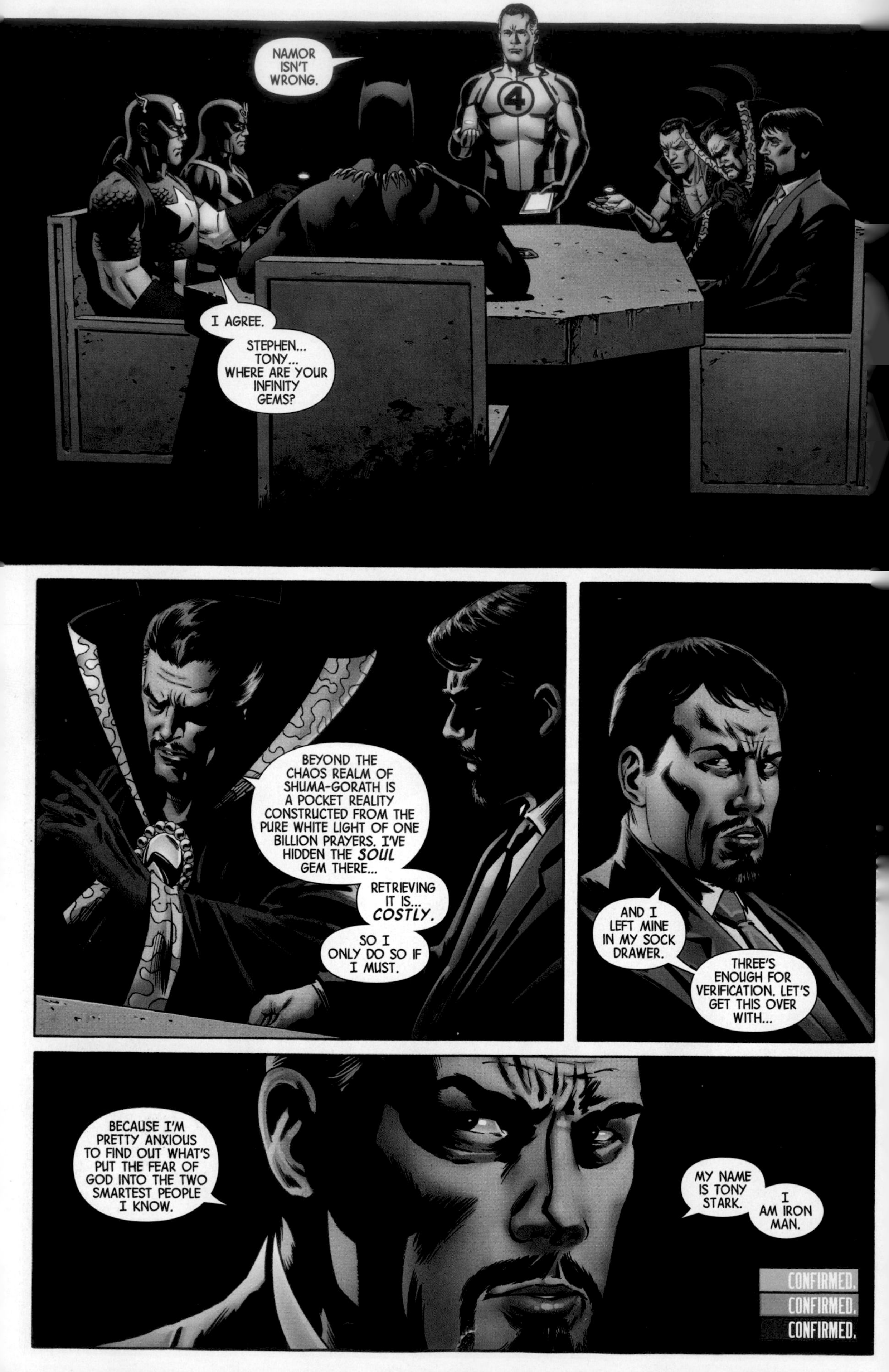
NAMOR ISN'T WRONG.
I AGREE.
STEPHEN... TONY... WHERE ARE YOUR INFINITY GEMS?
BEYOND THE CHAOS REALM OF SHUMA-GORATH IS A POCKET REALITY CONSTRUCTED FROM THE PURE WHITE LIGHT OF ONE BILLION PRAYERS. I'VE HIDDEN THE SOUL GEM THERE...
RETRIEVING IT IS... COSTLY.
SO I ONLY DO SO IF I MUST.
AND I LEFT MINE IN MY SOCK DRAWER.
THREE'S ENOUGH FOR VERIFICATION. LET'S GET THIS OVER WITH...
BECAUSE I'M PRETTY ANXIOUS TO FIND OUT WHAT'S PUT THE FEAR OF GOD INTO THE TWO SMARTEST PEOPLE I KNOW.
MY NAME IS TONY STARK.
I AM IRON MAN.
CONFIRMED.
CONFIRMED.
CONFIRMED.

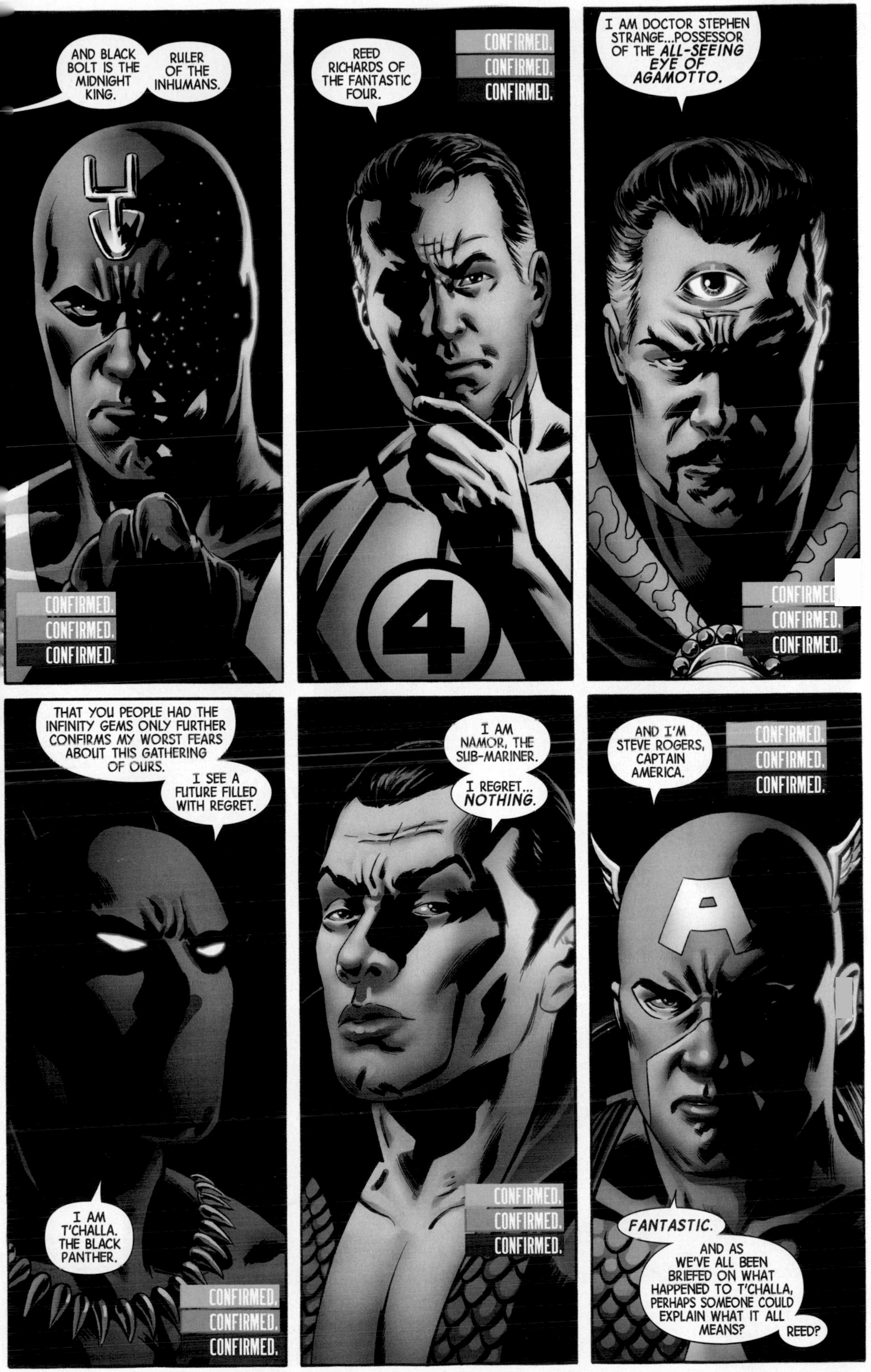
AND BLACK BOLT IS THE MIDNIGHT KING.
RULER OF THE INHUMANS.
CONFIRMED.
CONFIRMED.
CONFIRMED.
REED RICHARDS OF THE FANTASTIC FOUR.
CONFIRMED.
CONFIRMED.
CONFIRMED.
I AM DOCTOR STEPHEN STRANGE...POSSESSOR OF THE *ALL-SEEING EYE OF AGAMOTTO.*
CONFIRMED.
CONFIRMED.
CONFIRMED.
THAT YOU PEOPLE HAD THE INFINITY GEMS ONLY FURTHER CONFIRMS MY WORST FEARS ABOUT THIS GATHERING OF OURS.
I SEE A FUTURE FILLED WITH REGRET.
I AM T'CHALLA. THE BLACK PANTHER.
CONFIRMED.
CONFIRMED.
CONFIRMED.
I AM NAMOR, THE SUB-MARINER.
I REGRET... *NOTHING.*
CONFIRMED.
CONFIRMED.
CONFIRMED.
AND I'M STEVE ROGERS, CAPTAIN AMERICA.
CONFIRMED.
CONFIRMED.
CONFIRMED.
FANTASTIC.
AND AS WE'VE ALL BEEN BRIEFED ON WHAT HAPPENED TO T'CHALLA, PERHAPS SOMEONE COULD EXPLAIN WHAT IT ALL MEANS?
REED?

OF COURSE.

IT MIGHT BE BEST IF I START WITH THINGS WE ALL KNOW TO BE TRUE.

BE-DOOP!

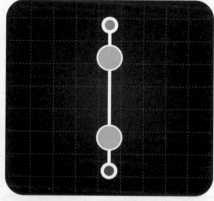

"LIFE AND DEATH.

"THE BIRTH AND HEAT DEATH OF EVERYTHING LIE AT OPPOSITE ENDS ON THE TIMELINE OF THE UNIVERSE.

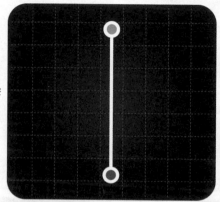

"THE BEGINNING AND END OF OUR EARTH ALSO EXISTS ON THIS TIMELINE AND, OF COURSE, FALLS WITHIN THESE TWO END POINTS.

"OUR WORLD WAS BORN AFTER THE UNIVERSE'S CREATION, AND OUR WORLD WILL DIE BEFORE THE UNIVERSE ENDS.

"WE ALSO KNOW THERE IS A MULTIVERSE OF REALITIES. AN INFINITE NUMBER OF EARTHS, INSIDE AN INFINITE NUMBER OF UNIVERSES, WHERE ANY MANNER OF DIVERGENT REALITY CAN EXIST.

"ENDLESS POSSIBILITIES...

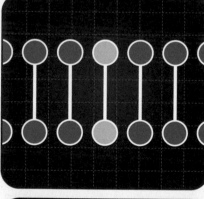

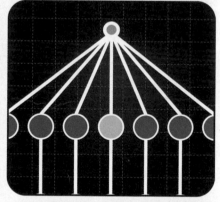

"HOWEVER, AS I MENTIONED EARLIER... *EVERYTHING DIES.*

"SO, REGARDLESS OF HOW MANY REALITIES THERE ARE, EVENTUALLY THEY ALL END UP IN THE SAME PLACE AND IN THE SAME STATE. EXTINGUISHED AT THE END OF EVERYTHING.

"AND HERE'S WHERE OUR PROBLEM LIES.

"I'VE LEARNED THAT SOMEWHERE, ON ONE OF THESE EARTHS, AN *EVENT* OCCURRED THAT CAUSED THE EARLY DEATH OF ONE OF THESE UNIVERSES.

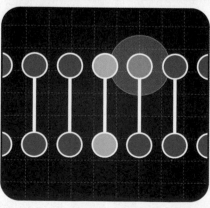

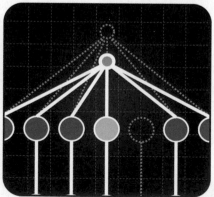

"THAT *UNTIMELY, UNNATURAL* EVENT THEN CAUSED A TINY CONTRACTION IN THE MULTIVERSE'S TIMELINE.

"NOW, EVERYTHING WOULD DIE EVER-SO-SLIGHTLY SOONER.

IN ADDITION, THAT TINY CONTRACTION CAUSED TWO UNIVERSES TO CRASH TOGETHER AT THE *INCURSION POINT* OF THE INITIAL EVENT.

AND THIS IS WHERE YOU REALLY WANT TO PAY ATTENTION... THAT *POINT* WAS *EARTH*.

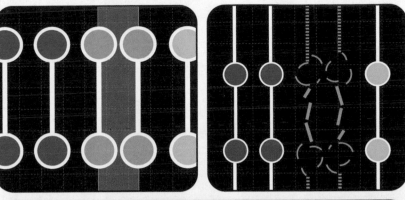

"THEY TOUCHED, AND DESTROYED EACH OTHER-- TAKING THEIR UNIVERSES WITH THEM--CAUSING YET ANOTHER CONTRACTION IN THE TIMELINE.

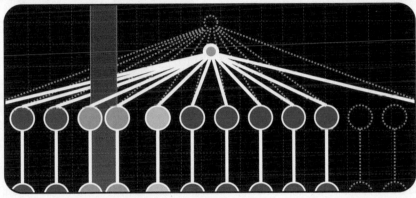

"WHICH IN TURN ACCELERATED THE SMASHING TOGETHER OF EVEN MORE EARTHS AND THEIR RESPECTIVE UNIVERSES.

"AND THAT'S WHAT T'CHALLA WITNESSED-- ANOTHER EARTH COLLIDING WITH OUR EARTH."

I DON'T UNDERSTAND. IF THIS IS WHAT HAPPENED, HOW ARE WE HERE?

THE WOMAN-- *THE BLACK SWAN*-- USED A DEVICE TO DESTROY THE OTHER EARTH, PREVENTING IMPACT.

IS THAT REALLY WHAT SHE CALLS HERSELF?

YES.

WELL THAT'S... *JUST PERFECT,* AND FOREBODING AS HELL.

WE HAVE TO FIND A WAY TO STOP THIS.

A MULTIVERSAL APOCALYPTIC DEATH SCENARIO...SURE, I'D SAY IT'S A SITUATION THAT NEEDS HANDLING.

OUR PROBLEM IS THAT WE HAVE TOO MANY UNKNOWNS.

WHAT'S THE SOURCE OF THE COLLAPSE? CAN THE CHAIN REACTION BE STOPPED? CAN IT EVEN BE SLOWED DOWN?

WE DO HAVE THE TECHNOLOGY THAT THE BLACK SWAN HAD ON HER PERSON.

THIS INCLUDES THE TRIGGER MECHANISM TO WHATEVER DESTROYED THE OTHER PLANET, SO THERE'S--

LET ME STOP THIS CONVERSATION RIGHT HERE.

WE ARE GOING TO HANDLE THIS EXACTLY LIKE WE NORMALLY WOULD.

WE WILL PREPARE, GATHER INTELLIGENCE, AND WHEN THE NEXT EPISODE OCCURS, USE THAT INFORMATION TO FIGURE OUT A WAY TO WIN.

BECAUSE THAT'S WHAT WE DO.

THERE'S A GOOD CHANCE THAT WON'T WORK, CAP.

WE WON'T HAVE ENOUGH TIME.

WHY NOT?

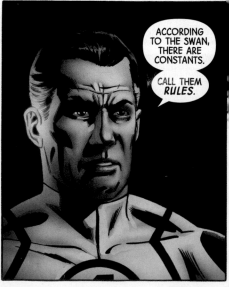

ACCORDING TO THE SWAN, THERE ARE CONSTANTS.

CALL THEM *RULES.*

"AS I STATED EARLIER, THE TIME WHEN TWO EARTHS BEGIN TO COLLIDE IS CALLED AN *INCURSION*, AND EVERY SINGLE ONE IS EXACTLY THE SAME.

"BEFORE THEY BEGIN, THERE IS A VERY SHORT PERIOD OF HARMONIC ALIGNMENT, WHICH IS WHAT ALLOWS THE TWO EARTHS TO EXIST IN THE SAME SPACE.

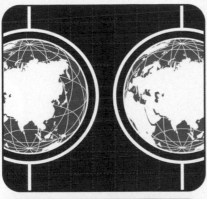 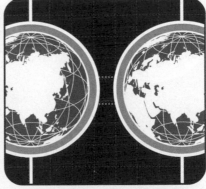

"THE SINGLE BIT OF GOOD NEWS HERE IS THAT WE SHOULD BE ABLE TO DETECT THIS, AND THEREFORE CREATE AN EARLY WARNING SYSTEM. SO, AT LEAST WE'LL KNOW WHEN ONE IS COMING.

"REGARDLESS, ONCE THE *INCURSION* ACTUALLY BEGINS, OUR TIME TO ACT GROWS VERY SHORT...

"AS EACH *INCURSION* LASTS EXACTLY 8 HOURS.

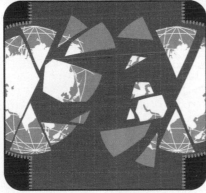 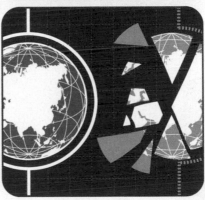

"AT THE END OF THOSE 8 HOURS, WHAT FOLLOWS IS EXTREMELY SIMPLE. EITHER BOTH WORLDS ARE DESTROYED, ALONG WITH THEIR RESPECTIVE UNIVERSES, AS THEY SMASH TOGETHER...

"...OR ONE EARTH IS DESTROYED, WHICH ELIMINATES THE INCURSION POINT BETWEEN THE TWO UNIVERSES, SPARING THEM BOTH.

"EIGHT HOURS. ONE EVENT-- TWO POSSIBLE OUTCOMES."

BE-*DOOP!*

NOW, ADMITTEDLY, THE BLACK SWAN COULD BE LYING--I DID NOT HAVE THAT MUCH TIME WITH HER AND I DEFINITELY THINK SHE'S LEAVING SOME THINGS OUT--BUT BIOMETRICS SHOWED NO SIGNS OF OUTRIGHT DECEPTION.

AND, OF COURSE, THERE'S THE MINOR POINT THAT SHE APPEARED TO DESTROY THE OTHER WORLD, THEREBY SPARING OURS AND SAVING HERSELF.

SO, FOR NOW, HER STORY CHECKS OUT.

EIGHT HOURS. THAT'S ALL WE'LL HAVE.

T'CHALLA?

AR

NOW ALL OF YOU UNDERSTAND.

I DON'T ASK FOR THE COUNSEL OF OTHER MEN--I DON'T NEED IT. I HAVE ALWAYS BEEN CAPABLE OF MAKING THE IMPOSSIBLE DECISION ON MY OWN. BUT THIS--IT IS BEYOND ME OR ANY SINGLE ONE OF US.

SO HERE WE ARE, AN UNHOLY ALLIANCE THAT JUST MIGHT BE THE EARTH'S ONLY HOPE.

HELP ME SAVE MY PEOPLE. HELP ME SAVE OUR WORLD--AND THE VERY *UNIVERSE* ITSELF.

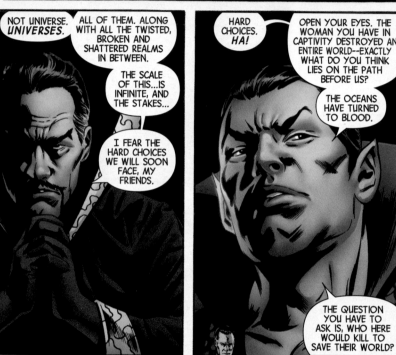

NOT UNIVERSE. *UNIVERSES.*

ALL OF THEM. ALONG WITH ALL THE TWISTED, BROKEN AND SHATTERED REALMS IN BETWEEN.

THE SCALE OF THIS...IS INFINITE, AND THE STAKES...

I FEAR THE HARD CHOICES WE WILL SOON FACE, MY FRIENDS.

HARD CHOICES. *HA!*

OPEN YOUR EYES. THE WOMAN YOU HAVE IN CAPTIVITY DESTROYED AN ENTIRE WORLD--EXACTLY WHAT DO YOU THINK LIES ON THE PATH BEFORE US?

THE OCEANS HAVE TURNED TO BLOOD.

THE QUESTION YOU HAVE TO ASK IS, WHO HERE WOULD KILL TO SAVE THEIR WORLD?

RRRUUMMBBLLEE

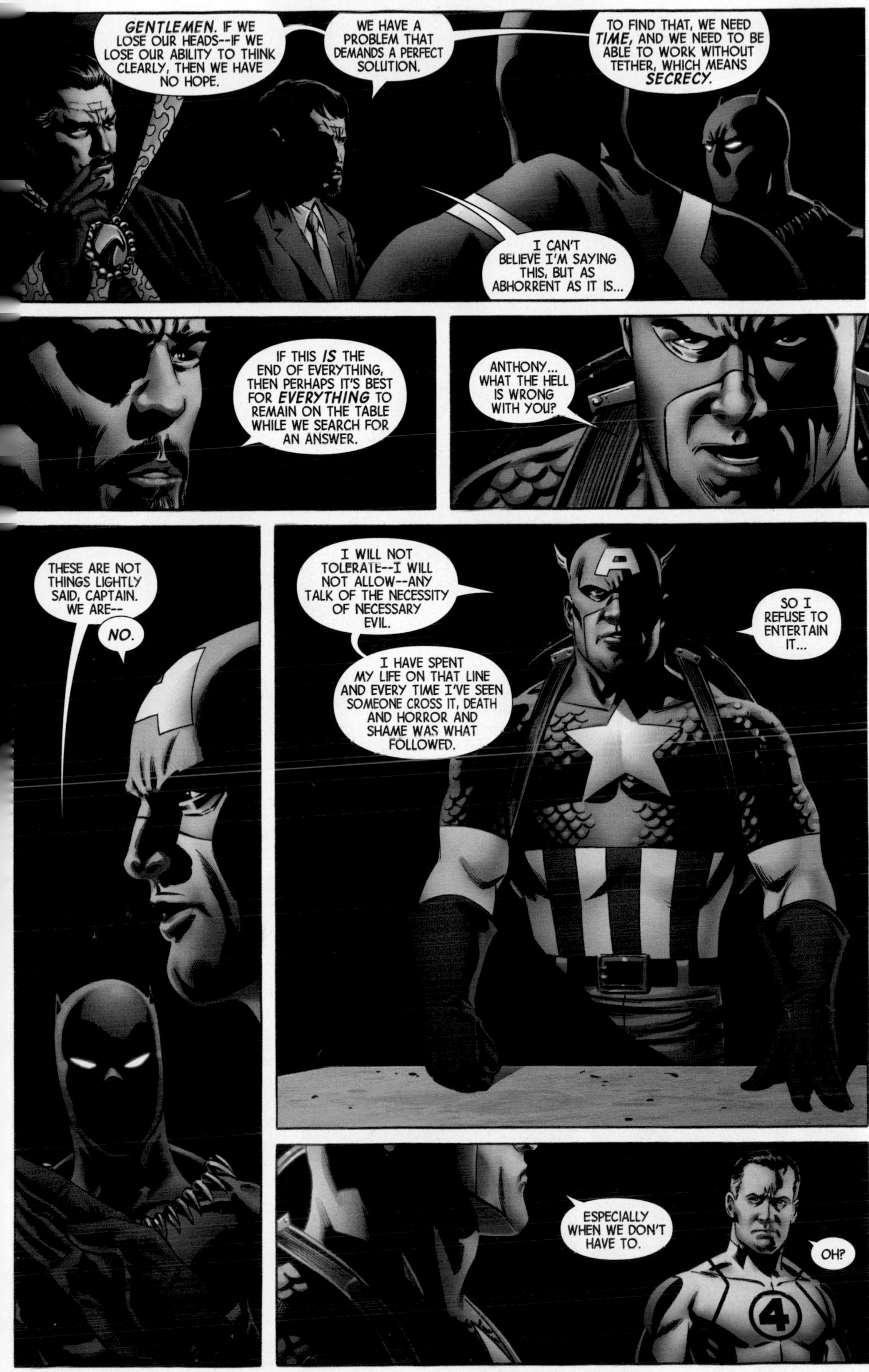
GENTLEMEN. IF WE LOSE OUR HEADS--IF WE LOSE OUR ABILITY TO THINK CLEARLY, THEN WE HAVE NO HOPE.
WE HAVE A PROBLEM THAT DEMANDS A PERFECT SOLUTION.
TO FIND THAT, WE NEED TIME, AND WE NEED TO BE ABLE TO WORK WITHOUT TETHER, WHICH MEANS SECRECY.
I CAN'T BELIEVE I'M SAYING THIS, BUT AS ABHORRENT AS IT IS...
IF THIS IS THE END OF EVERYTHING, THEN PERHAPS IT'S BEST FOR EVERYTHING TO REMAIN ON THE TABLE WHILE WE SEARCH FOR AN ANSWER.
ANTHONY... WHAT THE HELL IS WRONG WITH YOU?
THESE ARE NOT THINGS LIGHTLY SAID, CAPTAIN. WE ARE--
NO.
I WILL NOT TOLERATE--I WILL NOT ALLOW--ANY TALK OF THE NECESSITY OF NECESSARY EVIL.
I HAVE SPENT MY LIFE ON THAT LINE AND EVERY TIME I'VE SEEN SOMEONE CROSS IT, DEATH AND HORROR AND SHAME WAS WHAT FOLLOWED.
SO I REFUSE TO ENTERTAIN IT...
ESPECIALLY WHEN WE DON'T HAVE TO.
OH?

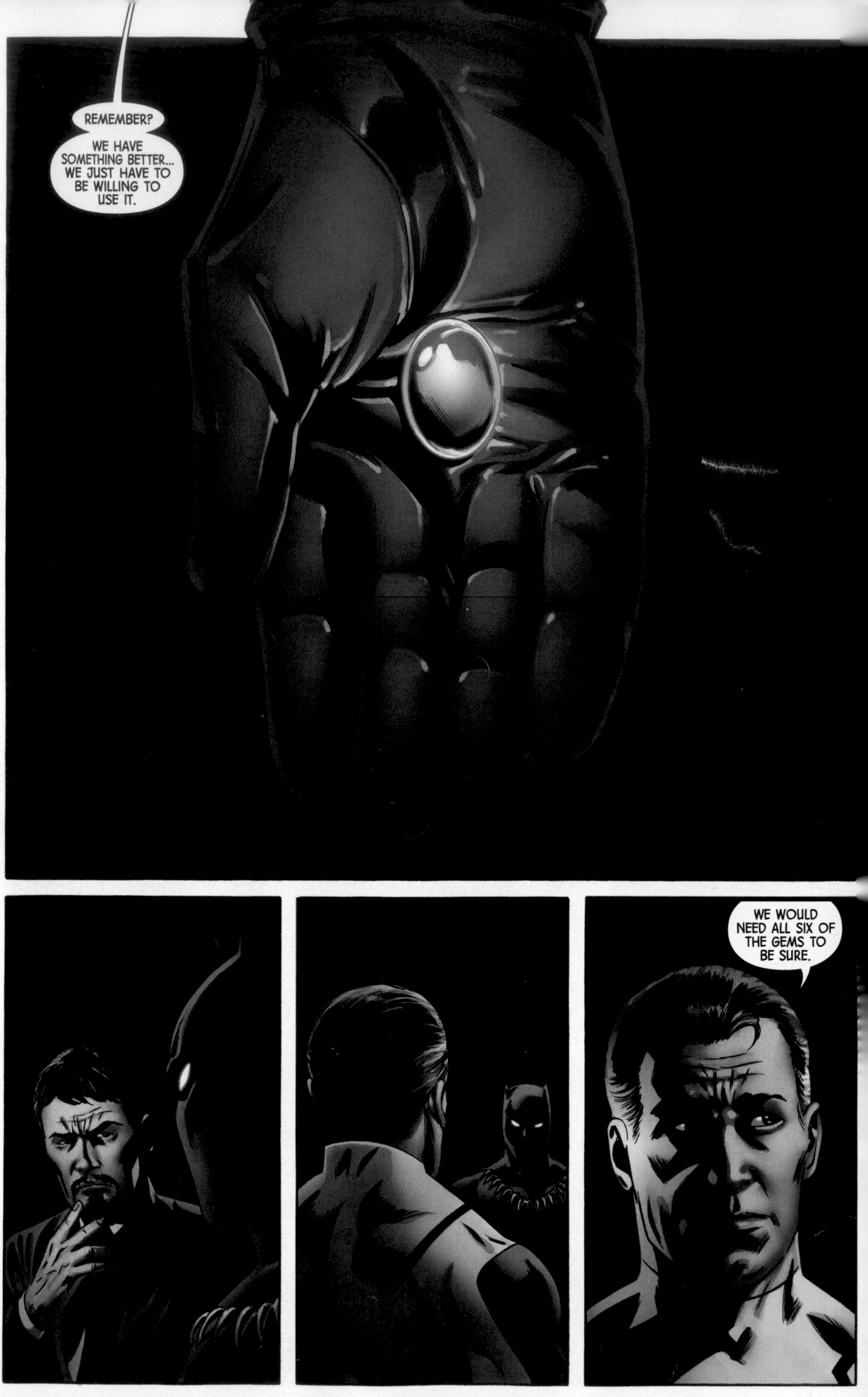
REMEMBER?
WE HAVE SOMETHING BETTER... WE JUST HAVE TO BE WILLING TO USE IT.
WE WOULD NEED ALL SIX OF THE GEMS TO BE SURE.

CHARLES XAVIER IS DEAD, AND THE LOCATION OF THE *MIND GEM* LOST WITH HIM.

NO. WE CAN USE THE FIVE WE HAVE TO FIND HIS--THE STONES *WANT* TO BE TOGETHER.

BE-
DOOP

SO WE AGREE? WE REASSEMBLE THE INFINITY GAUNTLET?

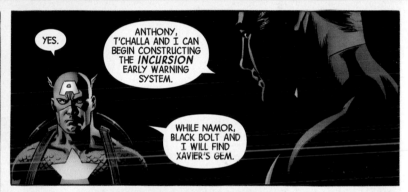

YES.

ANTHONY, T'CHALLA AND I CAN BEGIN CONSTRUCTING THE *INCURSION* EARLY WARNING SYSTEM.

WHILE NAMOR, BLACK BOLT AND I WILL FIND XAVIER'S GEM.

OKAY. GOOD.

NOW...I WANT EVERYONE TO LOOK AT ME.

YES, THIS IS MASSIVE. YES, IT IS *NIGHT*.

BUT REMEMBER, WE SHAPE THE WORLD... IT DOES NOT SHAPE US...

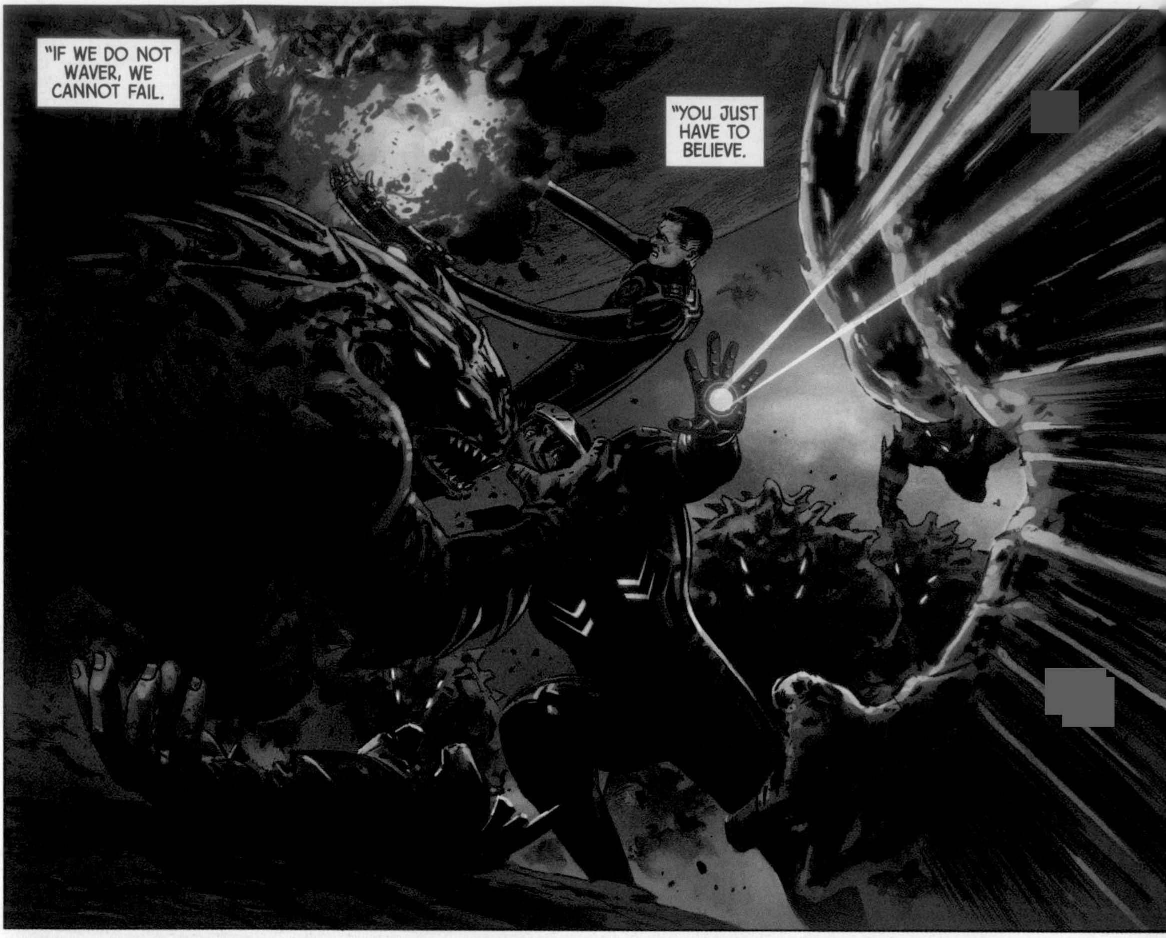
"IF WE DO NOT WAVER, WE CANNOT FAIL.
"YOU JUST HAVE TO BELIEVE.

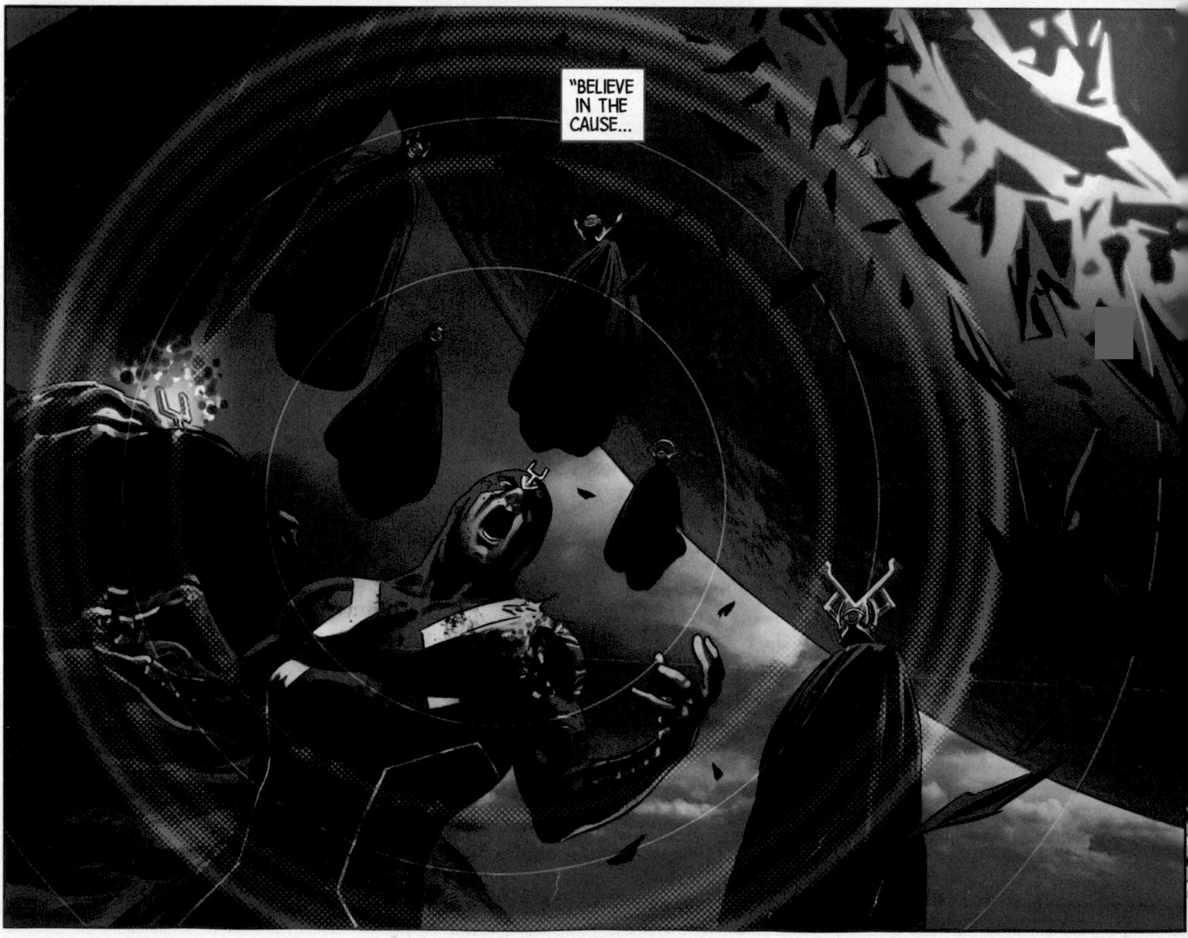
"BELIEVE IN THE CAUSE...

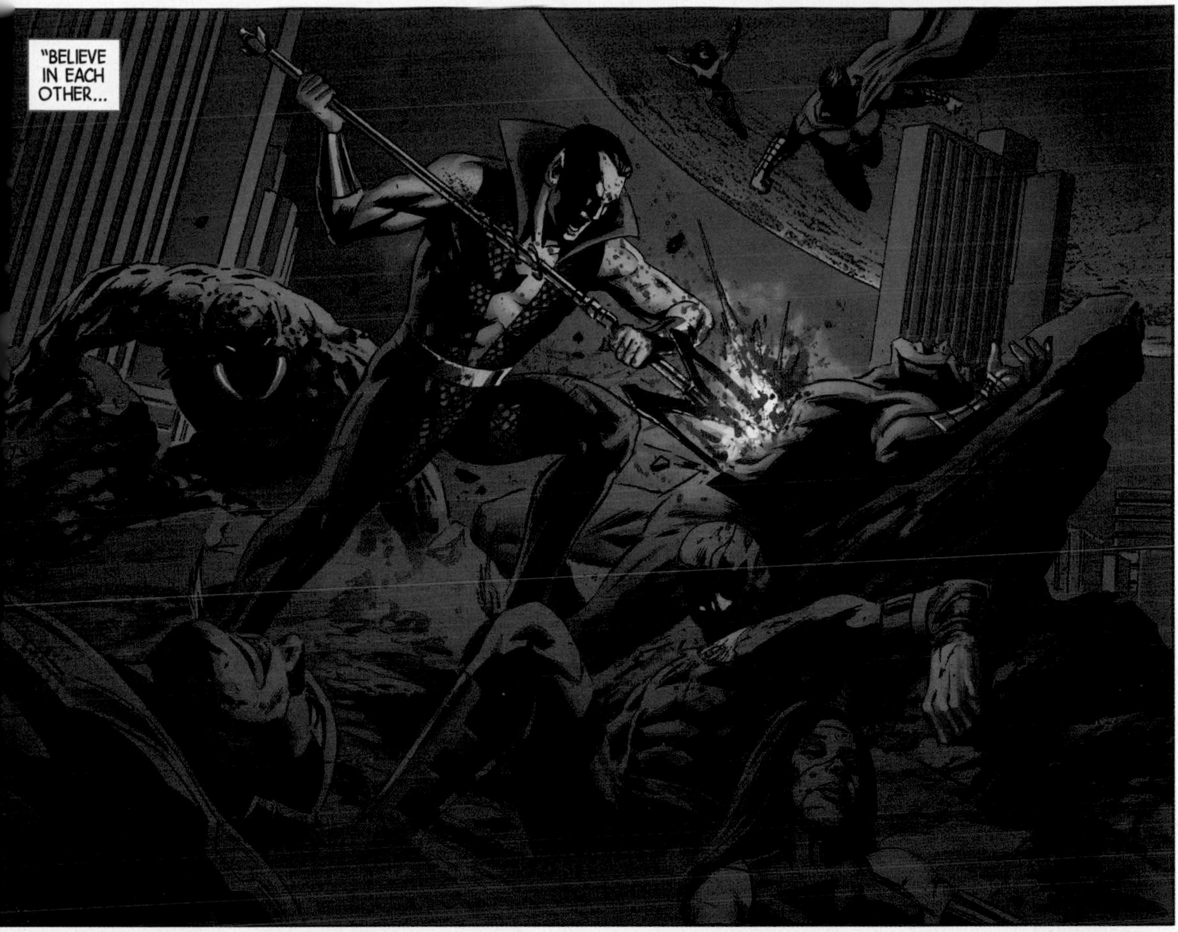
"BELIEVE IN EACH OTHER...

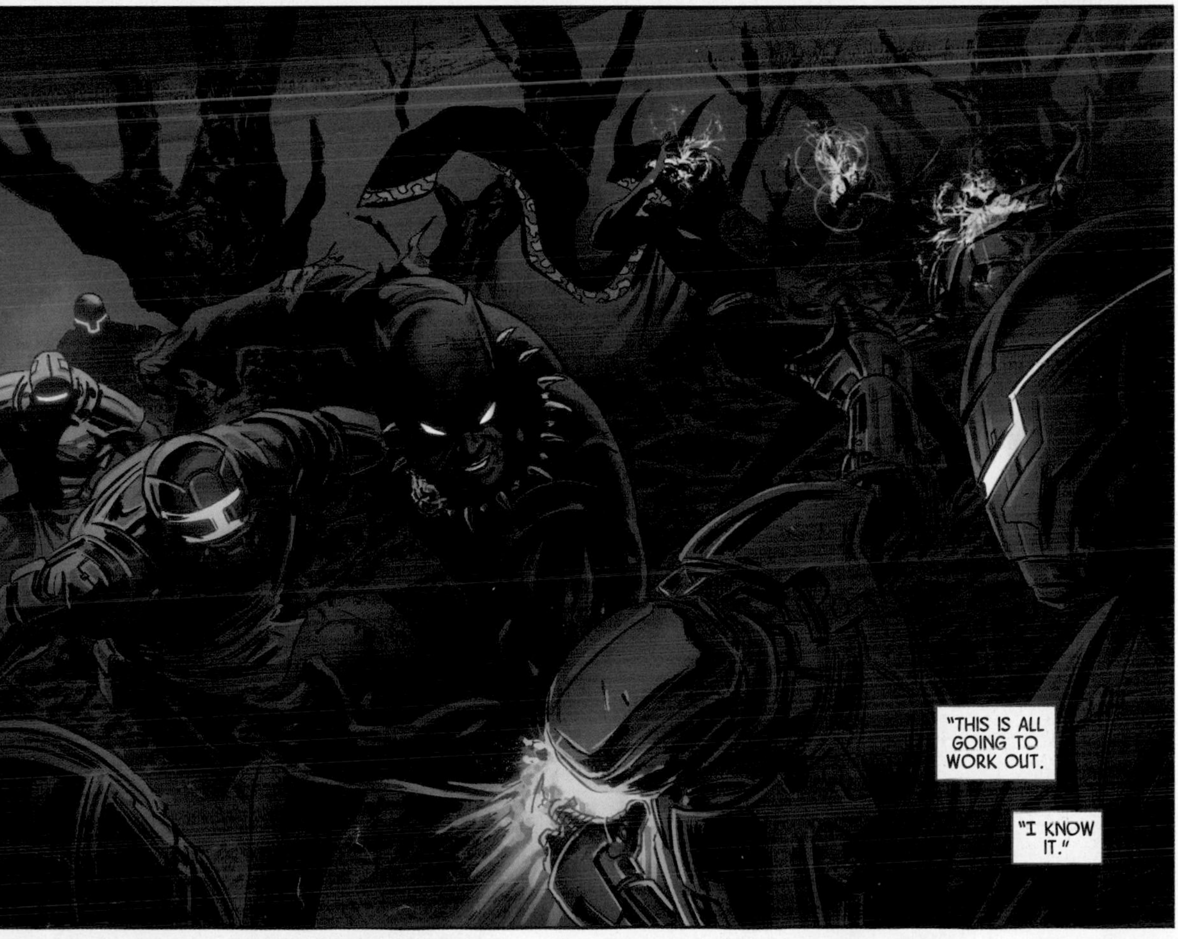
"THIS IS ALL GOING TO WORK OUT.
"I KNOW IT."

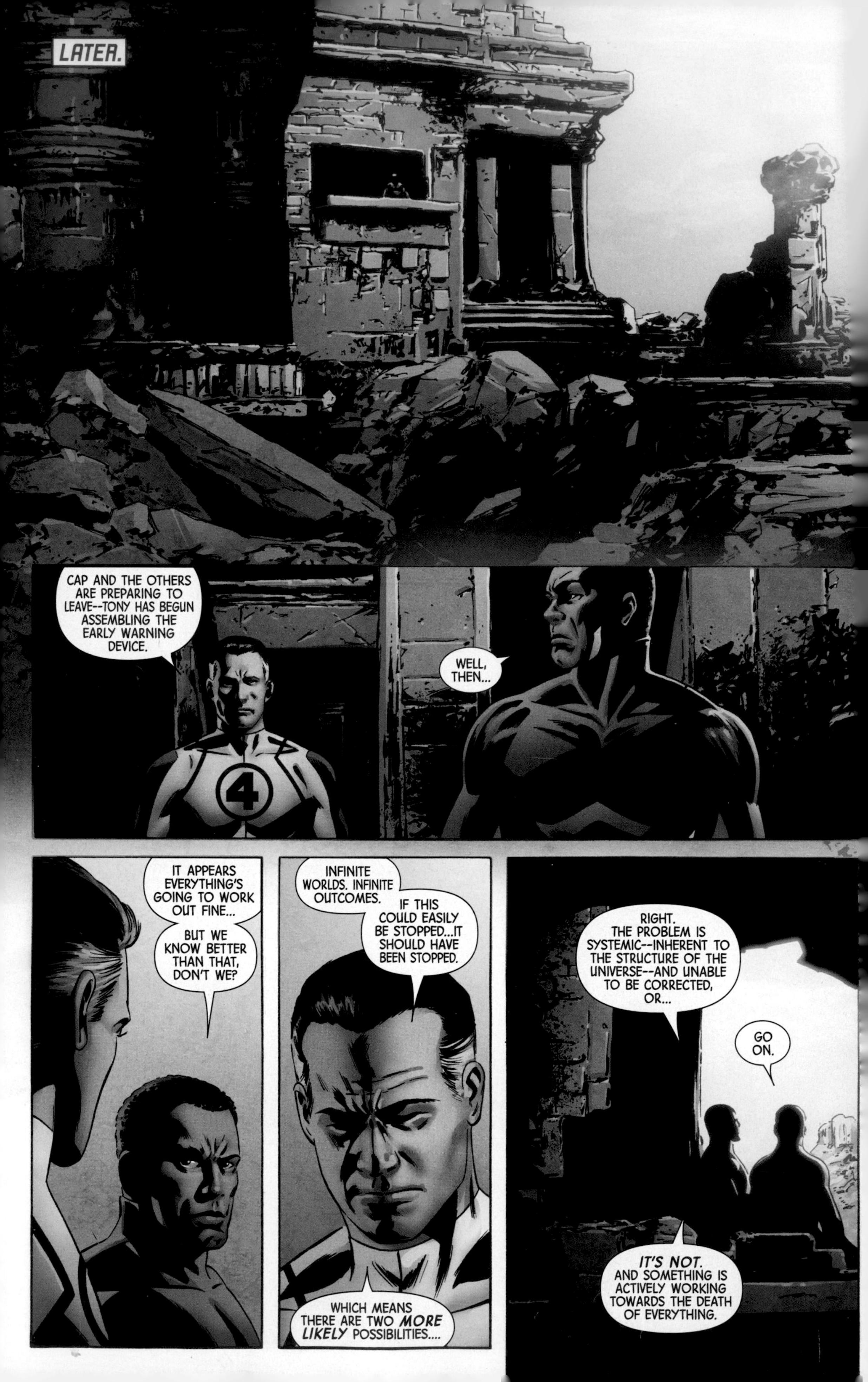
LATER.
CAP AND THE OTHERS ARE PREPARING TO LEAVE--TONY HAS BEGUN ASSEMBLING THE EARLY WARNING DEVICE.
WELL, THEN...
IT APPEARS EVERYTHING'S GOING TO WORK OUT FINE...
BUT WE KNOW BETTER THAN THAT, DON'T WE?
INFINITE WORLDS. INFINITE OUTCOMES.
IF THIS COULD EASILY BE STOPPED...IT SHOULD HAVE BEEN STOPPED.
WHICH MEANS THERE ARE TWO MORE LIKELY POSSIBILITIES....
RIGHT. THE PROBLEM IS SYSTEMIC--INHERENT TO THE STRUCTURE OF THE UNIVERSE--AND UNABLE TO BE CORRECTED, OR...
GO ON.
IT'S NOT. AND SOMETHING IS ACTIVELY WORKING TOWARDS THE DEATH OF EVERYTHING.

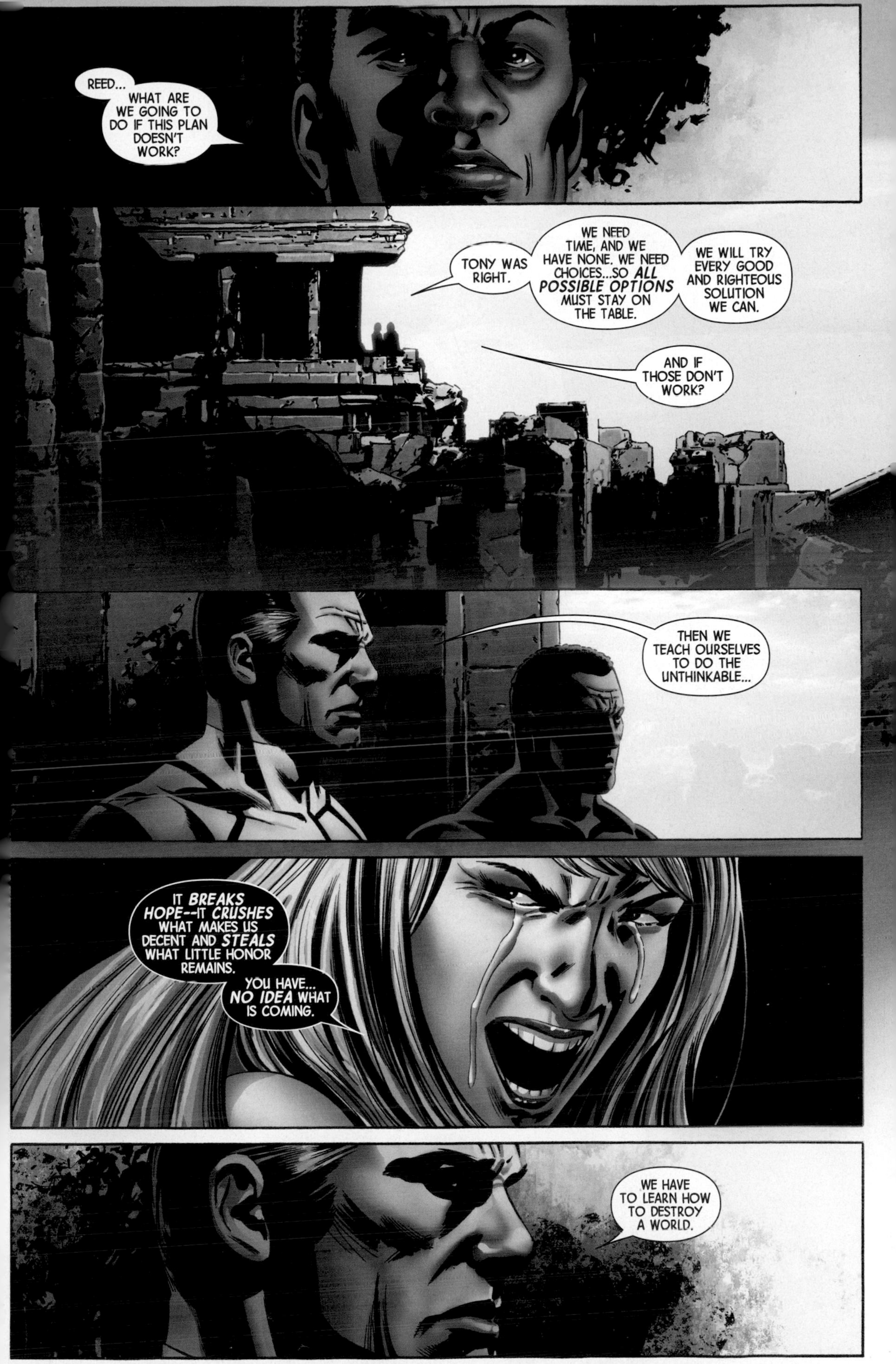
REED... WHAT ARE WE GOING TO DO IF THIS PLAN DOESN'T WORK?
TONY WAS RIGHT.
WE NEED TIME, AND WE HAVE NONE. WE NEED CHOICES...SO ALL POSSIBLE OPTIONS MUST STAY ON THE TABLE.
WE WILL TRY EVERY GOOD AND RIGHTEOUS SOLUTION WE CAN.
AND IF THOSE DON'T WORK?
THEN WE TEACH OURSELVES TO DO THE UNTHINKABLE...
IT BREAKS HOPE--IT CRUSHES WHAT MAKES US DECENT AND STEALS WHAT LITTLE HONOR REMAINS.
YOU HAVE... NO IDEA WHAT IS COMING.
WE HAVE TO LEARN HOW TO DESTROY A WORLD.

"INFINITY"

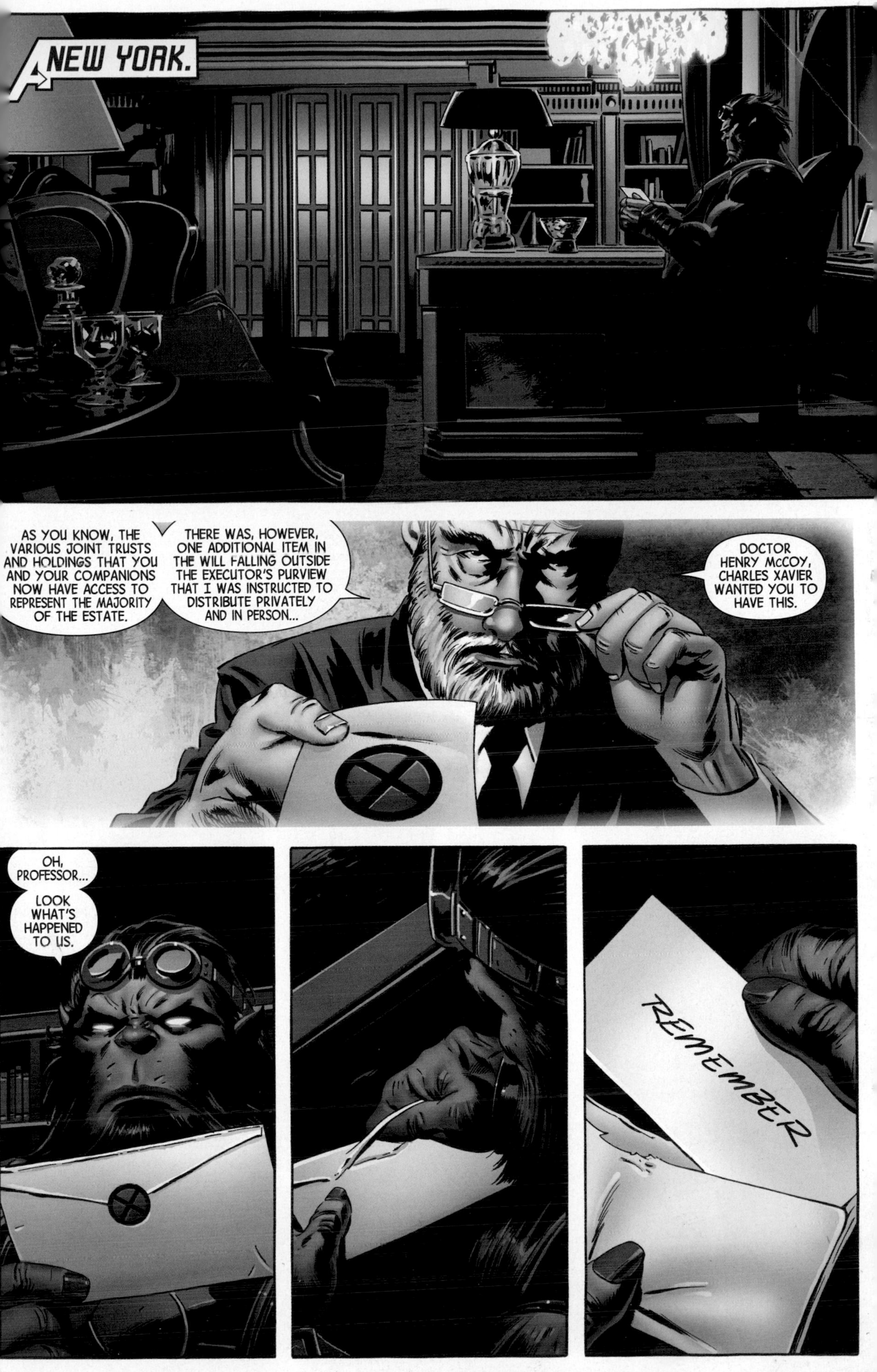
NEW YORK.
AS YOU KNOW, THE VARIOUS JOINT TRUSTS AND HOLDINGS THAT YOU AND YOUR COMPANIONS NOW HAVE ACCESS TO REPRESENT THE MAJORITY OF THE ESTATE.
THERE WAS, HOWEVER, ONE ADDITIONAL ITEM IN THE WILL FALLING OUTSIDE THE EXECUTOR'S PURVIEW THAT I WAS INSTRUCTED TO DISTRIBUTE PRIVATELY AND IN PERSON...
DOCTOR HENRY McCOY, CHARLES XAVIER WANTED YOU TO HAVE THIS.
OH, PROFESSOR...
LOOK WHAT'S HAPPENED TO US.
REMEMBER

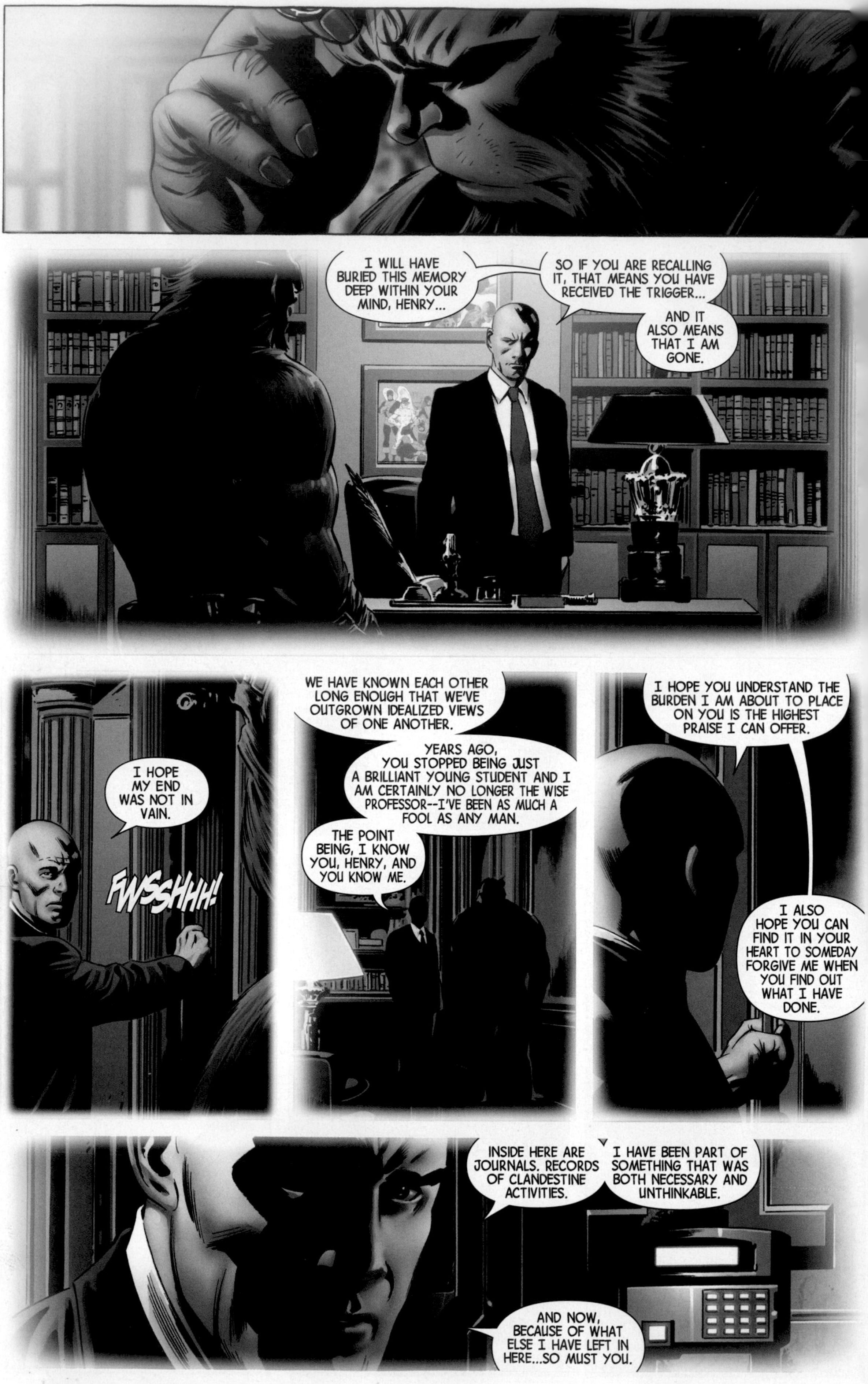
I WILL HAVE BURIED THIS MEMORY DEEP WITHIN YOUR MIND, HENRY...
SO IF YOU ARE RECALLING IT, THAT MEANS YOU HAVE RECEIVED THE TRIGGER...
AND IT ALSO MEANS THAT I AM GONE.
I HOPE MY END WAS NOT IN VAIN.
FWSSHHH!
WE HAVE KNOWN EACH OTHER LONG ENOUGH THAT WE'VE OUTGROWN IDEALIZED VIEWS OF ONE ANOTHER.
YEARS AGO, YOU STOPPED BEING JUST A BRILLIANT YOUNG STUDENT AND I AM CERTAINLY NO LONGER THE WISE PROFESSOR--I'VE BEEN AS MUCH A FOOL AS ANY MAN.
THE POINT BEING, I KNOW YOU, HENRY, AND YOU KNOW ME.
I HOPE YOU UNDERSTAND THE BURDEN I AM ABOUT TO PLACE ON YOU IS THE HIGHEST PRAISE I CAN OFFER.
I ALSO HOPE YOU CAN FIND IT IN YOUR HEART TO SOMEDAY FORGIVE ME WHEN YOU FIND OUT WHAT I HAVE DONE.
INSIDE HERE ARE JOURNALS. RECORDS OF CLANDESTINE ACTIVITIES.
I HAVE BEEN PART OF SOMETHING THAT WAS BOTH NECESSARY AND UNTHINKABLE.
AND NOW, BECAUSE OF WHAT ELSE I HAVE LEFT IN HERE...SO MUST YOU.

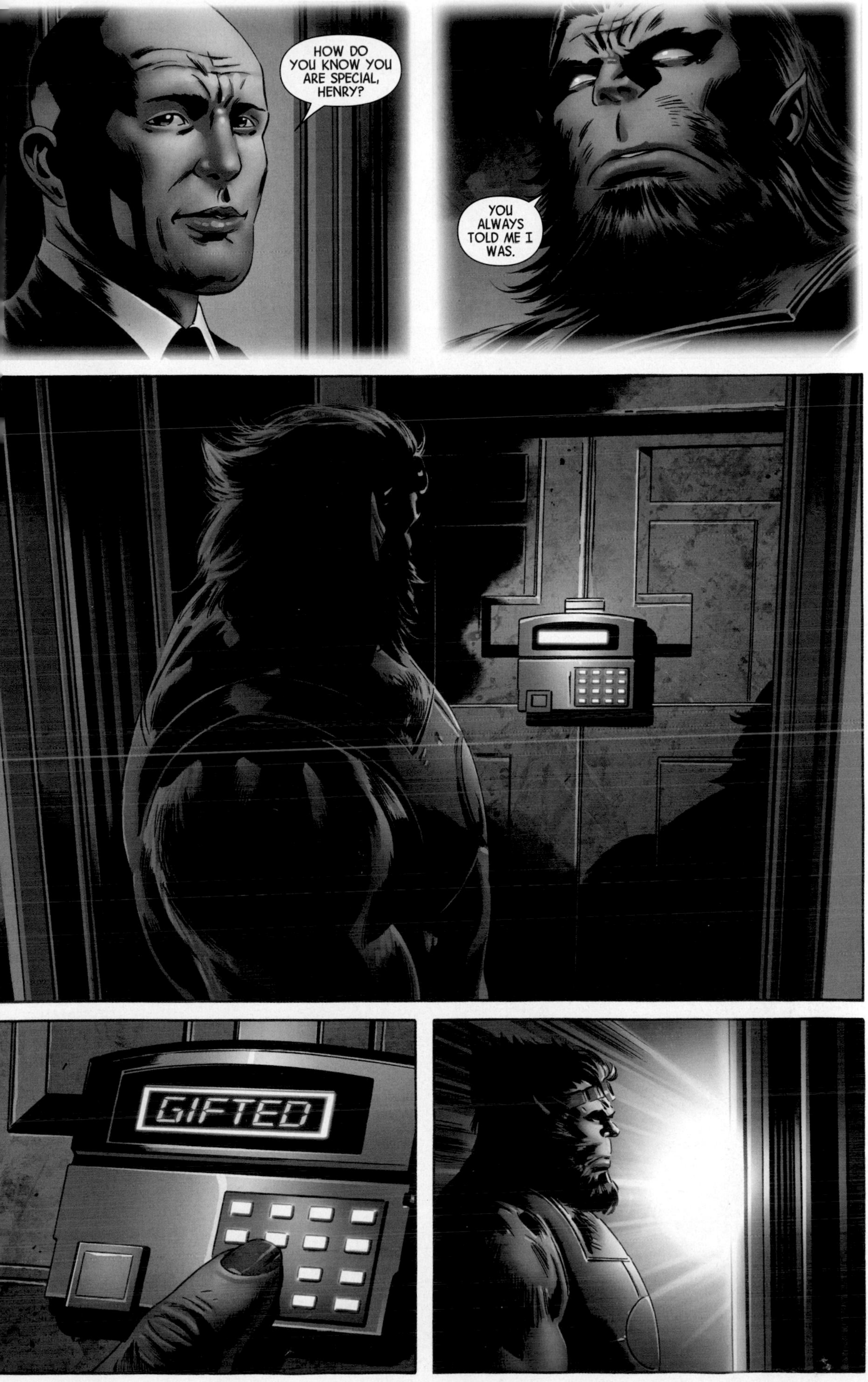
HOW DO YOU KNOW YOU ARE SPECIAL, HENRY?
YOU ALWAYS TOLD ME I WAS.
GIFTED

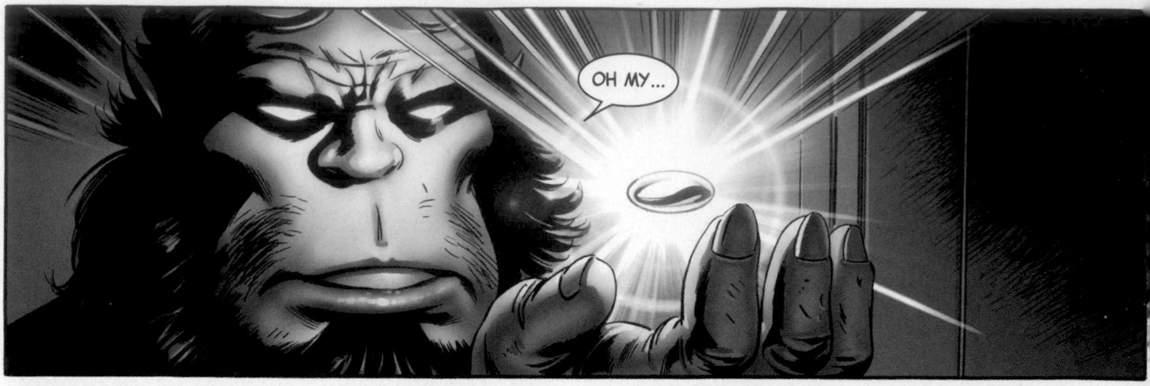
OH MY...

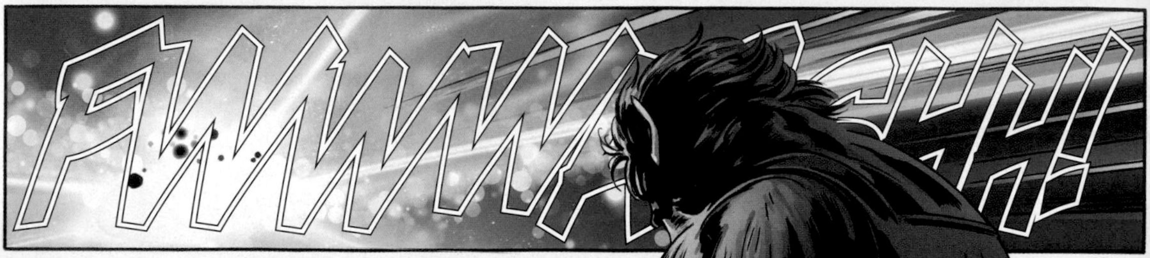

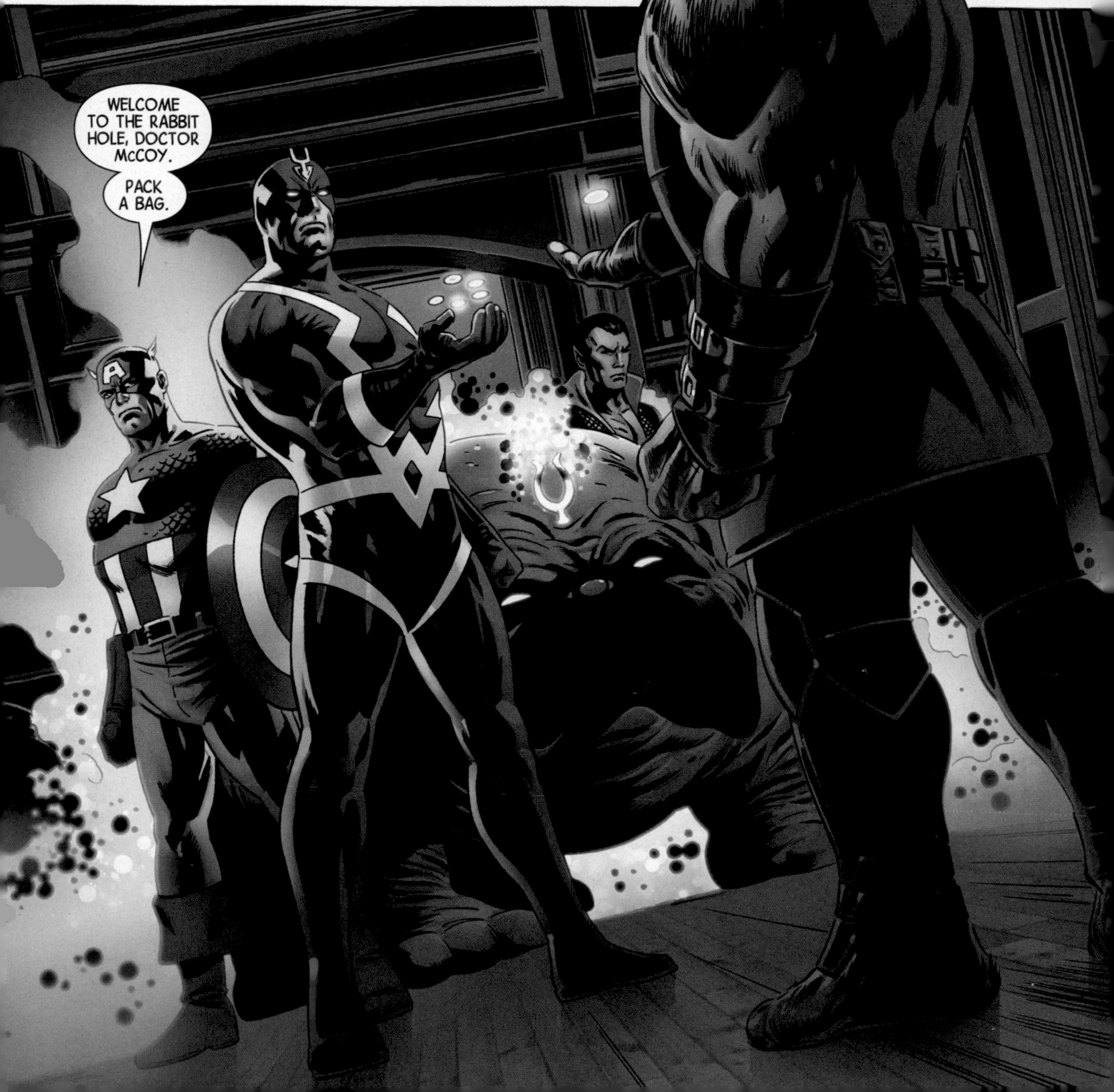
WELCOME TO THE RABBIT HOLE, DOCTOR McCOY.
PACK A BAG.

YOU'RE GOING TO FEEL A SLIGHT PINCH.

YEEEOOW!

COME NOW, HENRY...YOU'RE EMBARRASSING YOURSELF.

THE DEVICE WE'RE PLACING IN YOUR PALM SERVES SEVERAL FUNCTIONS, DOCTOR MCCOY.

THE FIRST IS AS A KIND OF LIMITED COMMUNICATION DEVICE--AN ALERT SYSTEM, IF YOU WILL.

THAT'S IT, STEPHEN...YOU CAN CLOSE HIM UP NOW.

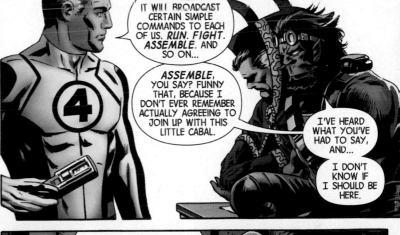

IT WILL BROADCAST CERTAIN SIMPLE COMMANDS TO EACH OF US. RUN. FIGHT. ASSEMBLE. AND SO ON...

ASSEMBLE, YOU SAY? FUNNY THAT, BECAUSE I DON'T EVER REMEMBER ACTUALLY AGREEING TO JOIN UP WITH THIS LITTLE CABAL.

I'VE HEARD WHAT YOU'VE HAD TO SAY, AND...

I DON'T KNOW IF I SHOULD BE HERE.

THE BEAST MAKES A GOOD POINT, RICHARDS. WE SHOULD TAKE WHAT WE NEED AND SEND HIM ON HIS WAY.

THIS ONE LACKS THE CONSTITUTION FOR HARD DECISIONS.

THE PROFESSOR LEFT THE GEM FOR ME-- ME, NOT YOU, NAMOR.

HE DID IT FOR A REASON.

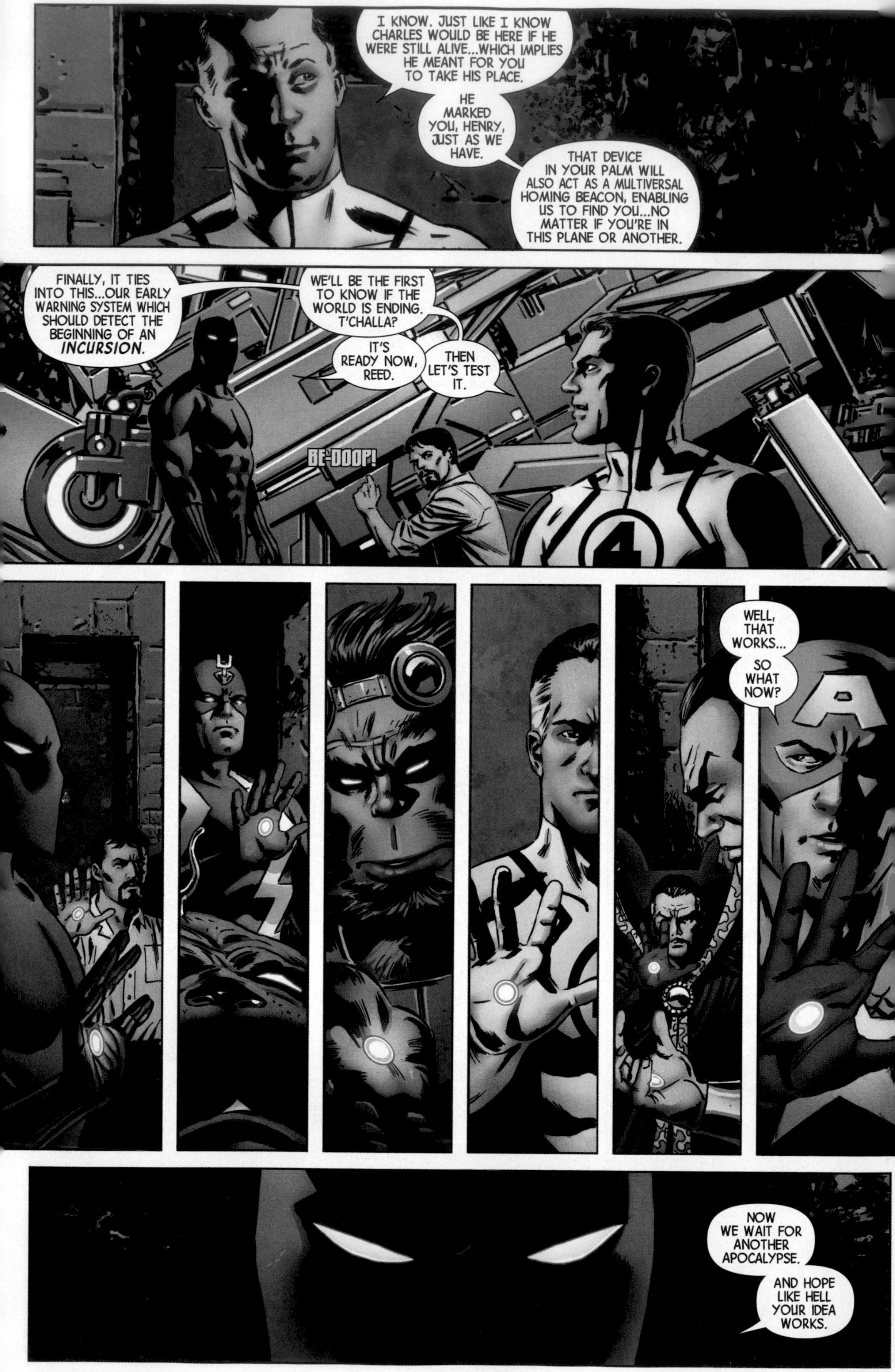
I KNOW. JUST LIKE I KNOW CHARLES WOULD BE HERE IF HE WERE STILL ALIVE...WHICH IMPLIES HE MEANT FOR YOU TO TAKE HIS PLACE.
HE MARKED YOU, HENRY, JUST AS WE HAVE.
THAT DEVICE IN YOUR PALM WILL ALSO ACT AS A MULTIVERSAL HOMING BEACON, ENABLING US TO FIND YOU...NO MATTER IF YOU'RE IN THIS PLANE OR ANOTHER.
FINALLY, IT TIES INTO THIS...OUR EARLY WARNING SYSTEM WHICH SHOULD DETECT THE BEGINNING OF AN INCURSION.
WE'LL BE THE FIRST TO KNOW IF THE WORLD IS ENDING. T'CHALLA?
IT'S READY NOW, REED.
THEN LET'S TEST IT.
BE-DOOP!
WELL, THAT WORKS...
SO WHAT NOW?
NOW WE WAIT FOR ANOTHER APOCALYPSE.
AND HOPE LIKE HELL YOUR IDEA WORKS.

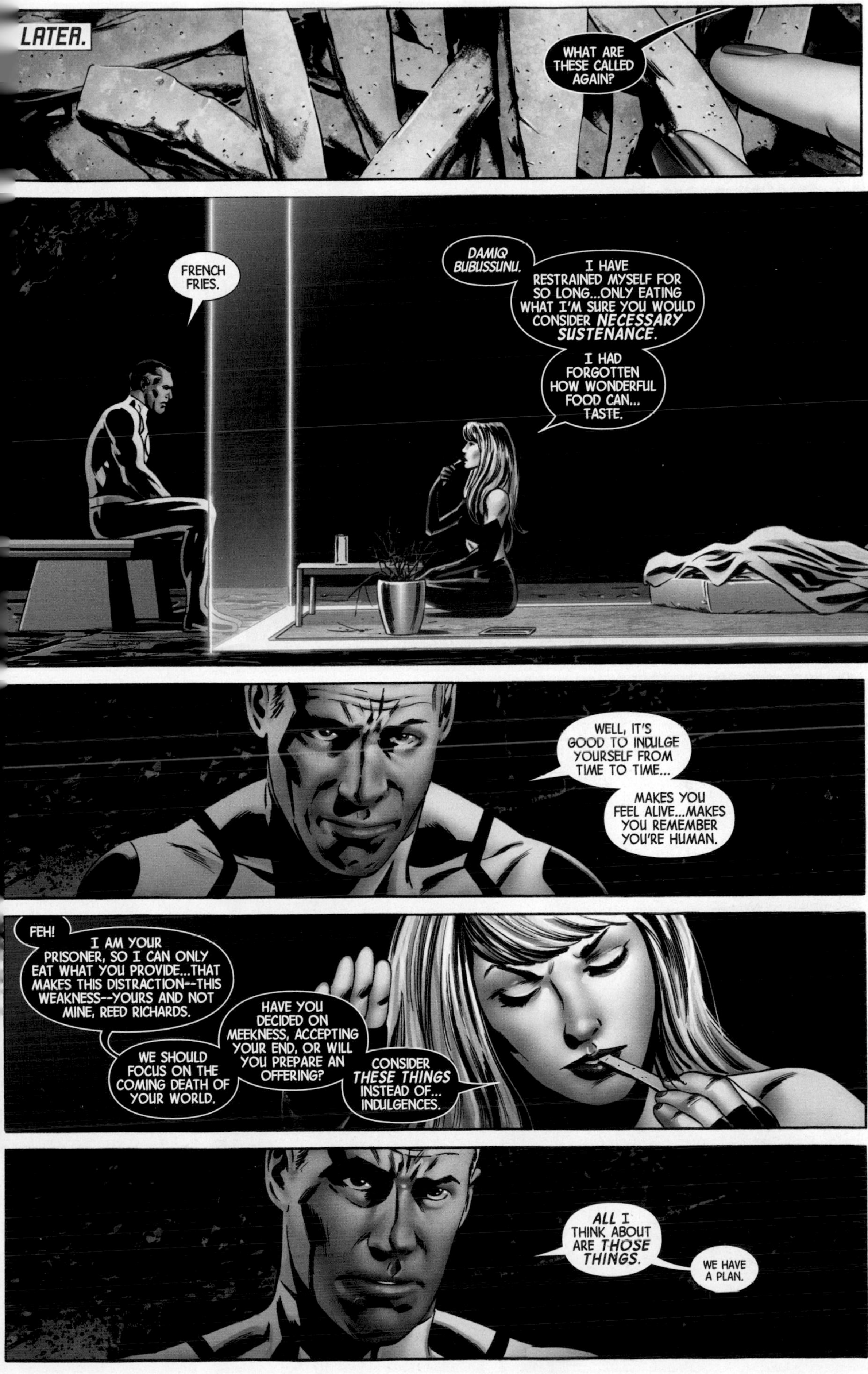
LATER.
WHAT ARE THESE CALLED AGAIN?
FRENCH FRIES.
DAMIQ BUBUSSUNU.
I HAVE RESTRAINED MYSELF FOR SO LONG...ONLY EATING WHAT I'M SURE YOU WOULD CONSIDER NECESSARY SUSTENANCE.
I HAD FORGOTTEN HOW WONDERFUL FOOD CAN... TASTE.
WELL, IT'S GOOD TO INDULGE YOURSELF FROM TIME TO TIME...
MAKES YOU FEEL ALIVE...MAKES YOU REMEMBER YOU'RE HUMAN.
FEH!
I AM YOUR PRISONER, SO I CAN ONLY EAT WHAT YOU PROVIDE...THAT MAKES THIS DISTRACTION--THIS WEAKNESS--YOURS AND NOT MINE, REED RICHARDS.
WE SHOULD FOCUS ON THE COMING DEATH OF YOUR WORLD.
HAVE YOU DECIDED ON MEEKNESS, ACCEPTING YOUR END, OR WILL YOU PREPARE AN OFFERING?
CONSIDER THESE THINGS INSTEAD OF... INDULGENCES.
ALL I THINK ABOUT ARE THOSE THINGS.
WE HAVE A PLAN.

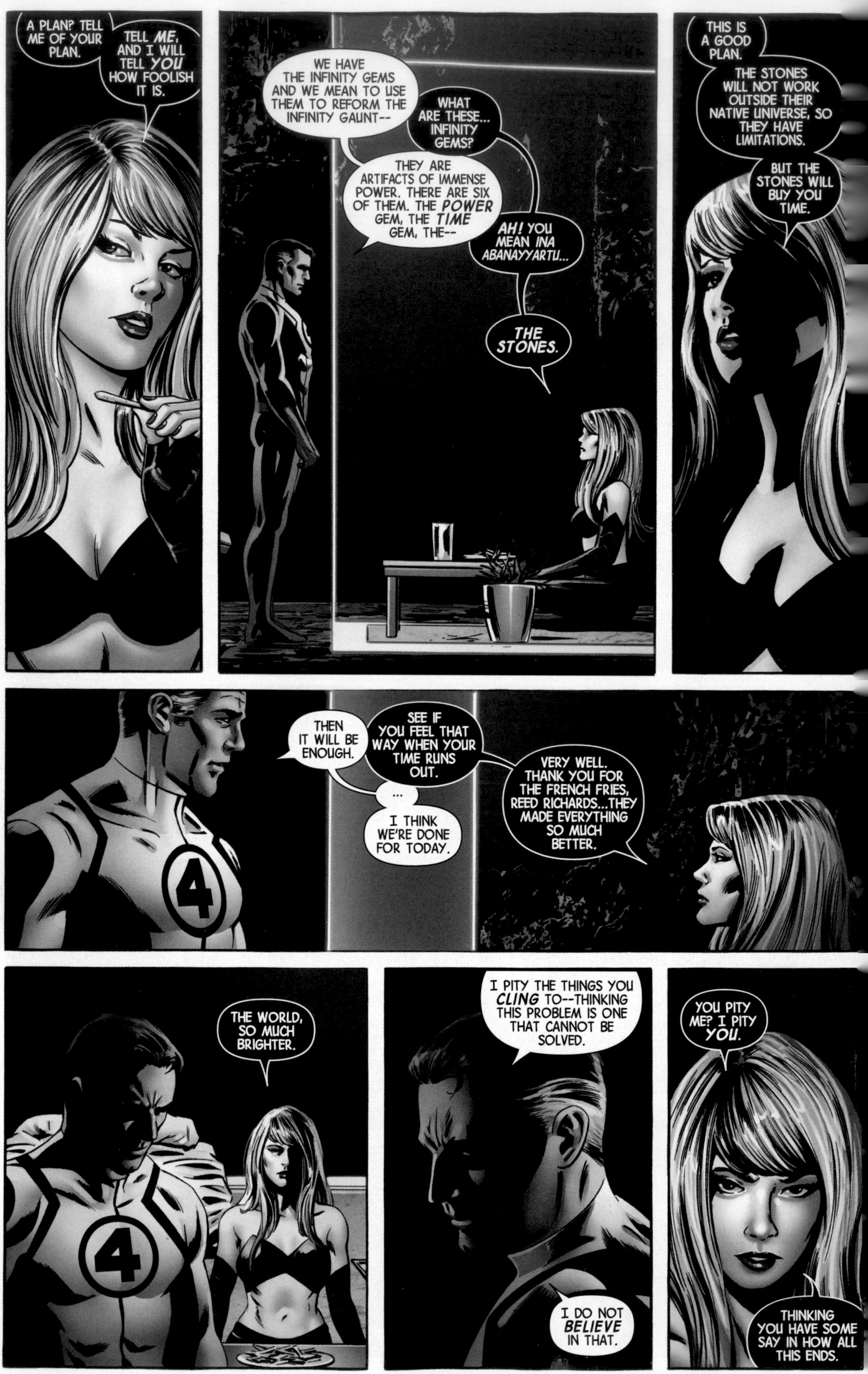
A PLAN? TELL ME OF YOUR PLAN.
TELL ME, AND I WILL TELL YOU HOW FOOLISH IT IS.
WE HAVE THE INFINITY GEMS AND WE MEAN TO USE THEM TO REFORM THE INFINITY GAUNT--
WHAT ARE THESE... INFINITY GEMS?
THEY ARE ARTIFACTS OF IMMENSE POWER. THERE ARE SIX OF THEM. THE POWER GEM, THE TIME GEM, THE--
AH! YOU MEAN INA ABANAYYARTU...
THE STONES.
THIS IS A GOOD PLAN.
THE STONES WILL NOT WORK OUTSIDE THEIR NATIVE UNIVERSE, SO THEY HAVE LIMITATIONS.
BUT THE STONES WILL BUY YOU TIME.
THEN IT WILL BE ENOUGH.
SEE IF YOU FEEL THAT WAY WHEN YOUR TIME RUNS OUT.
...
I THINK WE'RE DONE FOR TODAY.
VERY WELL. THANK YOU FOR THE FRENCH FRIES, REED RICHARDS...THEY MADE EVERYTHING SO MUCH BETTER.
THE WORLD, SO MUCH BRIGHTER.
I PITY THE THINGS YOU CLING TO--THINKING THIS PROBLEM IS ONE THAT CANNOT BE SOLVED.
I DO NOT BELIEVE IN THAT.
YOU PITY ME? I PITY YOU.
THINKING YOU HAVE SOME SAY IN HOW ALL THIS ENDS.

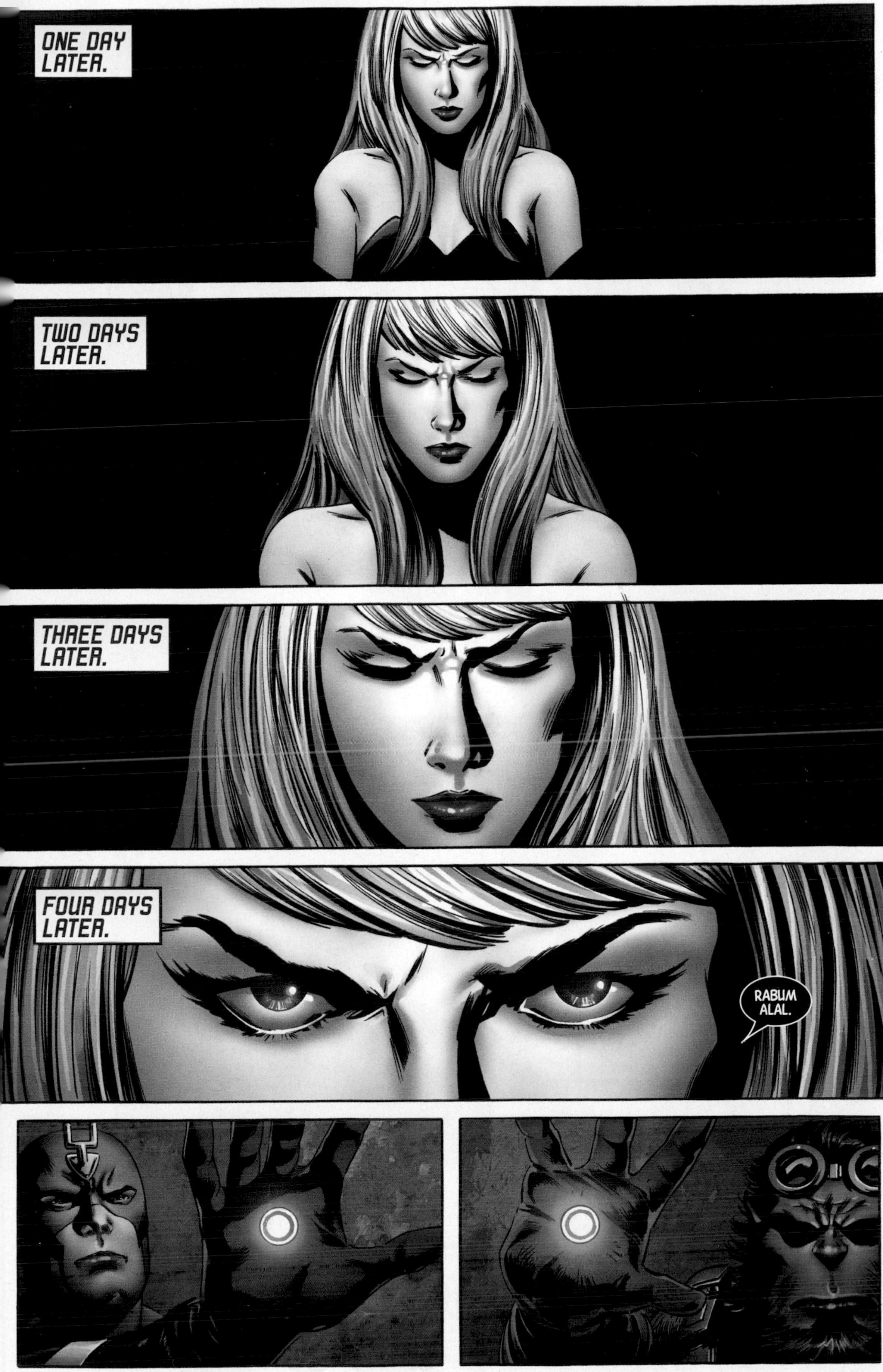
ONE DAY LATER.
TWO DAYS LATER.
THREE DAYS LATER.
FOUR DAYS LATER.
RABUM ALAL.

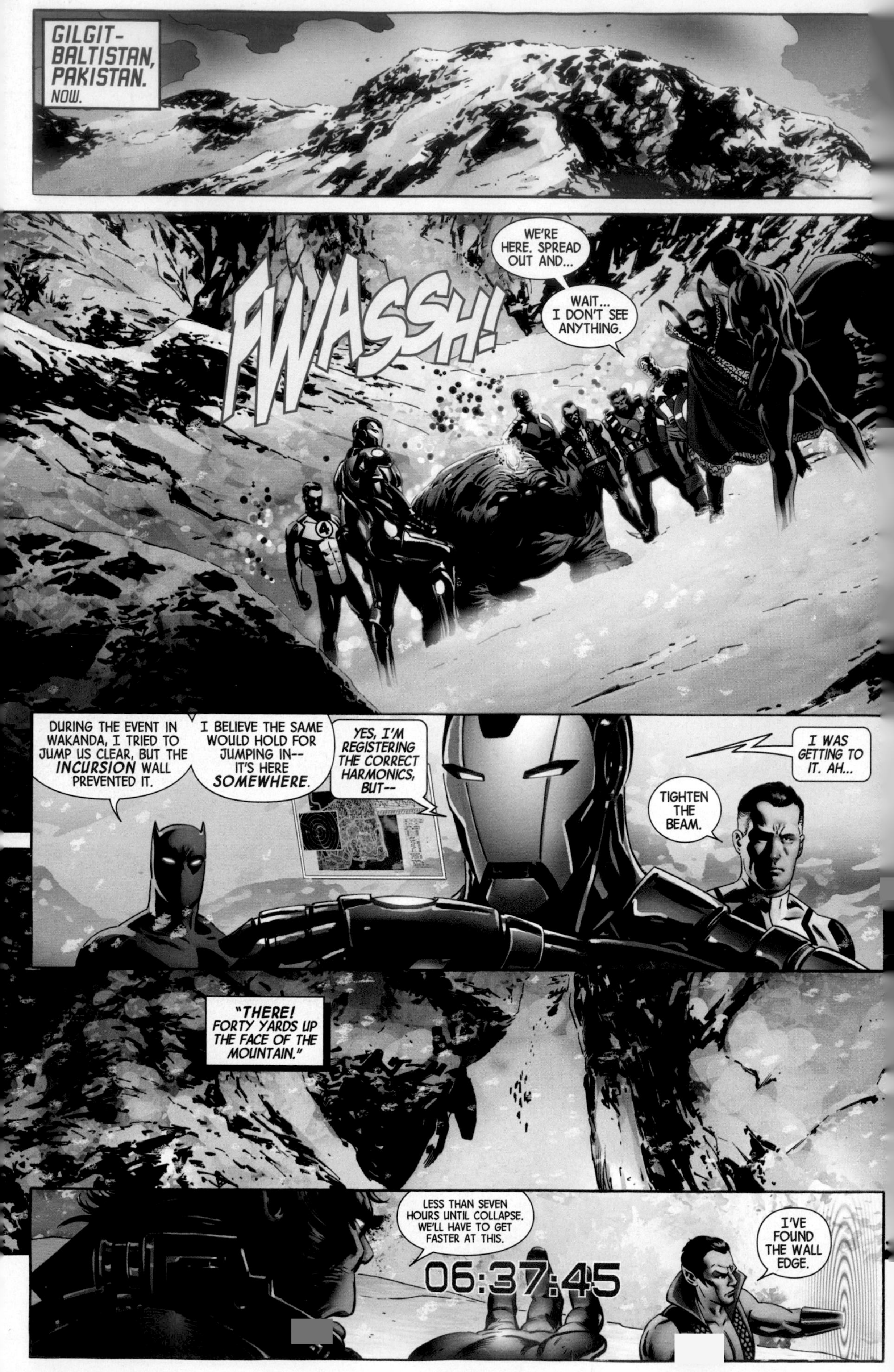
GILGIT-BALTISTAN, PAKISTAN. NOW.
FWASSH!
WE'RE HERE. SPREAD OUT AND...
WAIT... I DON'T SEE ANYTHING.
DURING THE EVENT IN WAKANDA, I TRIED TO JUMP US CLEAR, BUT THE INCURSION WALL PREVENTED IT.
I BELIEVE THE SAME WOULD HOLD FOR JUMPING IN-- IT'S HERE SOMEWHERE.
YES, I'M REGISTERING THE CORRECT HARMONICS, BUT--
I WAS GETTING TO IT. AH...
TIGHTEN THE BEAM.
"THERE! FORTY YARDS UP THE FACE OF THE MOUNTAIN."
LESS THAN SEVEN HOURS UNTIL COLLAPSE. WE'LL HAVE TO GET FASTER AT THIS.
06:37:45
I'VE FOUND THE WALL EDGE.

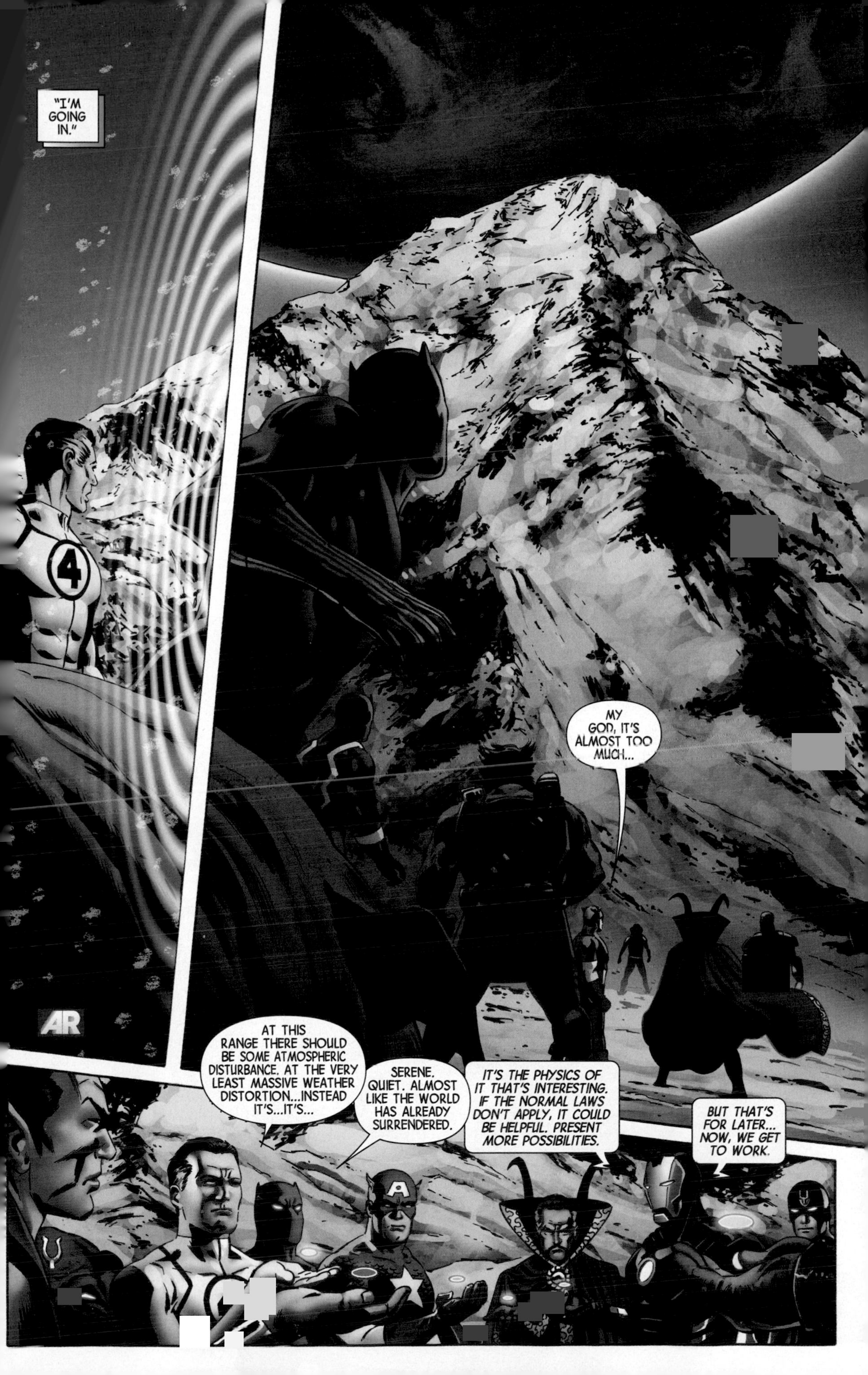
"I'M GOING IN."
MY GOD, IT'S ALMOST TOO MUCH...
AT THIS RANGE THERE SHOULD BE SOME ATMOSPHERIC DISTURBANCE. AT THE VERY LEAST MASSIVE WEATHER DISTORTION...INSTEAD IT'S...IT'S...
SERENE. QUIET. ALMOST LIKE THE WORLD HAS ALREADY SURRENDERED.
IT'S THE PHYSICS OF IT THAT'S INTERESTING. IF THE NORMAL LAWS DON'T APPLY, IT COULD BE HELPFUL. PRESENT MORE POSSIBILITIES.
BUT THAT'S FOR LATER... NOW, WE GET TO WORK.

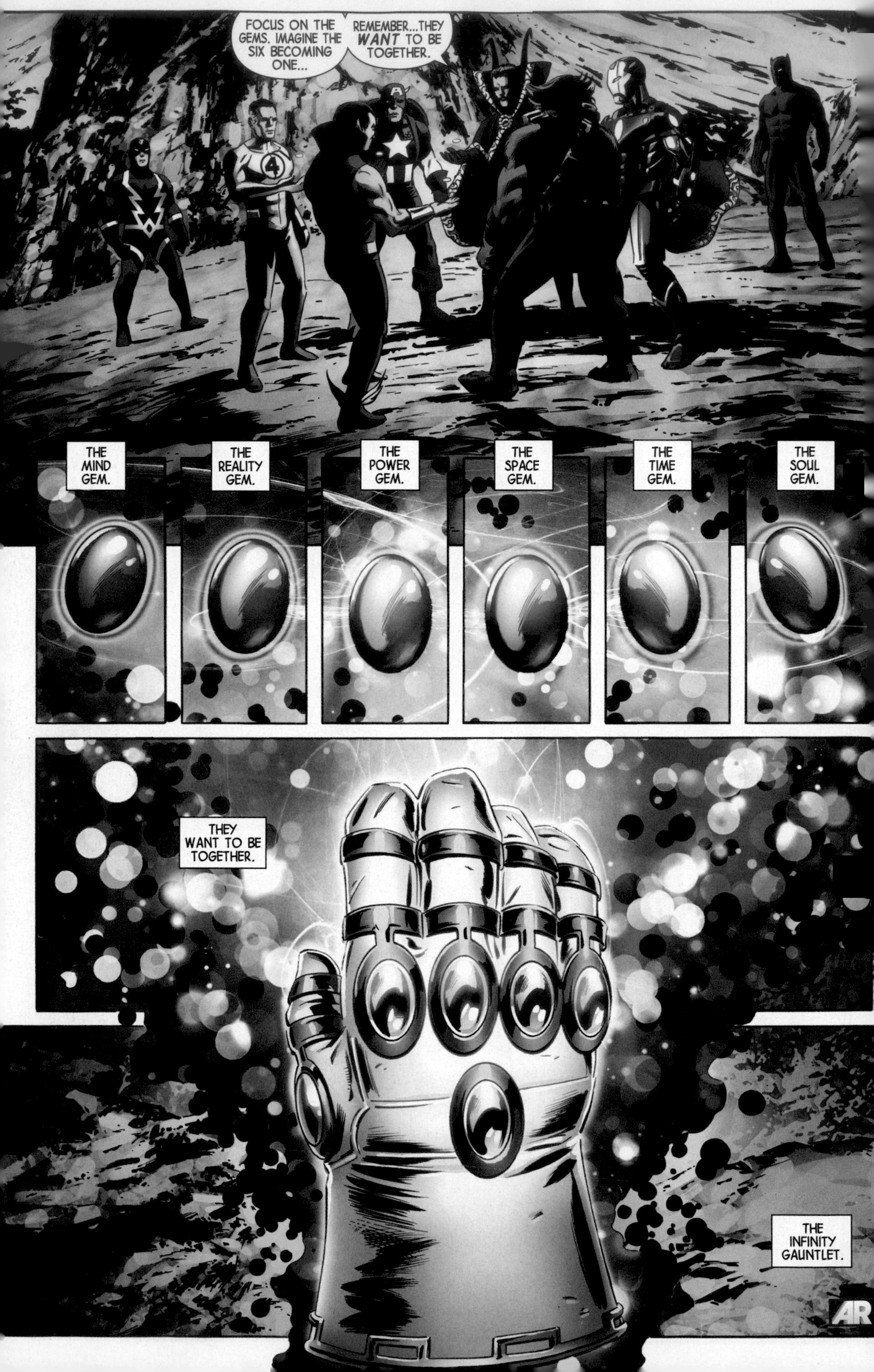

FOCUS ON THE GEMS. IMAGINE THE SIX BECOMING ONE...
REMEMBER...THEY *WANT* TO BE TOGETHER.
THE MIND GEM.
THE REALITY GEM.
THE POWER GEM.
THE SPACE GEM.
THE TIME GEM.
THE SOUL GEM.
THEY WANT TO BE TOGETHER.
THE INFINITY GAUNTLET.

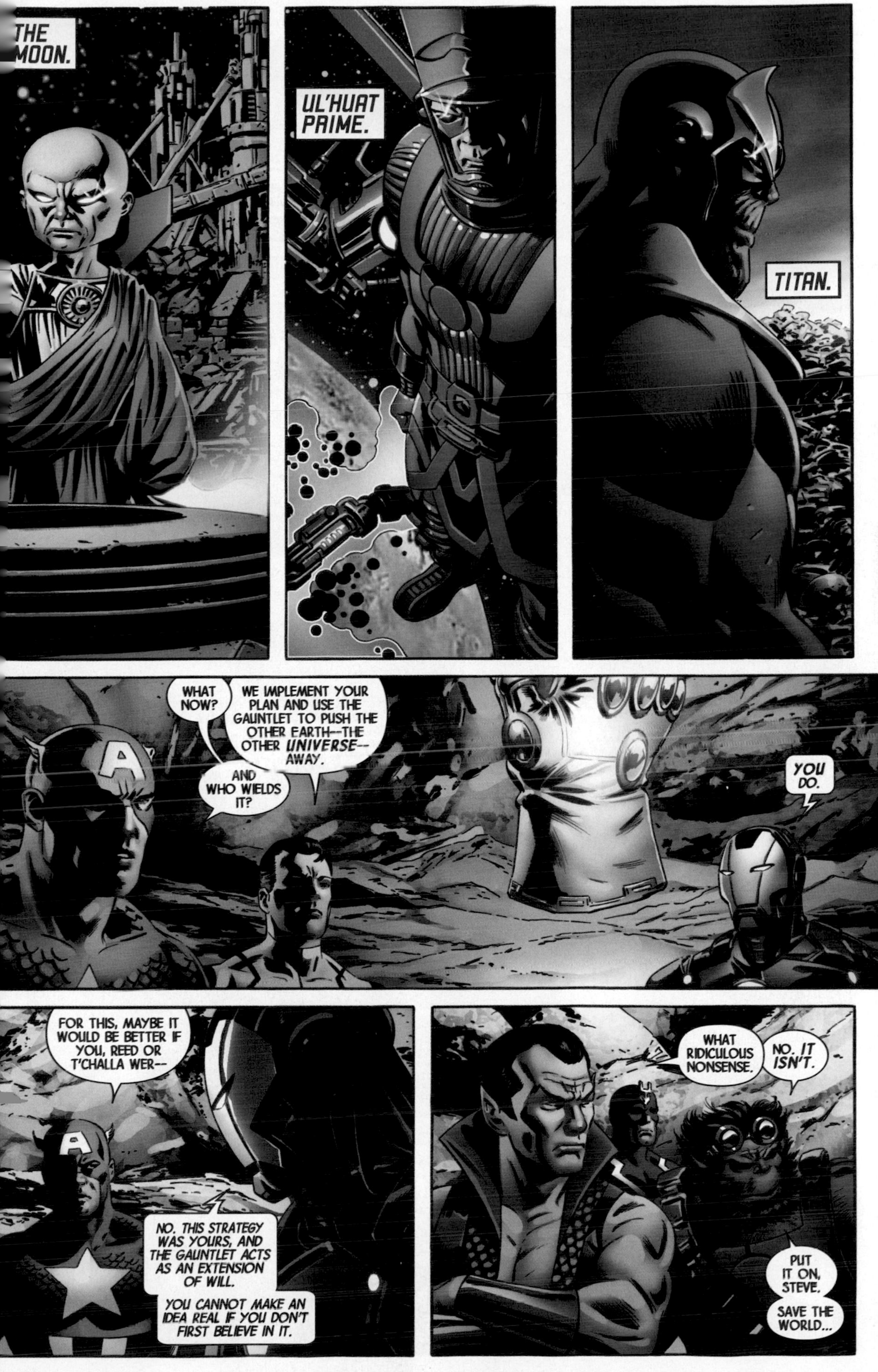
THE MOON.
UL'HUAT PRIME.
TITAN.
WHAT NOW?
WE IMPLEMENT YOUR PLAN AND USE THE GAUNTLET TO PUSH THE OTHER EARTH--THE OTHER UNIVERSE--AWAY.
AND WHO WIELDS IT?
YOU DO.
FOR THIS, MAYBE IT WOULD BE BETTER IF YOU, REED OR T'CHALLA WER--
NO. THIS STRATEGY WAS YOURS, AND THE GAUNTLET ACTS AS AN EXTENSION OF WILL.
YOU CANNOT MAKE AN IDEA REAL IF YOU DON'T FIRST BELIEVE IN IT.
WHAT RIDICULOUS NONSENSE.
NO. IT ISN'T.
PUT IT ON, STEVE.
SAVE THE WORLD...

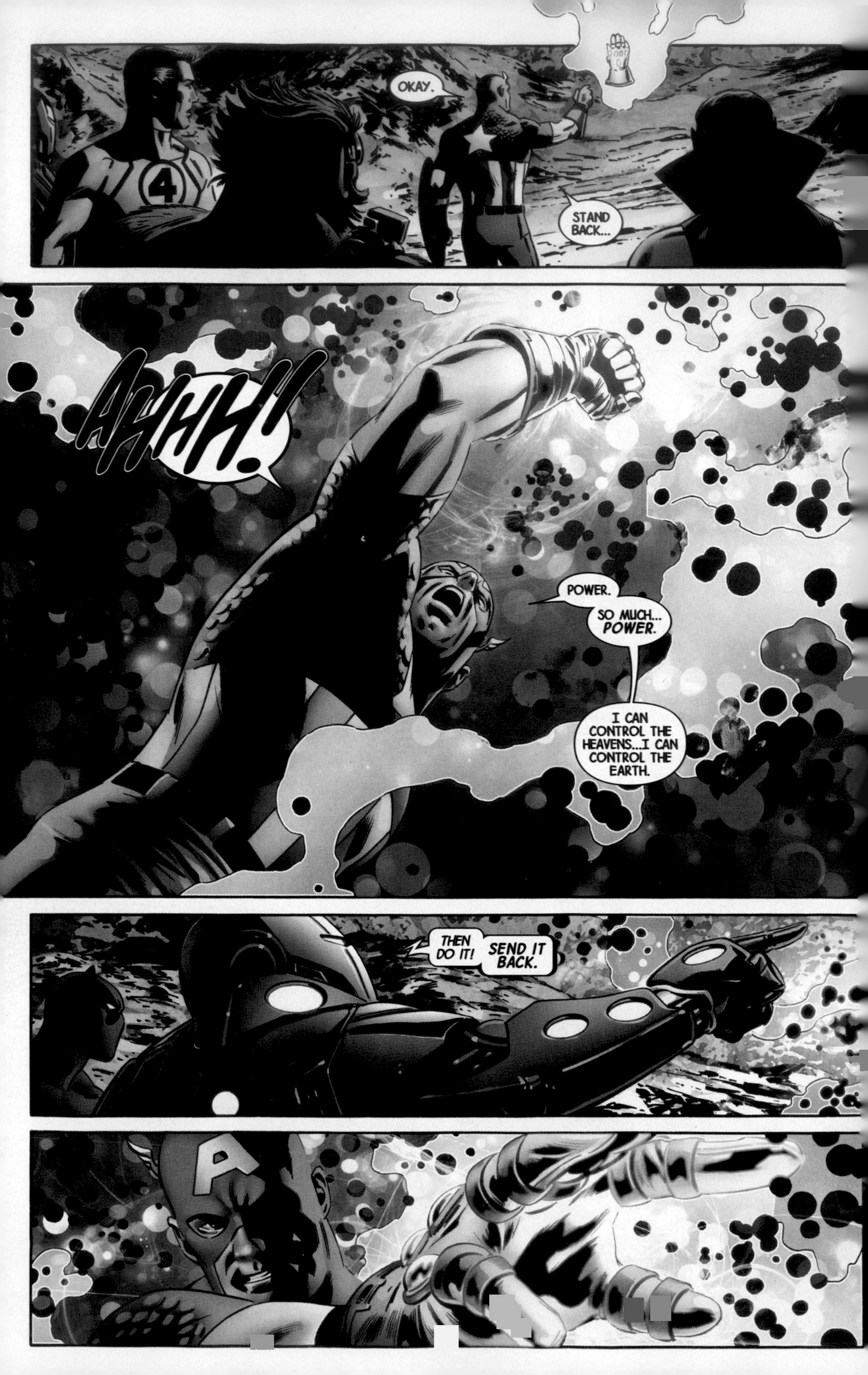
OKAY.
STAND BACK...
AHHH!
POWER.
SO MUCH... POWER.
I CAN CONTROL THE HEAVENS...I CAN CONTROL THE EARTH.
THEN DO IT!
SEND IT BACK.

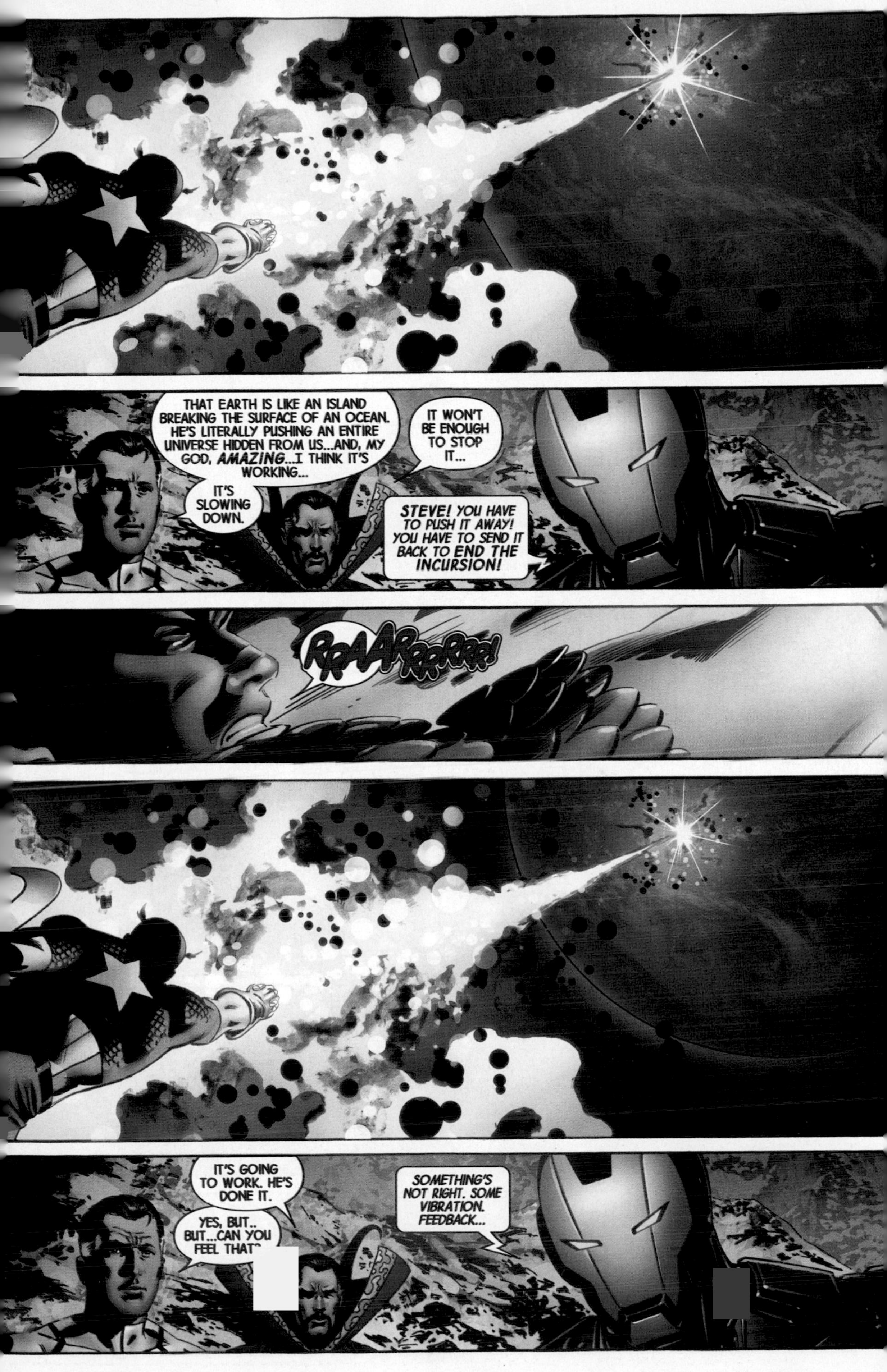
THAT EARTH IS LIKE AN ISLAND BREAKING THE SURFACE OF AN OCEAN. HE'S LITERALLY PUSHING AN ENTIRE UNIVERSE HIDDEN FROM US...AND, MY GOD, AMAZING...I THINK IT'S WORKING...
IT'S SLOWING DOWN.
IT WON'T BE ENOUGH TO STOP IT...
STEVE! YOU HAVE TO PUSH IT AWAY! YOU HAVE TO SEND IT BACK TO END THE INCURSION!
RRAAARRRRRRR!
IT'S GOING TO WORK. HE'S DONE IT.
YES, BUT.. BUT...CAN YOU FEEL THAT
SOMETHING'S NOT RIGHT. SOME VIBRATION. FEEDBACK...

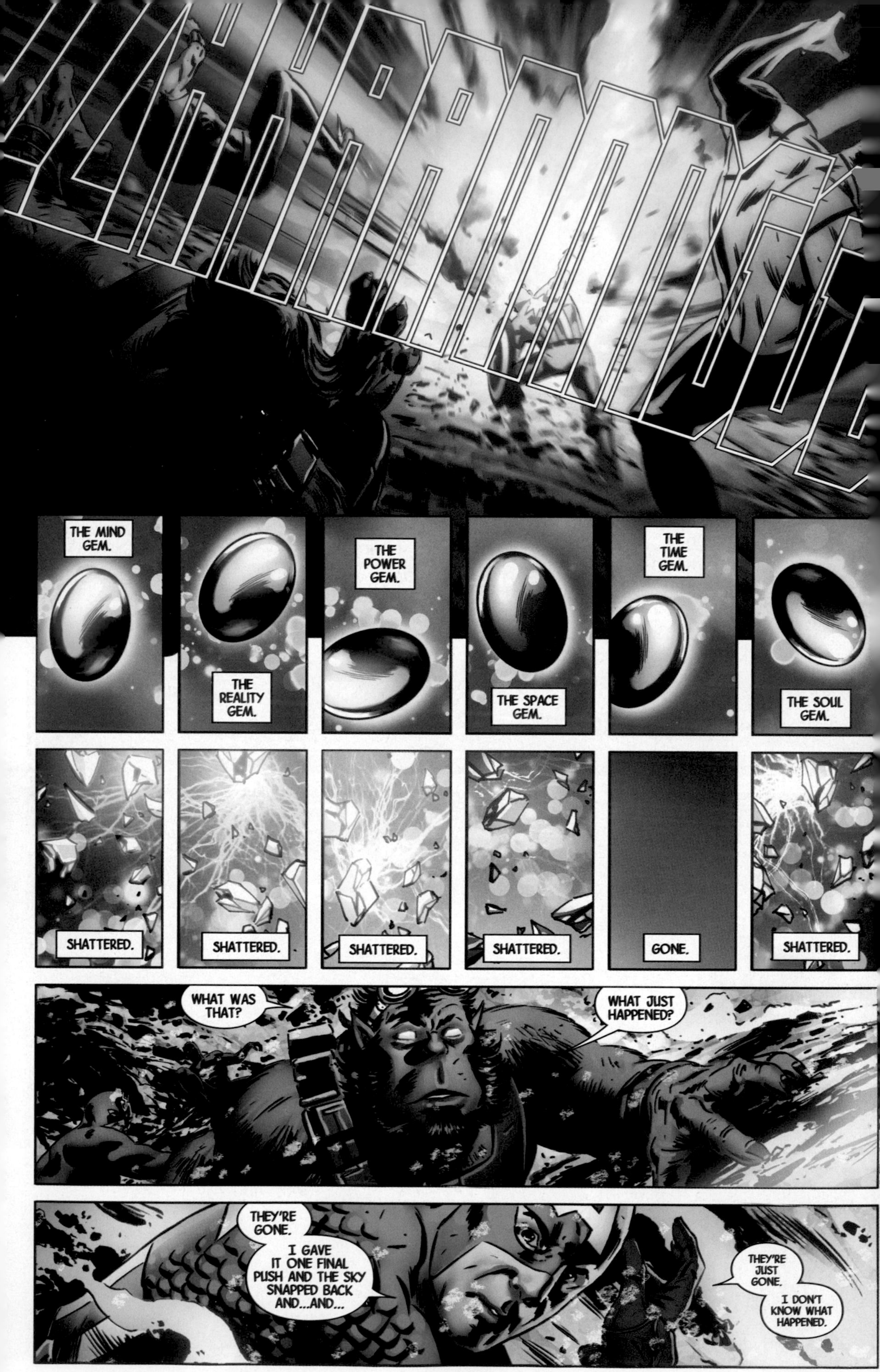
THE MIND GEM.
THE REALITY GEM.
THE POWER GEM.
THE SPACE GEM.
THE TIME GEM.
THE SOUL GEM.
SHATTERED.
SHATTERED.
SHATTERED.
SHATTERED.
GONE.
SHATTERED.
WHAT WAS THAT?
WHAT JUST HAPPENED?
THEY'RE GONE.
I GAVE IT ONE FINAL PUSH AND THE SKY SNAPPED BACK AND...AND...
THEY'RE JUST GONE.
I DON'T KNOW WHAT HAPPENED.

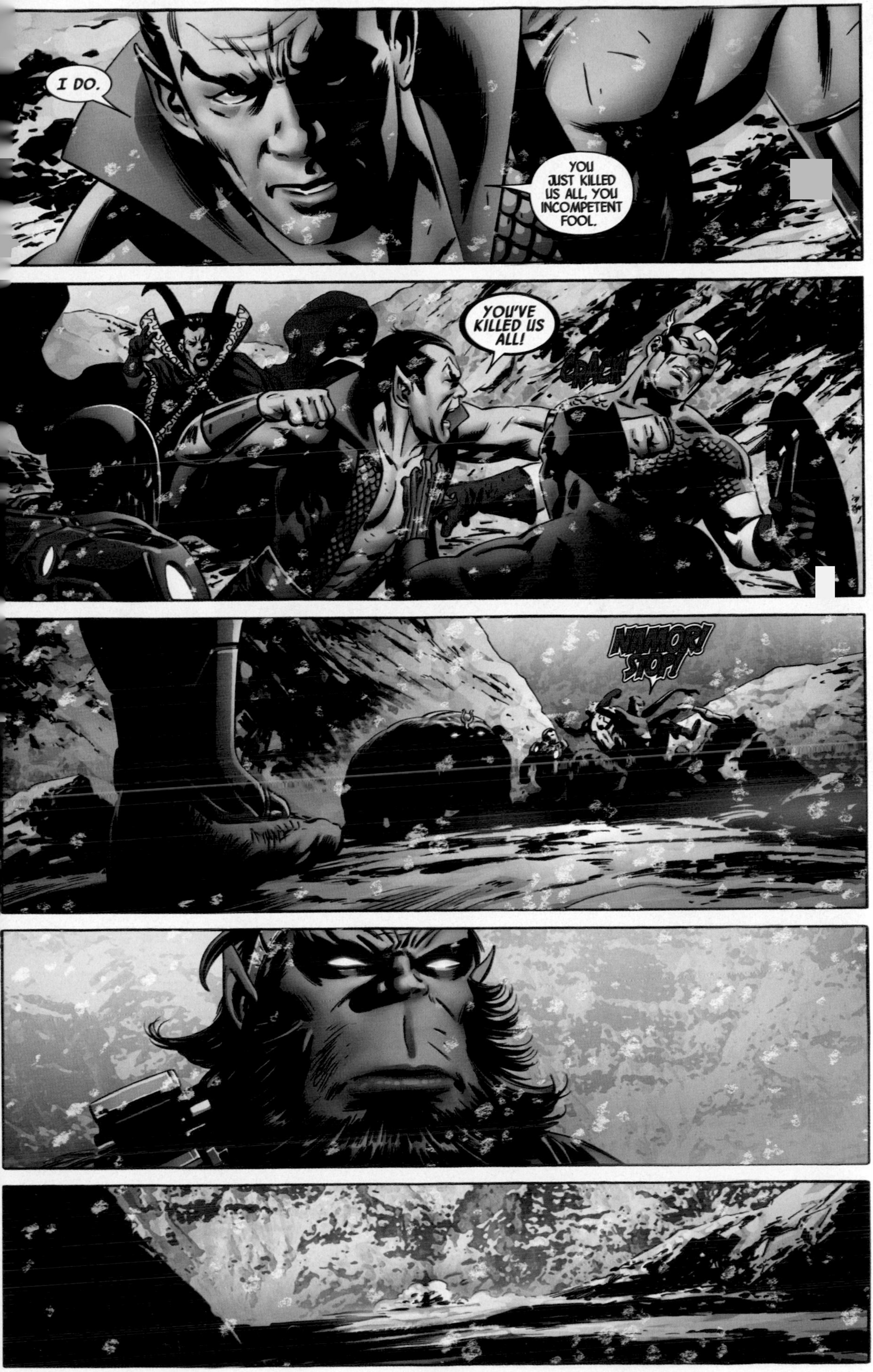
I DO.
YOU JUST KILLED US ALL, YOU INCOMPETENT FOOL.
YOU'VE KILLED US ALL!
CRACK
NAMOR! STOP!

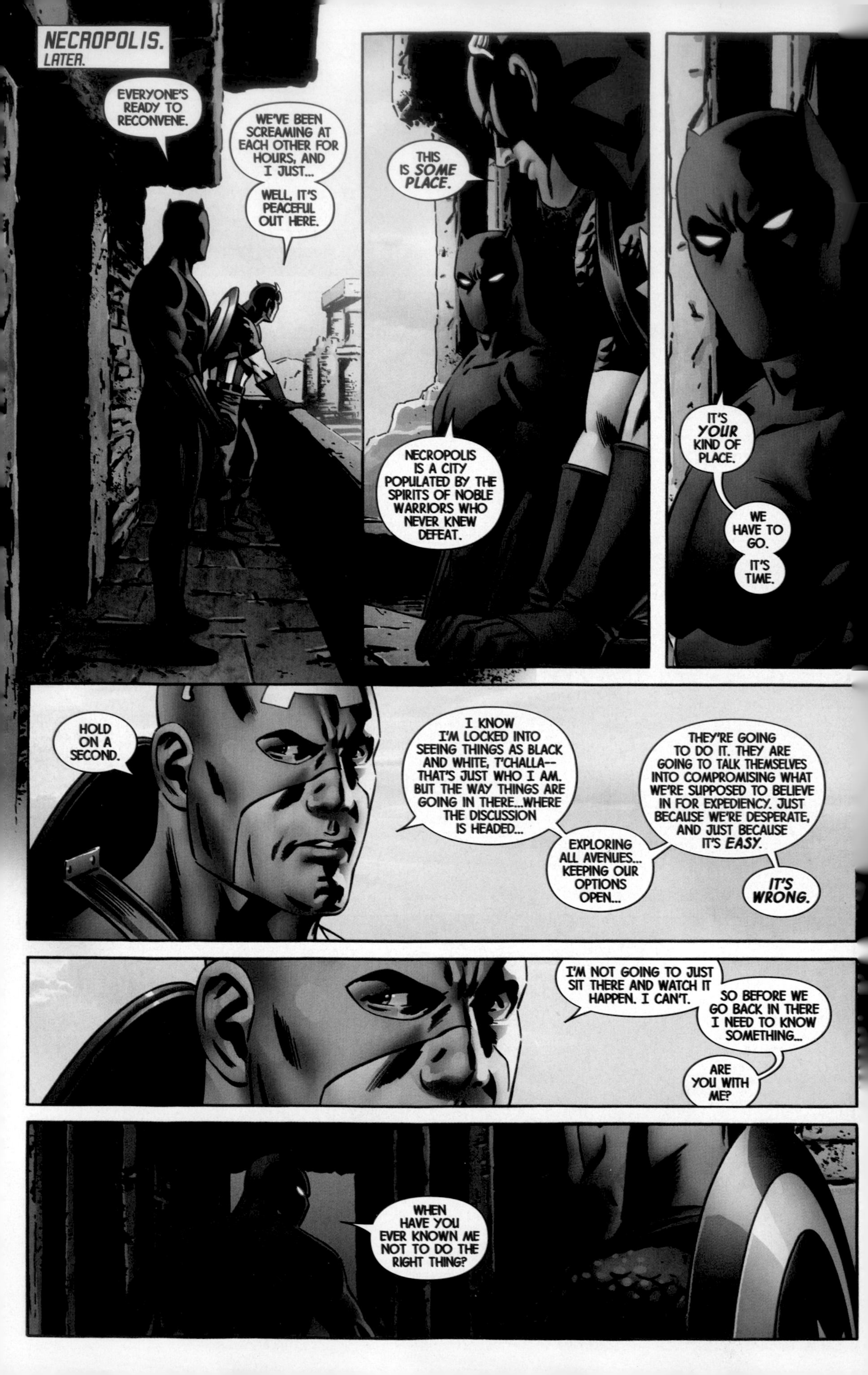
NECROPOLIS. LATER.
EVERYONE'S READY TO RECONVENE.
WE'VE BEEN SCREAMING AT EACH OTHER FOR HOURS, AND I JUST...
WELL, IT'S PEACEFUL OUT HERE.
THIS IS SOME PLACE.
NECROPOLIS IS A CITY POPULATED BY THE SPIRITS OF NOBLE WARRIORS WHO NEVER KNEW DEFEAT.
IT'S YOUR KIND OF PLACE.
WE HAVE TO GO.
IT'S TIME.
HOLD ON A SECOND.
I KNOW I'M LOCKED INTO SEEING THINGS AS BLACK AND WHITE, T'CHALLA-- THAT'S JUST WHO I AM. BUT THE WAY THINGS ARE GOING IN THERE...WHERE THE DISCUSSION IS HEADED...
EXPLORING ALL AVENUES... KEEPING OUR OPTIONS OPEN...
THEY'RE GOING TO DO IT. THEY ARE GOING TO TALK THEMSELVES INTO COMPROMISING WHAT WE'RE SUPPOSED TO BELIEVE IN FOR EXPEDIENCY. JUST BECAUSE WE'RE DESPERATE, AND JUST BECAUSE IT'S EASY.
IT'S WRONG.
I'M NOT GOING TO JUST SIT THERE AND WATCH IT HAPPEN. I CAN'T.
SO BEFORE WE GO BACK IN THERE I NEED TO KNOW SOMETHING...
ARE YOU WITH ME?
WHEN HAVE YOU EVER KNOWN ME NOT TO DO THE RIGHT THING?

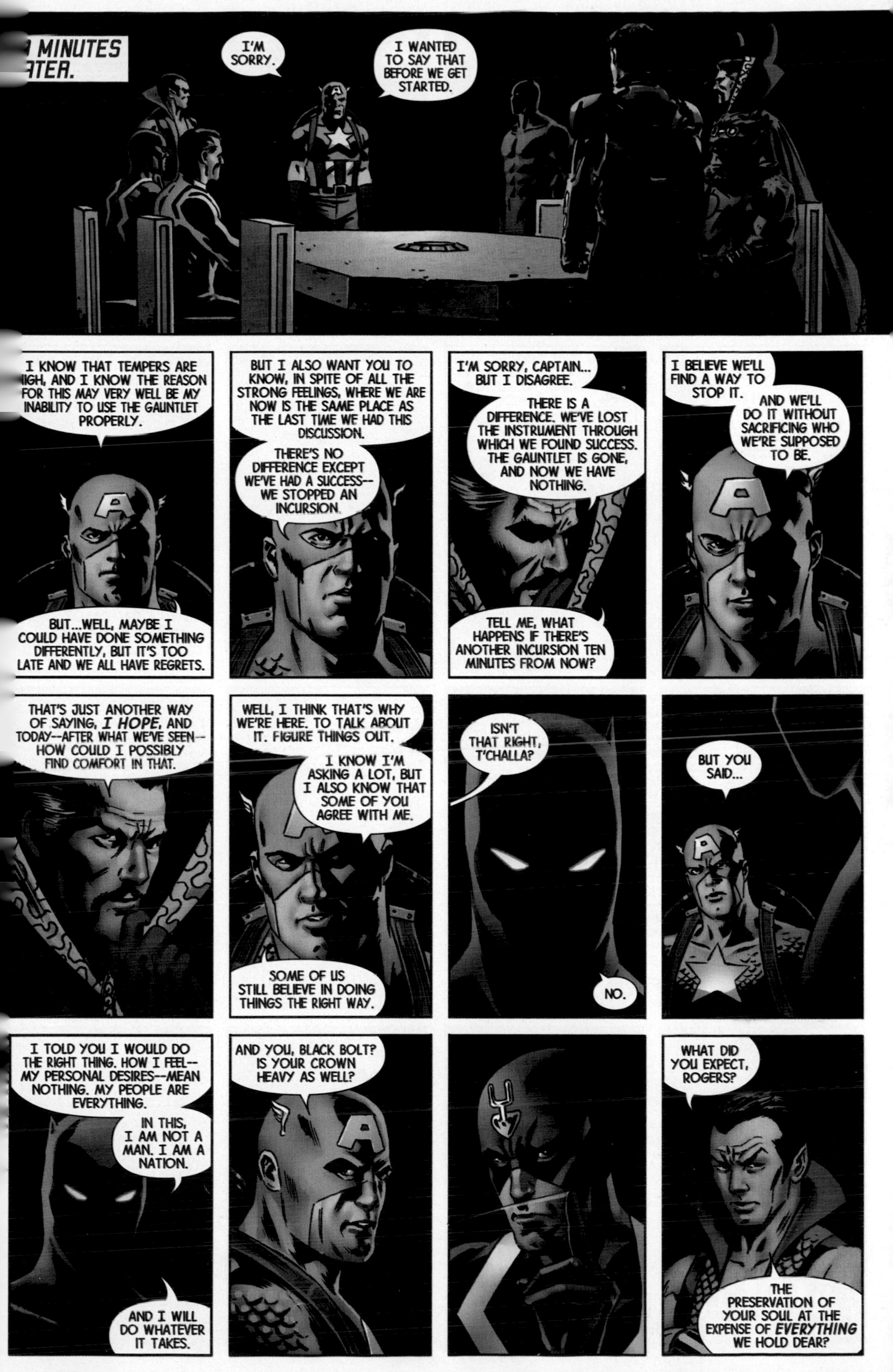
MINUTES LATER.
I'M SORRY.
I WANTED TO SAY THAT BEFORE WE GET STARTED.
I KNOW THAT TEMPERS ARE HIGH, AND I KNOW THE REASON FOR THIS MAY VERY WELL BE MY INABILITY TO USE THE GAUNTLET PROPERLY.
BUT...WELL, MAYBE I COULD HAVE DONE SOMETHING DIFFERENTLY, BUT IT'S TOO LATE AND WE ALL HAVE REGRETS.
BUT I ALSO WANT YOU TO KNOW, IN SPITE OF ALL THE STRONG FEELINGS, WHERE WE ARE NOW IS THE SAME PLACE AS THE LAST TIME WE HAD THIS DISCUSSION.
THERE'S NO DIFFERENCE EXCEPT WE'VE HAD A SUCCESS--WE STOPPED AN INCURSION.
I'M SORRY, CAPTAIN... BUT I DISAGREE.
THERE IS A DIFFERENCE. WE'VE LOST THE INSTRUMENT THROUGH WHICH WE FOUND SUCCESS. THE GAUNTLET IS GONE, AND NOW WE HAVE NOTHING.
TELL ME, WHAT HAPPENS IF THERE'S ANOTHER INCURSION TEN MINUTES FROM NOW?
I BELIEVE WE'LL FIND A WAY TO STOP IT.
AND WE'LL DO IT WITHOUT SACRIFICING WHO WE'RE SUPPOSED TO BE.
THAT'S JUST ANOTHER WAY OF SAYING, *I HOPE*, AND TODAY--AFTER WHAT WE'VE SEEN--HOW COULD I POSSIBLY FIND COMFORT IN THAT.
WELL, I THINK THAT'S WHY WE'RE HERE. TO TALK ABOUT IT. FIGURE THINGS OUT.
I KNOW I'M ASKING A LOT, BUT I ALSO KNOW THAT SOME OF YOU AGREE WITH ME.
SOME OF US STILL BELIEVE IN DOING THINGS THE RIGHT WAY.
ISN'T THAT RIGHT, T'CHALLA?
NO.
BUT YOU SAID...
I TOLD YOU I WOULD DO THE RIGHT THING. HOW I FEEL--MY PERSONAL DESIRES--MEAN NOTHING. MY PEOPLE ARE EVERYTHING.
IN THIS, I AM NOT A MAN. I AM A NATION.
AND I WILL DO WHATEVER IT TAKES.
AND YOU, BLACK BOLT? IS YOUR CROWN HEAVY AS WELL?
WHAT DID YOU EXPECT, ROGERS?
THE PRESERVATION OF YOUR SOUL AT THE EXPENSE OF *EVERYTHING* WE HOLD DEAR?

WHAT ABOUT YOU, HANK? CAN YOU STILL FIND HUMANITY IN THAT GIANT HEART OF YOURS?

WELL, FAR BE IT FROM ME TO ACT OBSTINATE IN THE FACE OF THE HISTORY YOU GENTLEMEN SHARE.

BUT ARE YOU SERIOUSLY ASKING A MUTANT WHAT HE'S PREPARED TO DO TO STAVE OFF EXTINCTION?

STEVE, IF I MAY.

YOUR DEMEANOR UNDERMINES THE CASE YOU'RE MAKING...

YOU'RE ACTING LIKE THE DECISIONS WE'RE FACING AREN'T DIFFICULT FOR US AS WELL.

IT'S, WELL, QUITE INSULTING.

YOU WILL LOSE YOURSELF IN THIS, REED.

YOU'LL WAKE UP ONE DAY AND HAVE NO IDEA WHO IS LOOKING BACK AT YOU IN THE MIRROR.

YOU SEEM SURPRISED THAT I WOULD BE WILLING TO SACRIFICE MYSELF FOR MY FAMILY.

WHY?

I'M SORRY...

BUT I WON'T ALLOW THIS TO HAPPEN.

I KNOW YOU PEOPLE.

YOU'RE GOING TO BUILD A MACHINE OR SOME KIND OF WEAPON WITHOUT THINKING IF YOU SHOULD—JUST BECAUSE YOU MIGHT NEED IT.

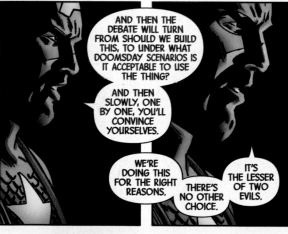

AND THEN THE DEBATE WILL TURN FROM SHOULD WE BUILD THIS, TO UNDER WHAT DOOMSDAY SCENARIOS IS IT ACCEPTABLE TO USE THE THING?

AND THEN SLOWLY, ONE BY ONE, YOU'LL CONVINCE YOURSELVES.

WE'RE DOING THIS FOR THE RIGHT REASONS.

THERE'S NO OTHER CHOICE.

IT'S THE LESSER OF TWO EVILS.

ISN'T THAT RIGHT, BROTHER?

DAMMIT, STEVE.

WHY DO YOU ALWAYS HAVE TO BE THIS WAY?

I'M SORRY...

I'LL FIND SOME WAY TO MAKE THIS RIGHT.

WHAT?

DO IT, STEPHEN.

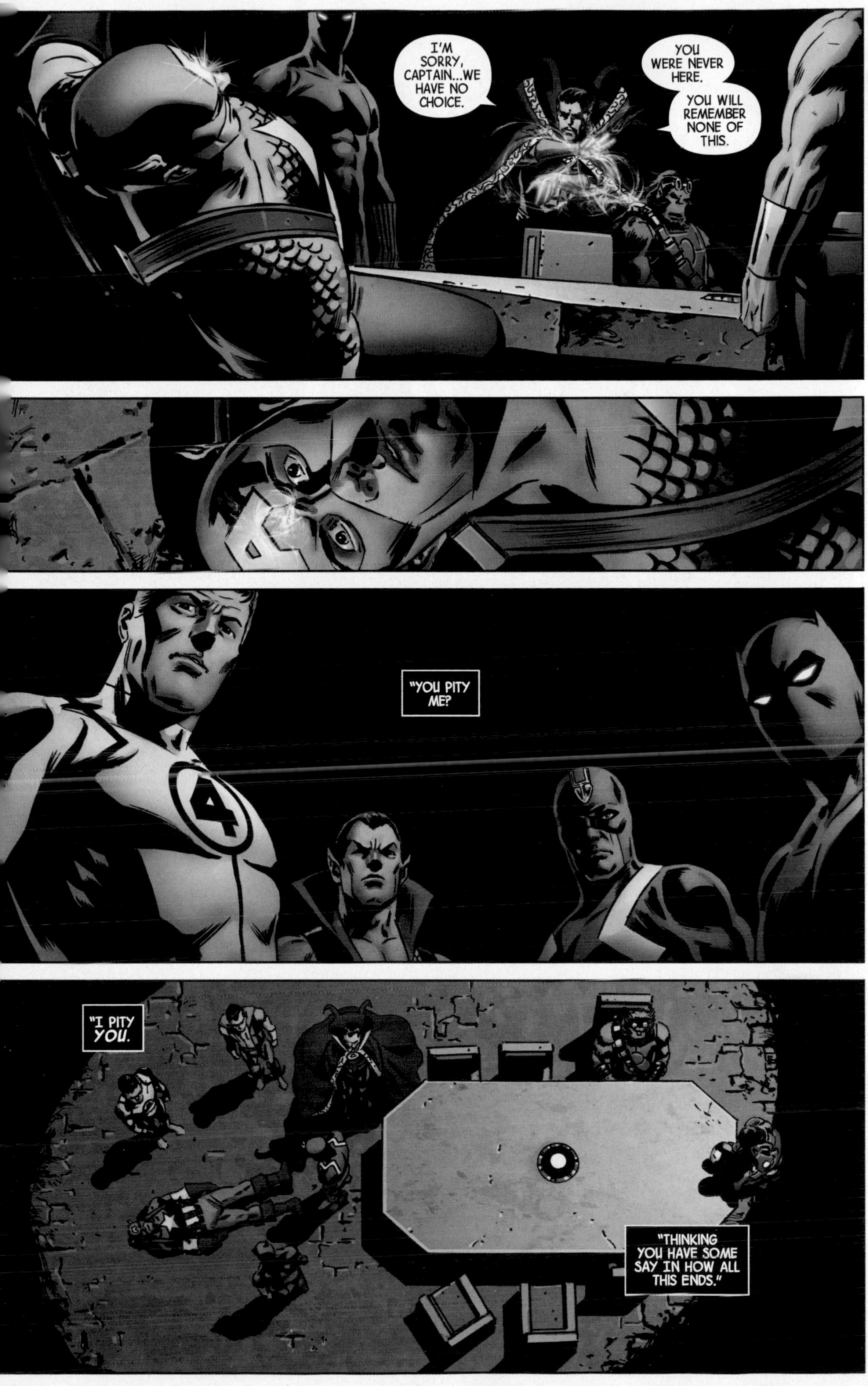
I'M SORRY, CAPTAIN...WE HAVE NO CHOICE.
YOU WERE NEVER HERE.
YOU WILL REMEMBER NONE OF THIS.
"YOU PITY ME?
"I PITY YOU.
"THINKING YOU HAVE SOME SAY IN HOW ALL THIS ENDS."

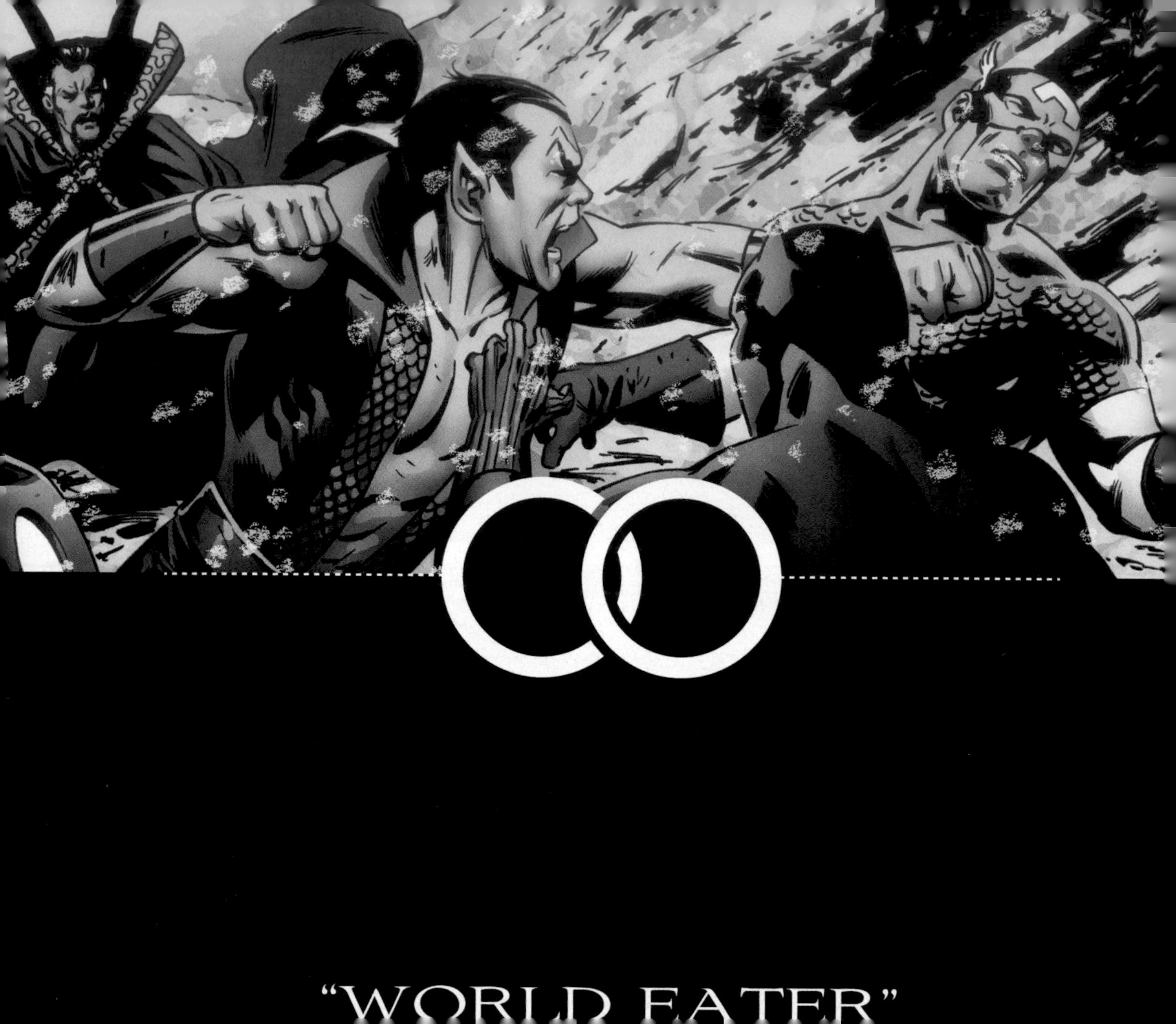

"WORLD EATER"

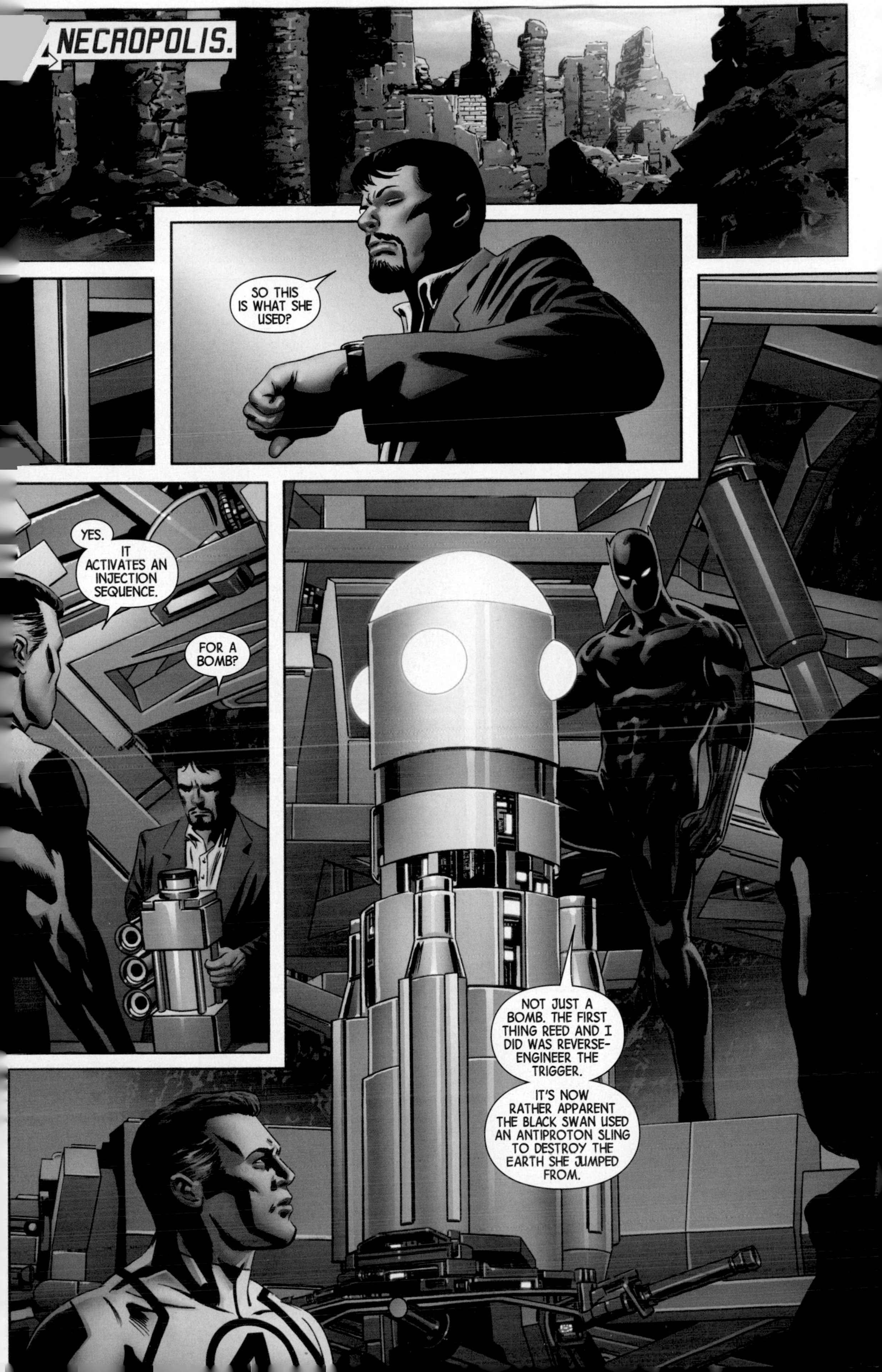
NECROPOLIS.
SO THIS IS WHAT SHE USED?
YES.
IT ACTIVATES AN INJECTION SEQUENCE.
FOR A BOMB?
NOT JUST A BOMB. THE FIRST THING REED AND I DID WAS REVERSE-ENGINEER THE TRIGGER.
IT'S NOW RATHER APPARENT THE BLACK SWAN USED AN ANTIPROTON SLING TO DESTROY THE EARTH SHE JUMPED FROM.

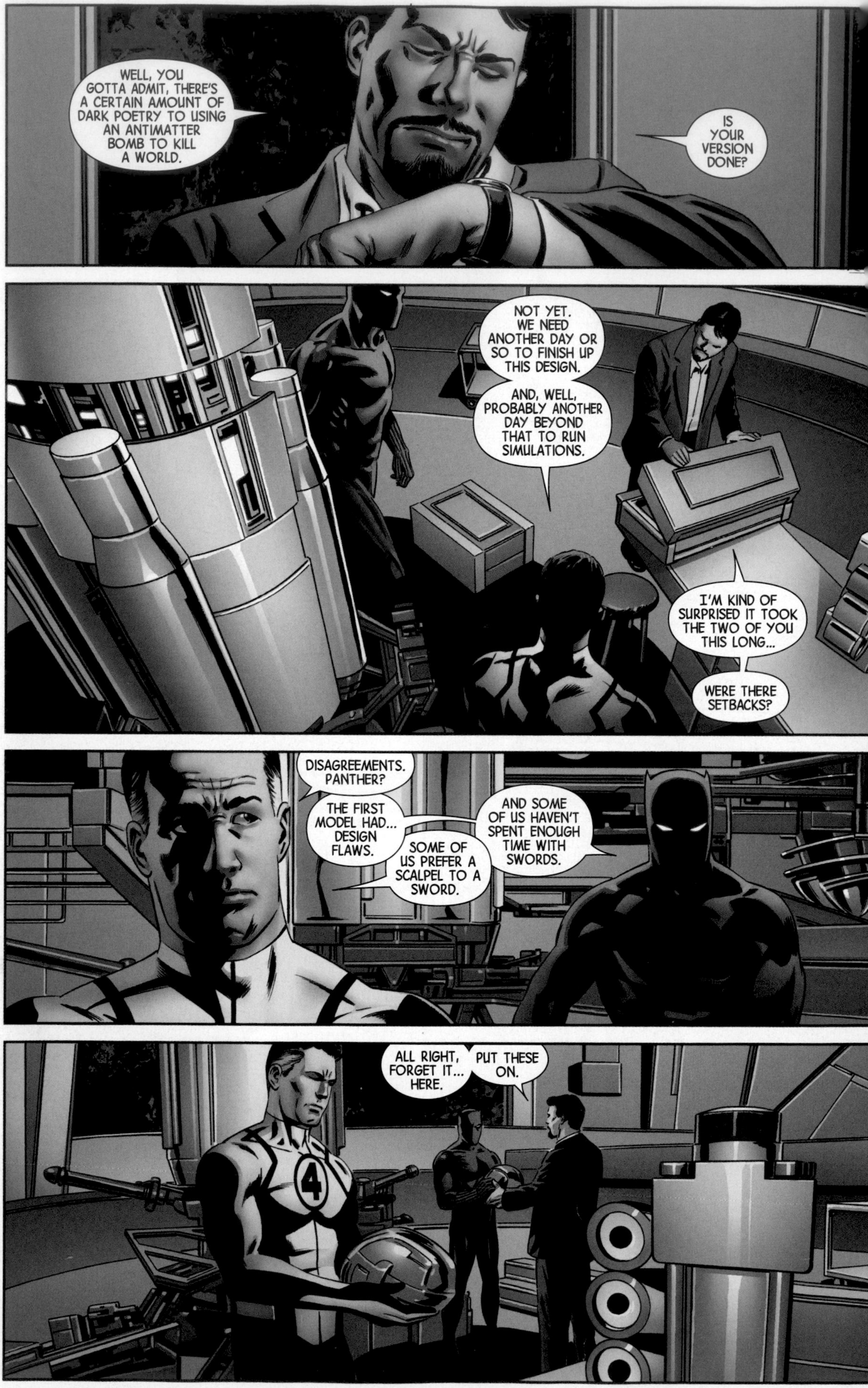
WELL, YOU GOTTA ADMIT, THERE'S A CERTAIN AMOUNT OF DARK POETRY TO USING AN ANTIMATTER BOMB TO KILL A WORLD.
IS YOUR VERSION DONE?
NOT YET. WE NEED ANOTHER DAY OR SO TO FINISH UP THIS DESIGN.
AND, WELL, PROBABLY ANOTHER DAY BEYOND THAT TO RUN SIMULATIONS.
I'M KIND OF SURPRISED IT TOOK THE TWO OF YOU THIS LONG...
WERE THERE SETBACKS?
DISAGREEMENTS. PANTHER?
THE FIRST MODEL HAD... DESIGN FLAWS.
AND SOME OF US HAVEN'T SPENT ENOUGH TIME WITH SWORDS.
SOME OF US PREFER A SCALPEL TO A SWORD.
ALL RIGHT, FORGET IT... HERE.
PUT THESE ON.

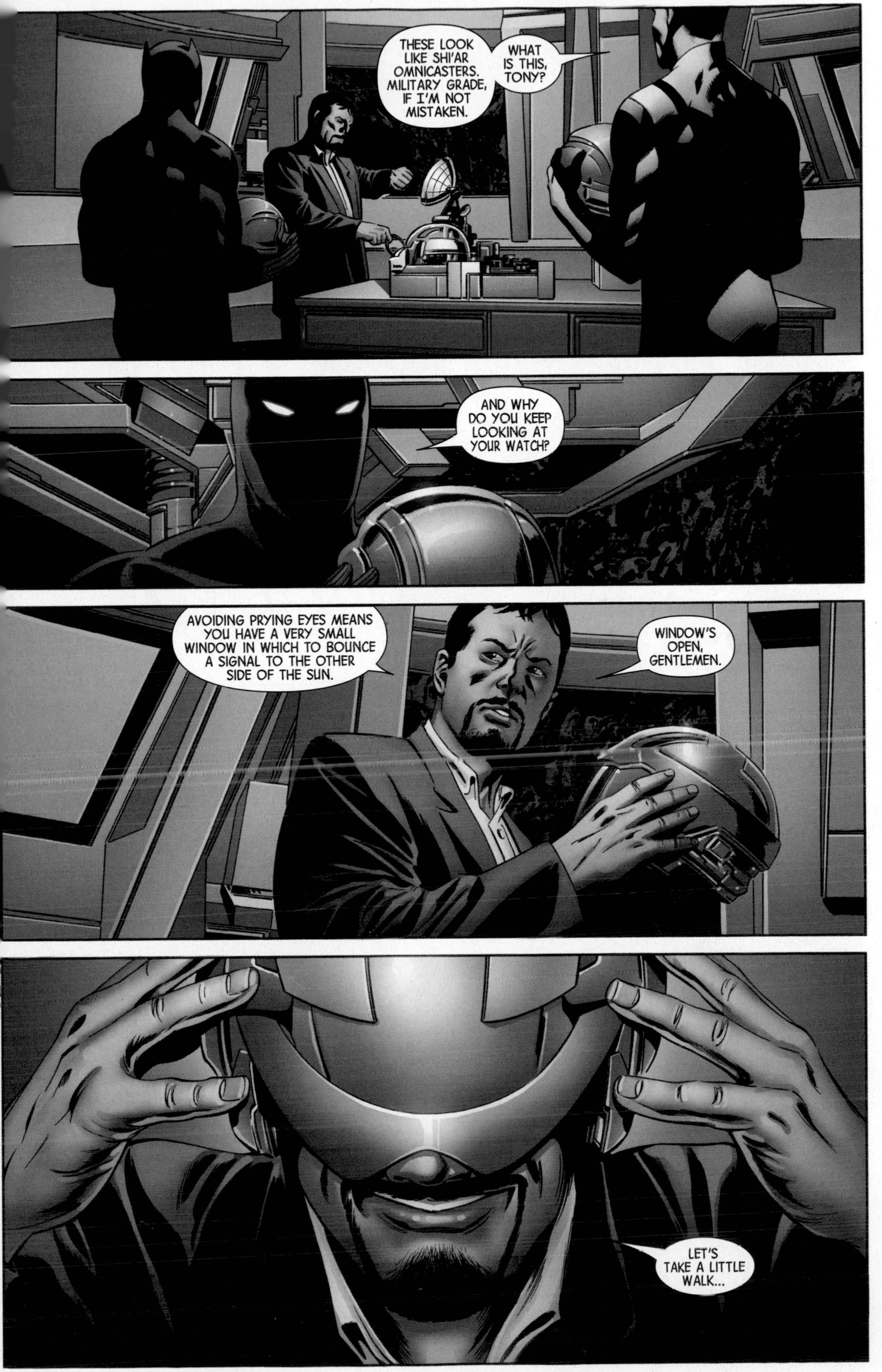
THESE LOOK LIKE SHI'AR OMNICASTERS. MILITARY GRADE, IF I'M NOT MISTAKEN.
WHAT IS THIS, TONY?
AND WHY DO YOU KEEP LOOKING AT YOUR WATCH?
AVOIDING PRYING EYES MEANS YOU HAVE A VERY SMALL WINDOW IN WHICH TO BOUNCE A SIGNAL TO THE OTHER SIDE OF THE SUN.
WINDOW'S OPEN, GENTLEMEN.
LET'S TAKE A LITTLE WALK...

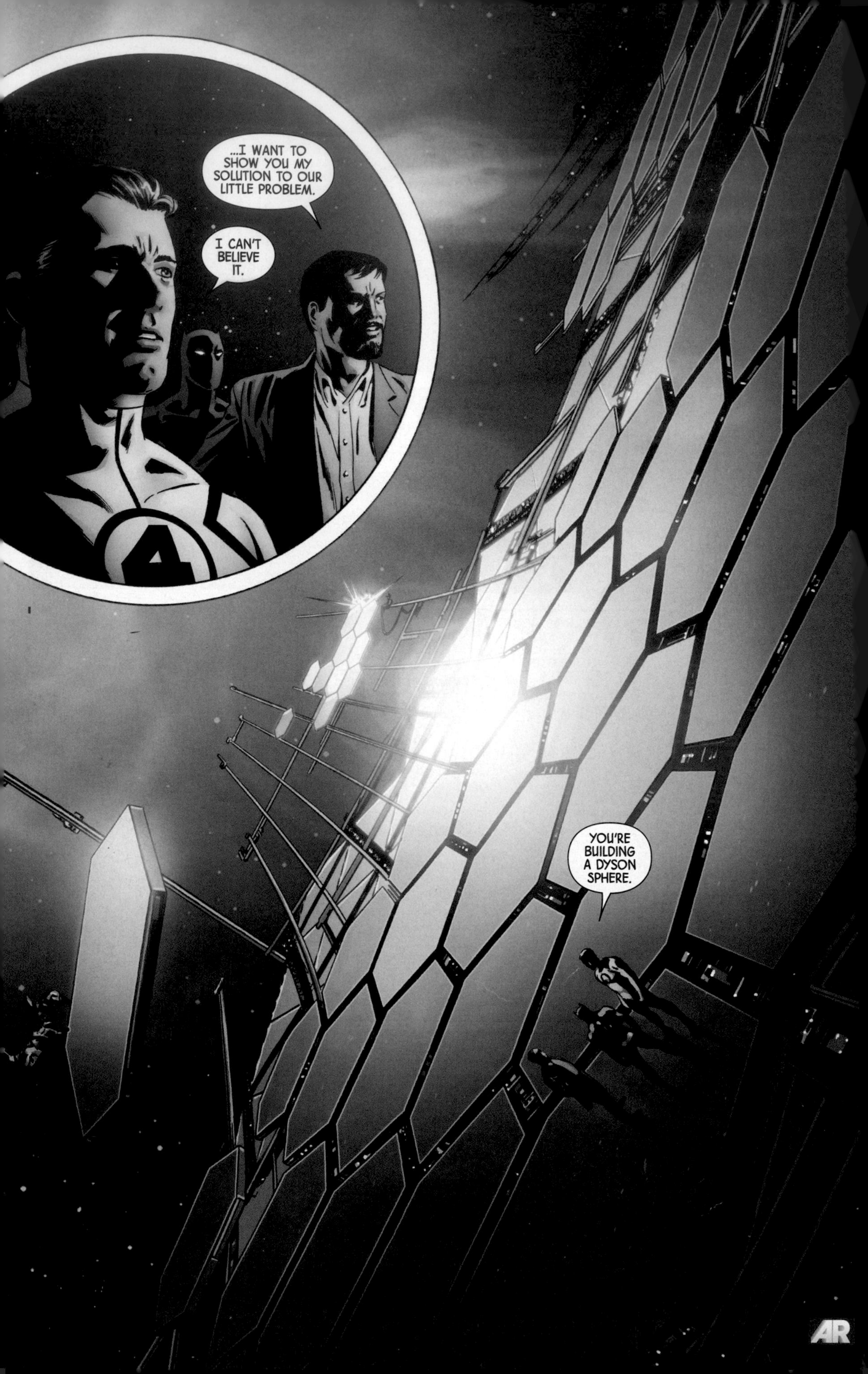
...I WANT TO SHOW YOU MY SOLUTION TO OUR LITTLE PROBLEM.
I CAN'T BELIEVE IT.
YOU'RE BUILDING A DYSON SPHERE.
AR

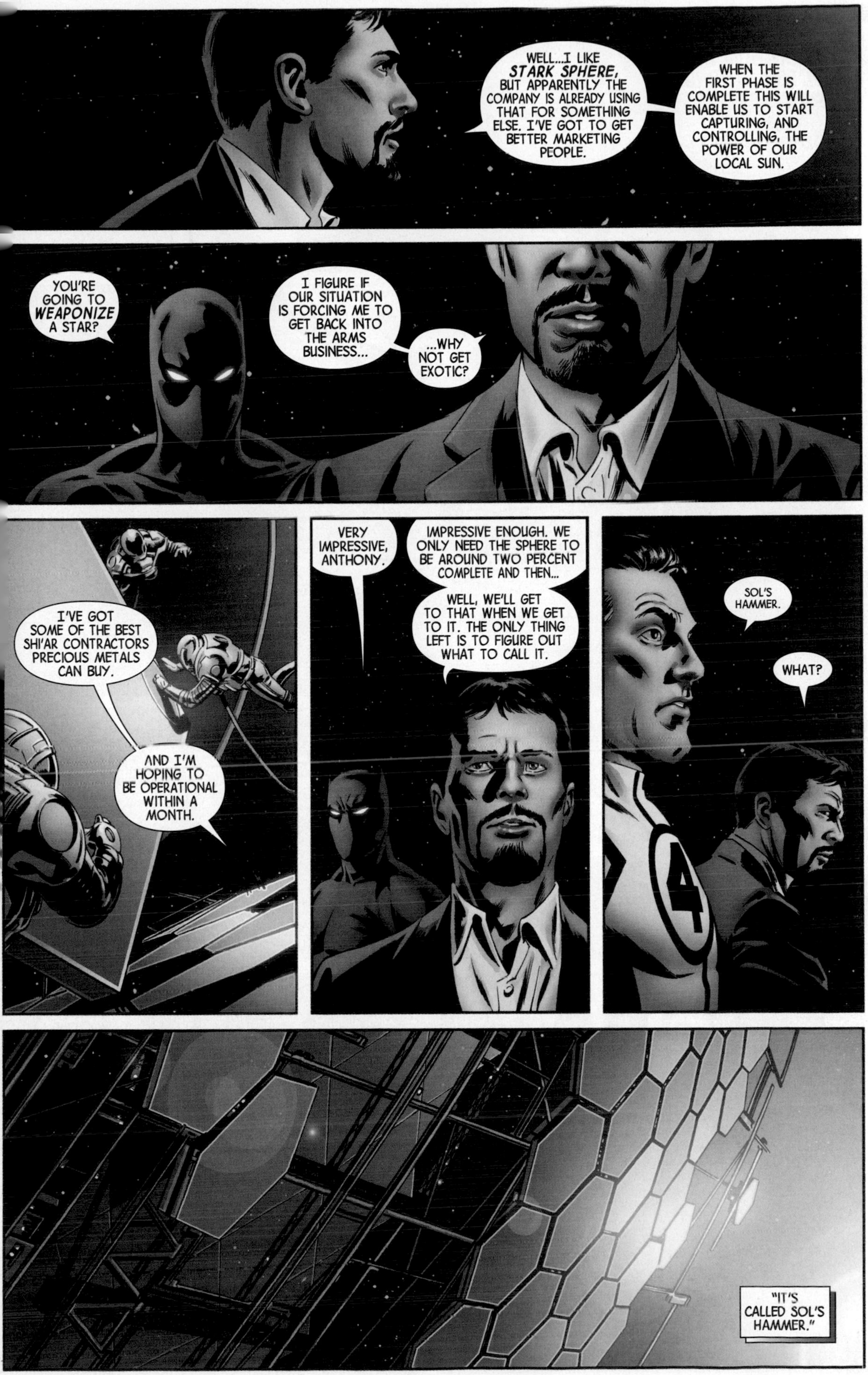
WELL...I LIKE STARK SPHERE, BUT APPARENTLY THE COMPANY IS ALREADY USING THAT FOR SOMETHING ELSE. I'VE GOT TO GET BETTER MARKETING PEOPLE.
WHEN THE FIRST PHASE IS COMPLETE THIS WILL ENABLE US TO START CAPTURING, AND CONTROLLING, THE POWER OF OUR LOCAL SUN.
YOU'RE GOING TO WEAPONIZE A STAR?
I FIGURE IF OUR SITUATION IS FORCING ME TO GET BACK INTO THE ARMS BUSINESS...
...WHY NOT GET EXOTIC?
I'VE GOT SOME OF THE BEST SHI'AR CONTRACTORS PRECIOUS METALS CAN BUY.
AND I'M HOPING TO BE OPERATIONAL WITHIN A MONTH.
VERY IMPRESSIVE, ANTHONY.
IMPRESSIVE ENOUGH. WE ONLY NEED THE SPHERE TO BE AROUND TWO PERCENT COMPLETE AND THEN...
WELL, WE'LL GET TO THAT WHEN WE GET TO IT. THE ONLY THING LEFT IS TO FIGURE OUT WHAT TO CALL IT.
SOL'S HAMMER.
WHAT?
"IT'S CALLED SOL'S HAMMER."

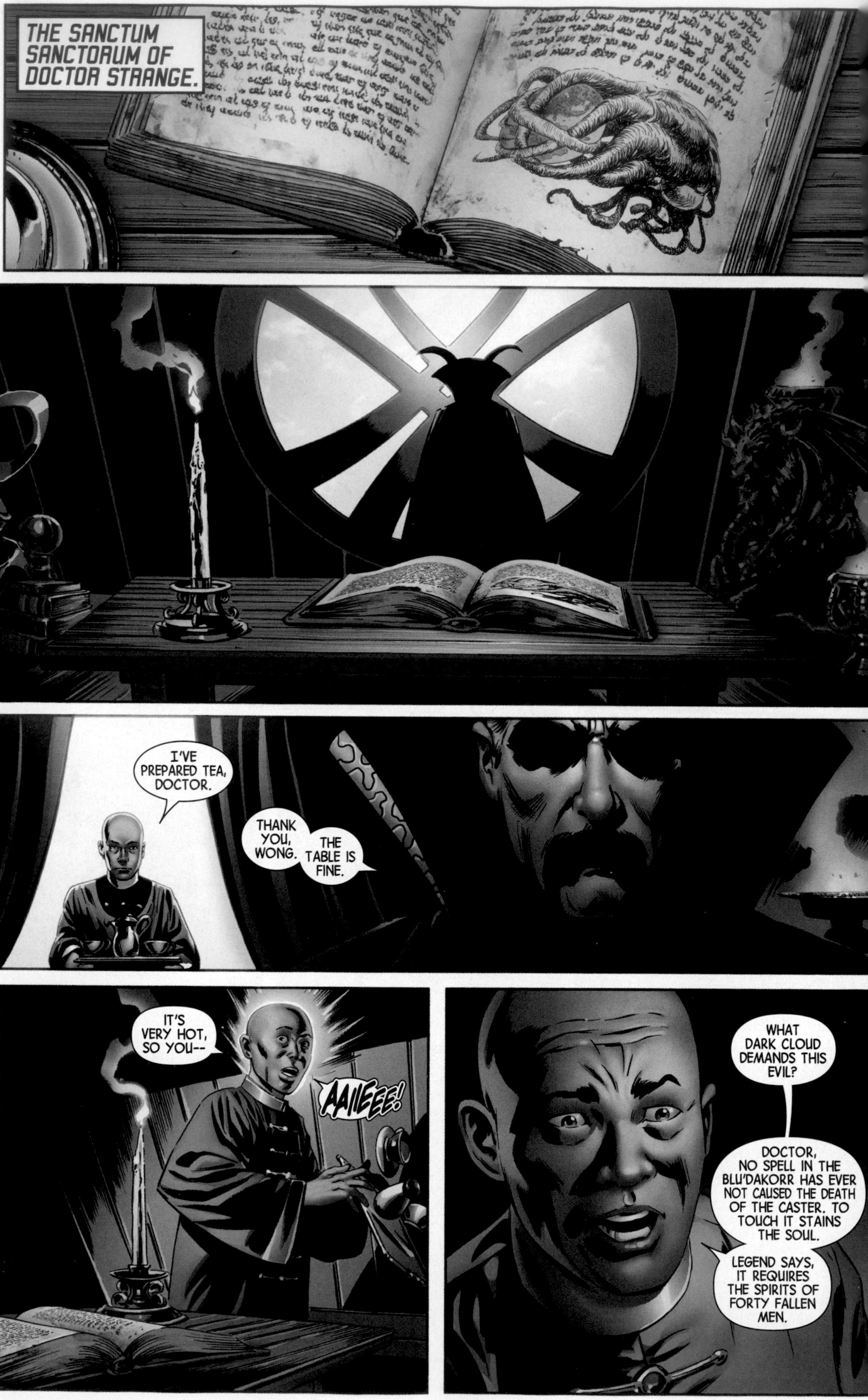
THE SANCTUM SANCTORUM OF DOCTOR STRANGE.
I'VE PREPARED TEA, DOCTOR.
THANK YOU, WONG.
THE TABLE IS FINE.
IT'S VERY HOT, SO YOU--
AAIIEEE!
WHAT DARK CLOUD DEMANDS THIS EVIL?
DOCTOR, NO SPELL IN THE BLU'DAKORR HAS EVER NOT CAUSED THE DEATH OF THE CASTER. TO TOUCH IT STAINS THE SOUL.
LEGEND SAYS, IT REQUIRES THE SPIRITS OF FORTY FALLEN MEN.

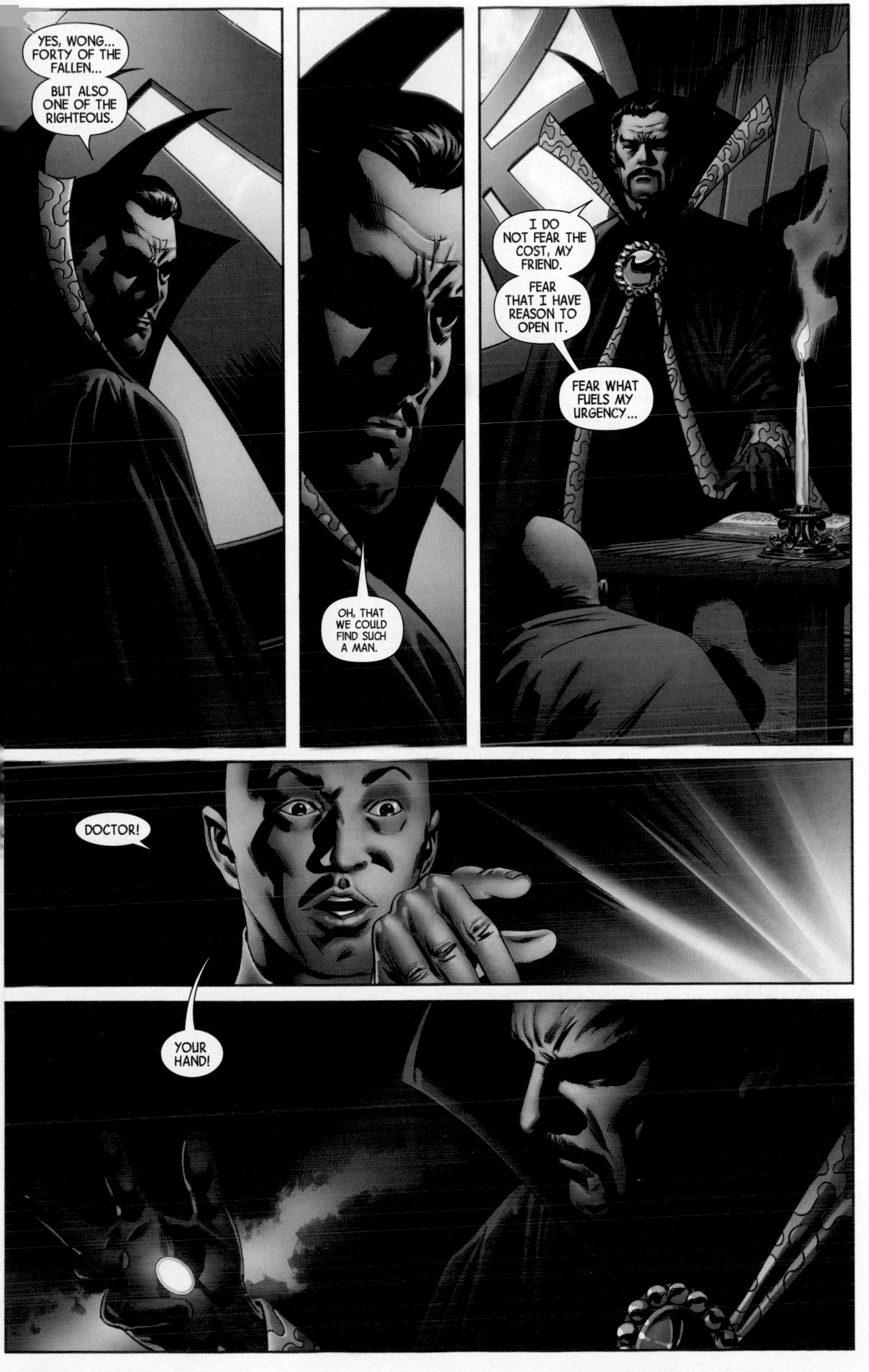

YES, WONG... FORTY OF THE FALLEN...
BUT ALSO ONE OF THE RIGHTEOUS.
OH, THAT WE COULD FIND SUCH A MAN.
I DO NOT FEAR THE COST, MY FRIEND.
FEAR THAT I HAVE REASON TO OPEN IT.
FEAR WHAT FUELS MY URGENCY...
DOCTOR!
YOUR HAND!

AND FEAR MOST OF ALL... TIME SLIPPING AWAY.

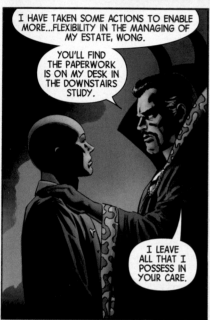

I HAVE TAKEN SOME ACTIONS TO ENABLE MORE...FLEXIBILITY IN THE MANAGING OF MY ESTATE, WONG.

YOU'LL FIND THE PAPERWORK IS ON MY DESK IN THE DOWNSTAIRS STUDY.

I LEAVE ALL THAT I POSSESS IN YOUR CARE.

YOU UNNERVE ME, STEPHEN.

MY FRIEND, FROM THIS POINT FORWARD TREAT EACH MOMENT OF EACH DAY AS IF IT WERE YOUR LAST.

AS IT VERY WELL MAY BE.

AM I GOING TO SEE YOU AGAIN?

I CARRY THE BLOOD BIBLE, WONG...

IT WOULD SEEM UNLIKELY.

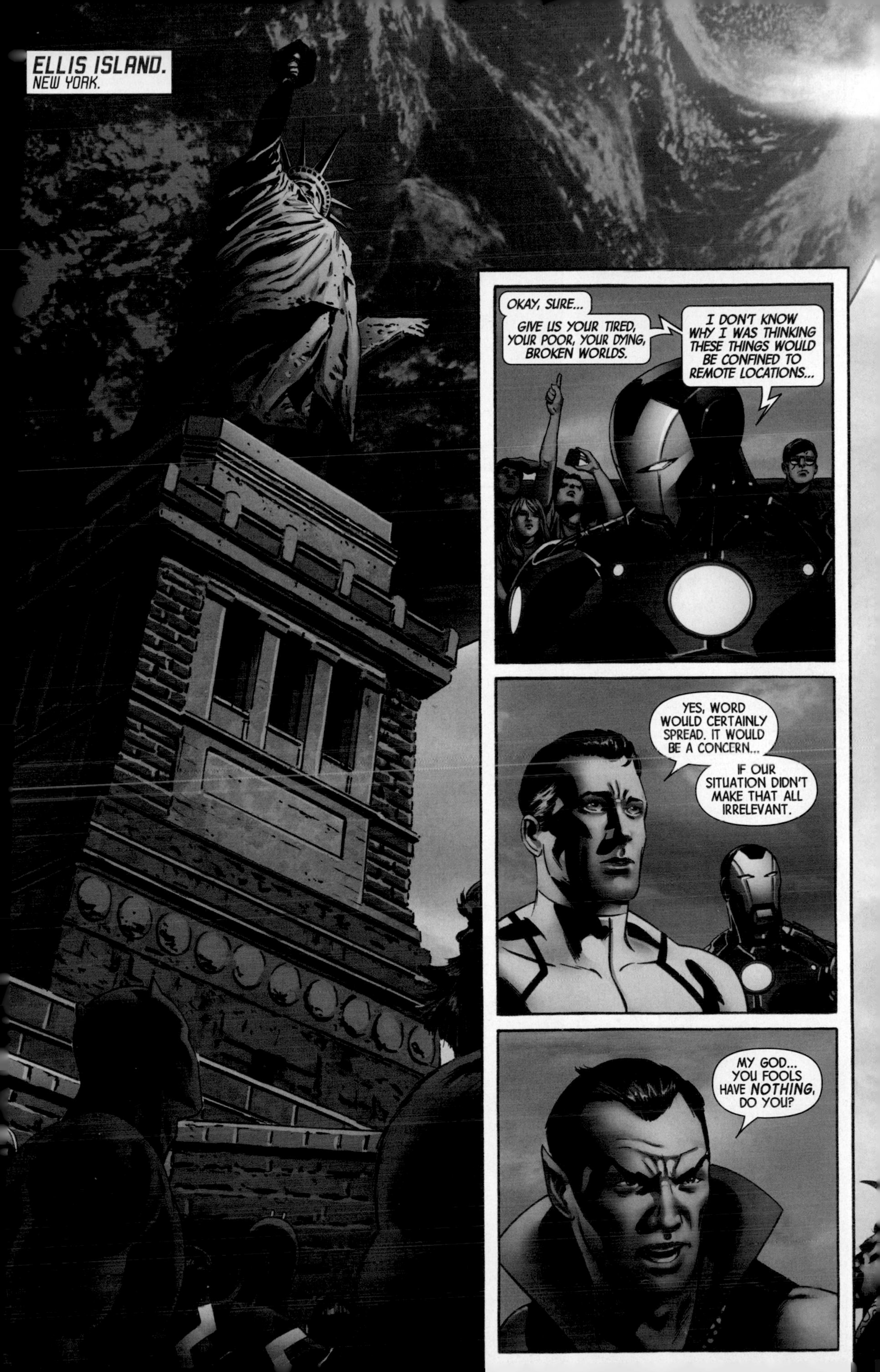
ELLIS ISLAND.
NEW YORK.
OKAY, SURE... GIVE US YOUR TIRED, YOUR POOR, YOUR DYING, BROKEN WORLDS.
I DON'T KNOW WHY I WAS THINKING THESE THINGS WOULD BE CONFINED TO REMOTE LOCATIONS...
YES, WORD WOULD CERTAINLY SPREAD. IT WOULD BE A CONCERN...
IF OUR SITUATION DIDN'T MAKE THAT ALL IRRELEVANT.
MY GOD... YOU FOOLS HAVE NOTHING, DO YOU?

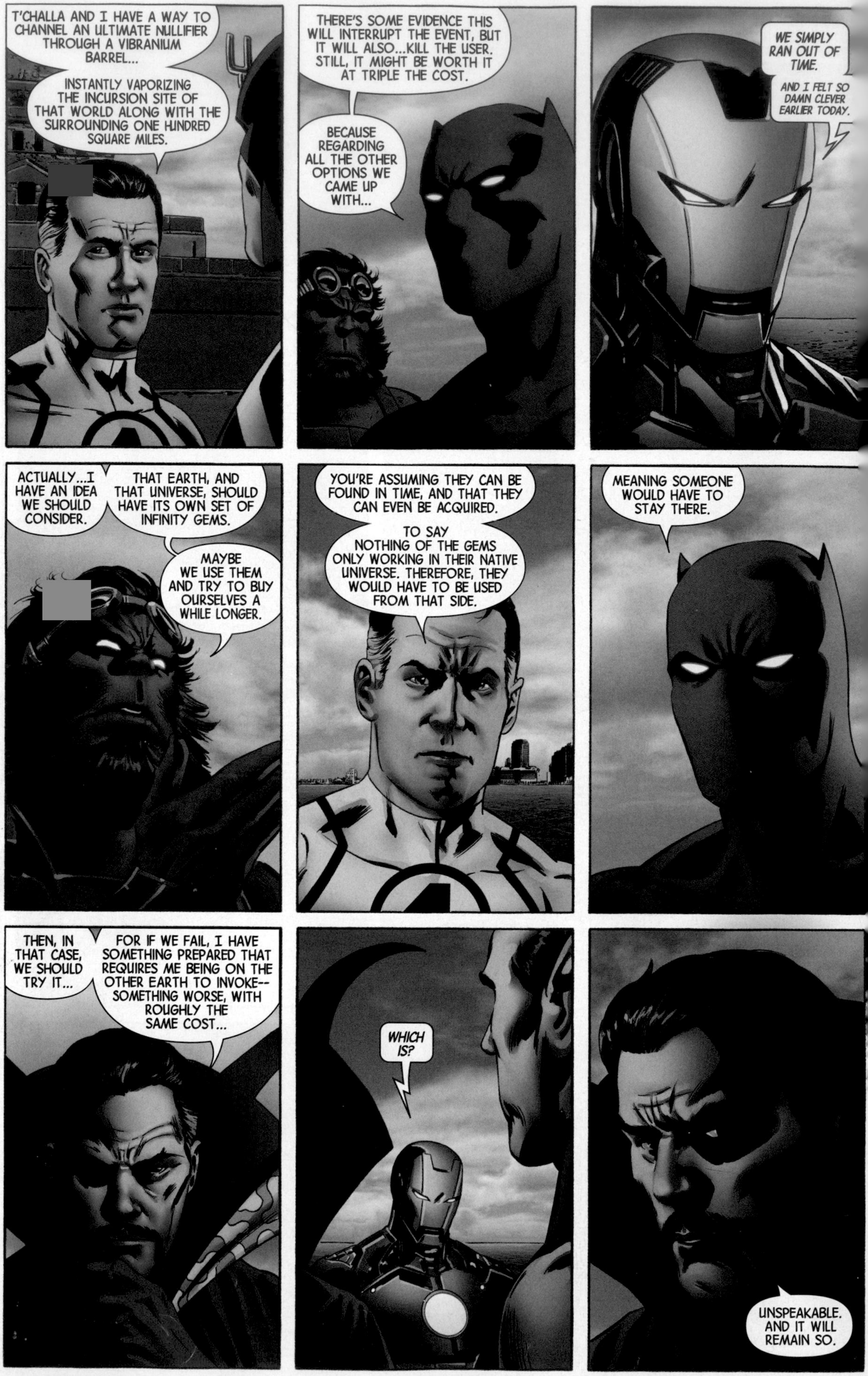
T'CHALLA AND I HAVE A WAY TO CHANNEL AN ULTIMATE NULLIFIER THROUGH A VIBRANIUM BARREL...
INSTANTLY VAPORIZING THE INCURSION SITE OF THAT WORLD ALONG WITH THE SURROUNDING ONE HUNDRED SQUARE MILES.
THERE'S SOME EVIDENCE THIS WILL INTERRUPT THE EVENT, BUT IT WILL ALSO...KILL THE USER. STILL, IT MIGHT BE WORTH IT AT TRIPLE THE COST.
BECAUSE REGARDING ALL THE OTHER OPTIONS WE CAME UP WITH...
WE SIMPLY RAN OUT OF TIME.
AND I FELT SO DAMN CLEVER EARLIER TODAY.
ACTUALLY...I HAVE AN IDEA WE SHOULD CONSIDER.
THAT EARTH, AND THAT UNIVERSE, SHOULD HAVE ITS OWN SET OF INFINITY GEMS.
MAYBE WE USE THEM AND TRY TO BUY OURSELVES A WHILE LONGER.
YOU'RE ASSUMING THEY CAN BE FOUND IN TIME, AND THAT THEY CAN EVEN BE ACQUIRED.
TO SAY NOTHING OF THE GEMS ONLY WORKING IN THEIR NATIVE UNIVERSE. THEREFORE, THEY WOULD HAVE TO BE USED FROM THAT SIDE.
MEANING SOMEONE WOULD HAVE TO STAY THERE.
THEN, IN THAT CASE, WE SHOULD TRY IT...
FOR IF WE FAIL, I HAVE SOMETHING PREPARED THAT REQUIRES ME BEING ON THE OTHER EARTH TO INVOKE-- SOMETHING WORSE, WITH ROUGHLY THE SAME COST...
WHICH IS?
UNSPEAKABLE. AND IT WILL REMAIN SO.

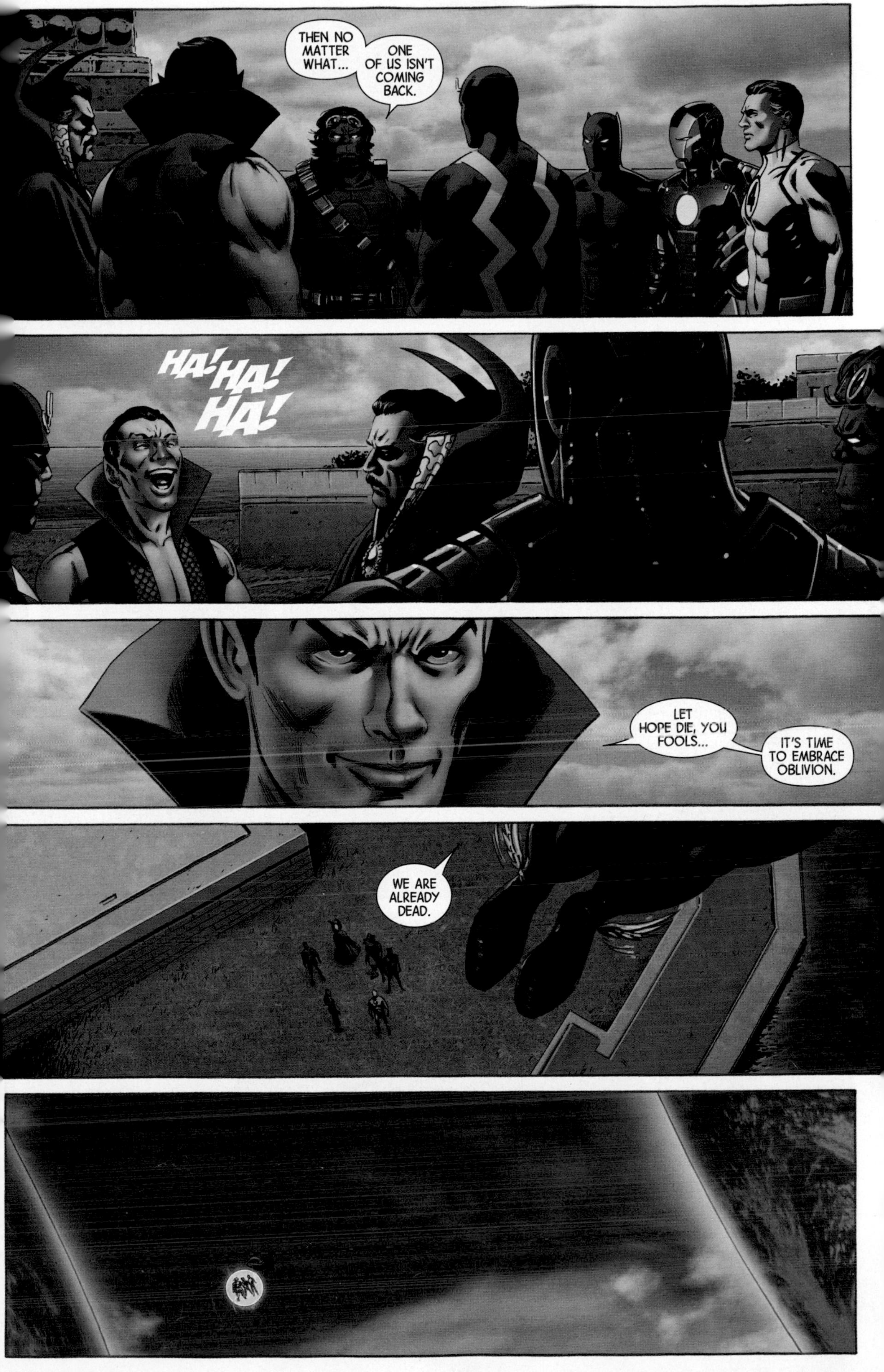
THEN NO MATTER WHAT...
ONE OF US ISN'T COMING BACK.
HA! HA! HA!
LET HOPE DIE, YOU FOOLS...
IT'S TIME TO EMBRACE OBLIVION.
WE ARE ALREADY DEAD.

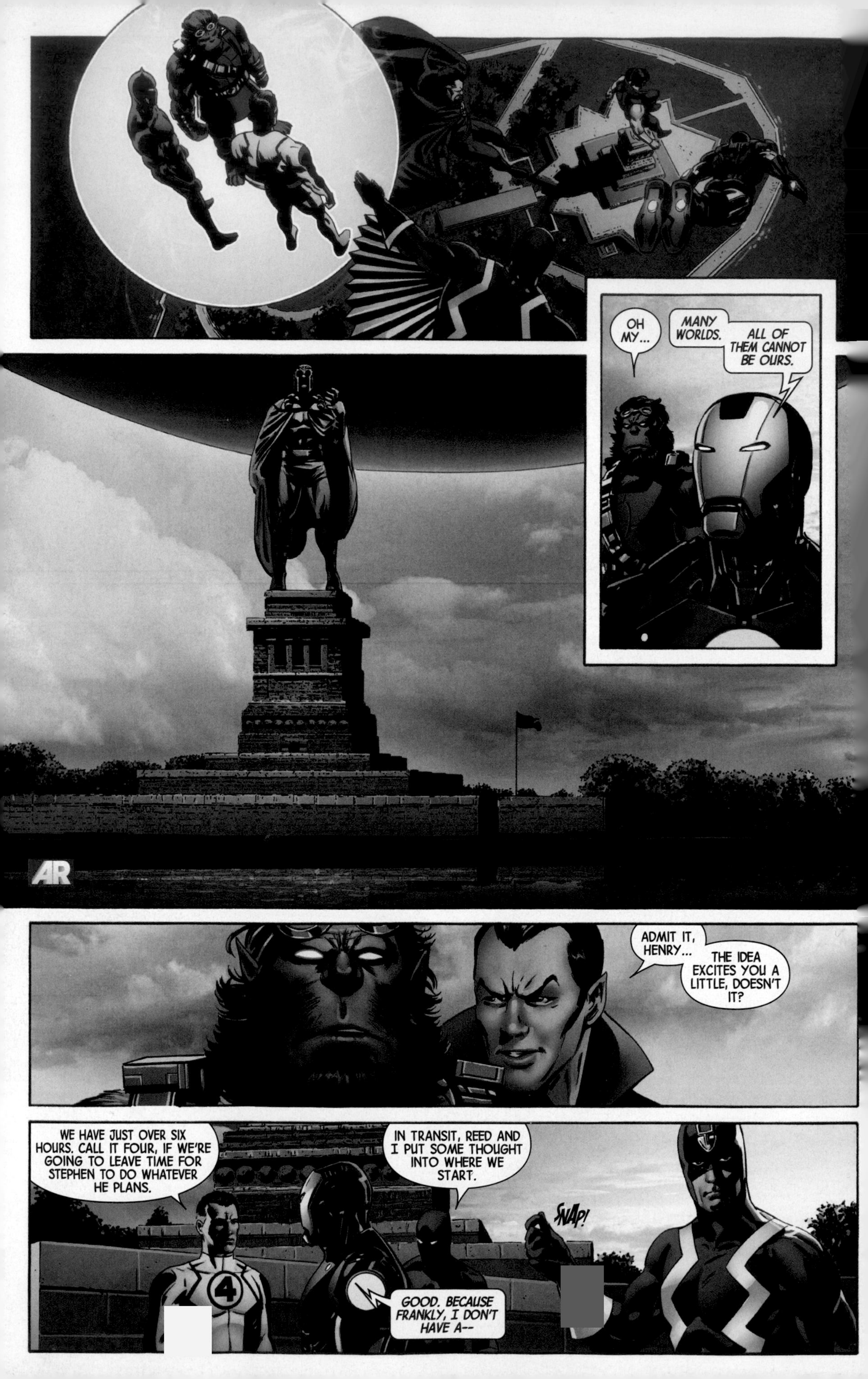
OH MY...
MANY WORLDS.
ALL OF THEM CANNOT BE OURS.
ADMIT IT, HENRY...
THE IDEA EXCITES YOU A LITTLE, DOESN'T IT?
WE HAVE JUST OVER SIX HOURS. CALL IT FOUR, IF WE'RE GOING TO LEAVE TIME FOR STEPHEN TO DO WHATEVER HE PLANS.
IN TRANSIT, REED AND I PUT SOME THOUGHT INTO WHERE WE START.
SNAP!
GOOD. BECAUSE FRANKLY, I DON'T HAVE A--

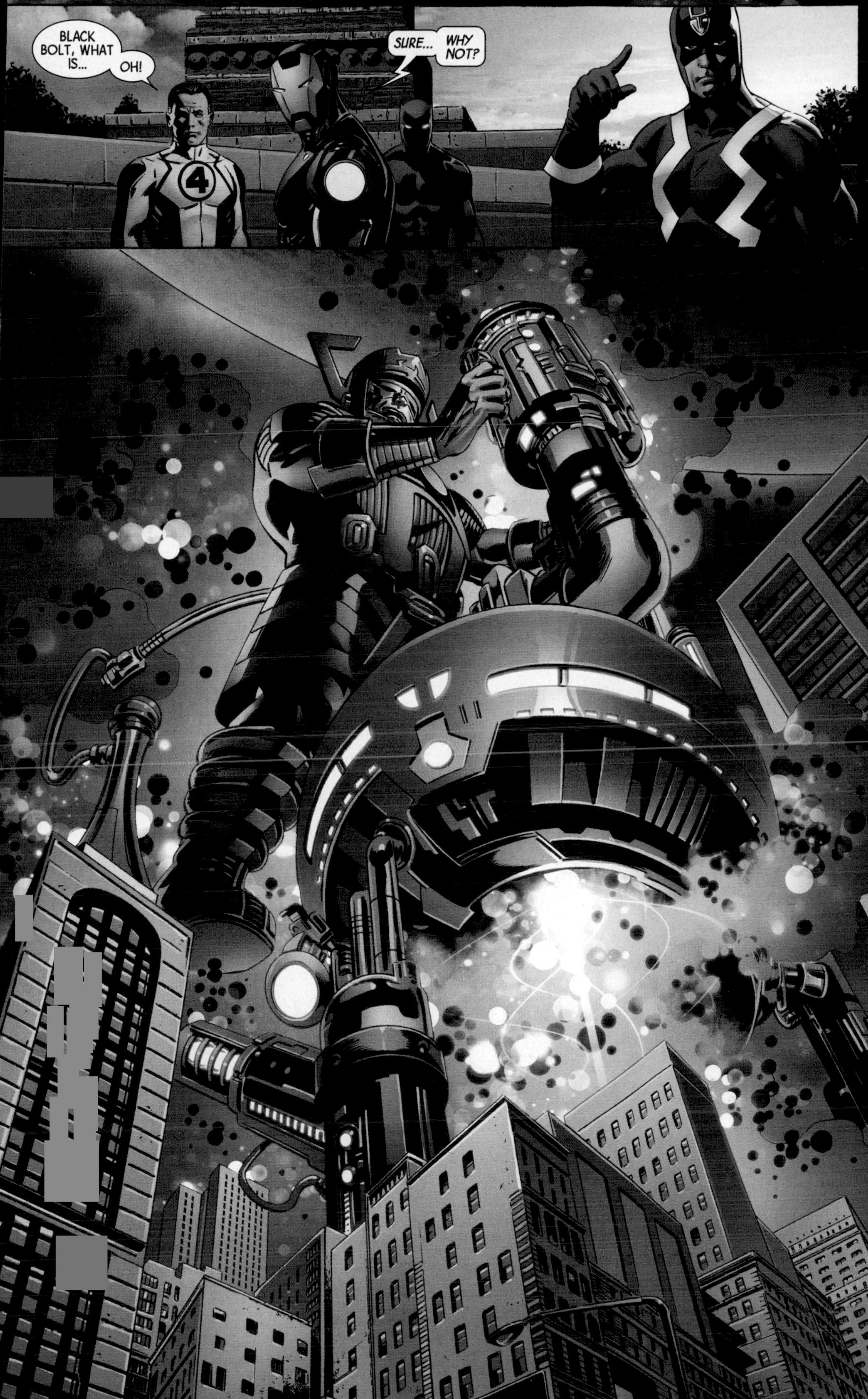
BLACK BOLT, WHAT IS... OH!
SURE... WHY NOT?

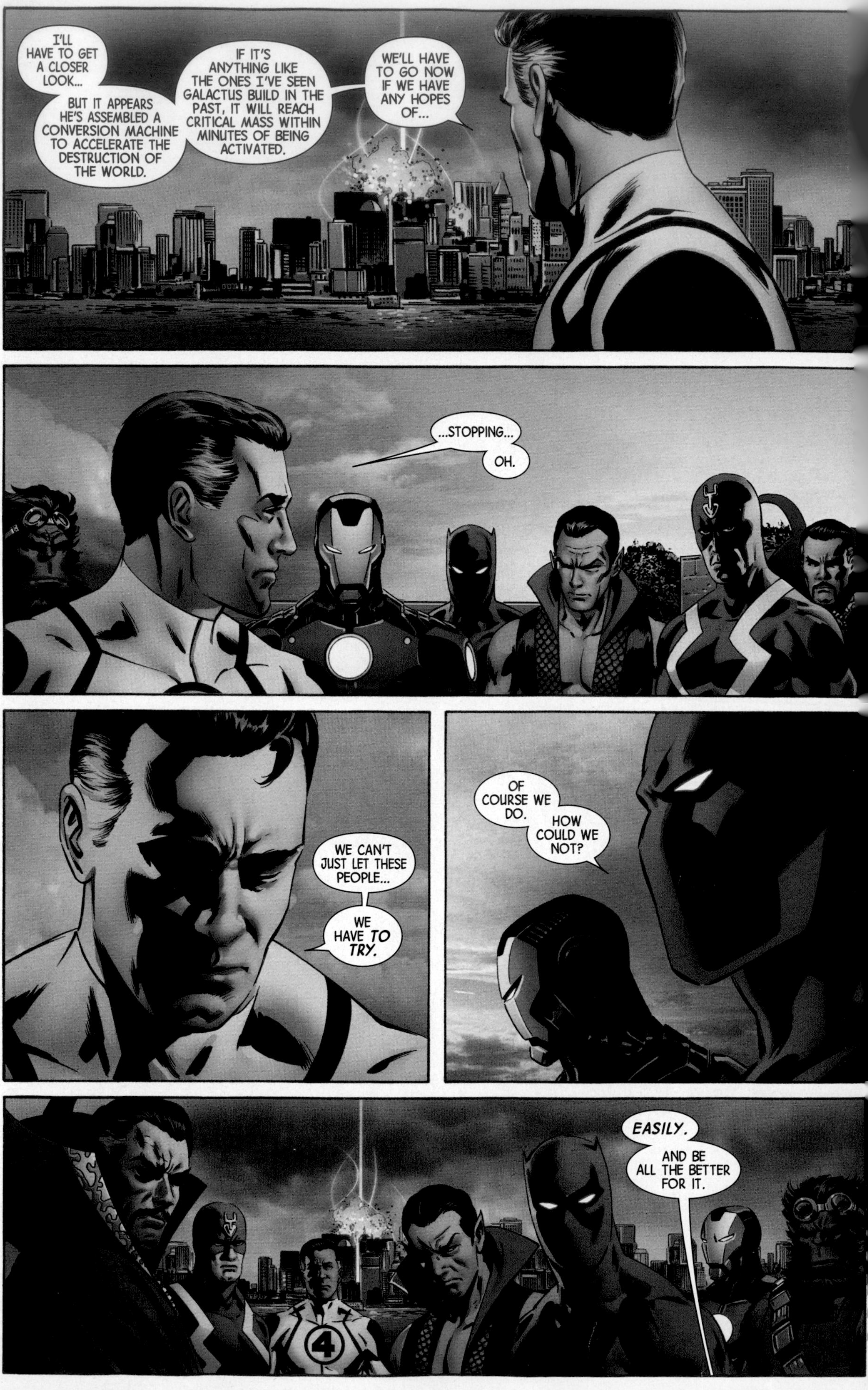
I'LL HAVE TO GET A CLOSER LOOK...
BUT IT APPEARS HE'S ASSEMBLED A CONVERSION MACHINE TO ACCELERATE THE DESTRUCTION OF THE WORLD.
IF IT'S ANYTHING LIKE THE ONES I'VE SEEN GALACTUS BUILD IN THE PAST, IT WILL REACH CRITICAL MASS WITHIN MINUTES OF BEING ACTIVATED.
WE'LL HAVE TO GO NOW IF WE HAVE ANY HOPES OF...
...STOPPING...
OH.
WE CAN'T JUST LET THESE PEOPLE...
WE HAVE *TO TRY.*
OF COURSE WE DO.
HOW COULD WE NOT?
EASILY.
AND BE ALL THE BETTER FOR IT.

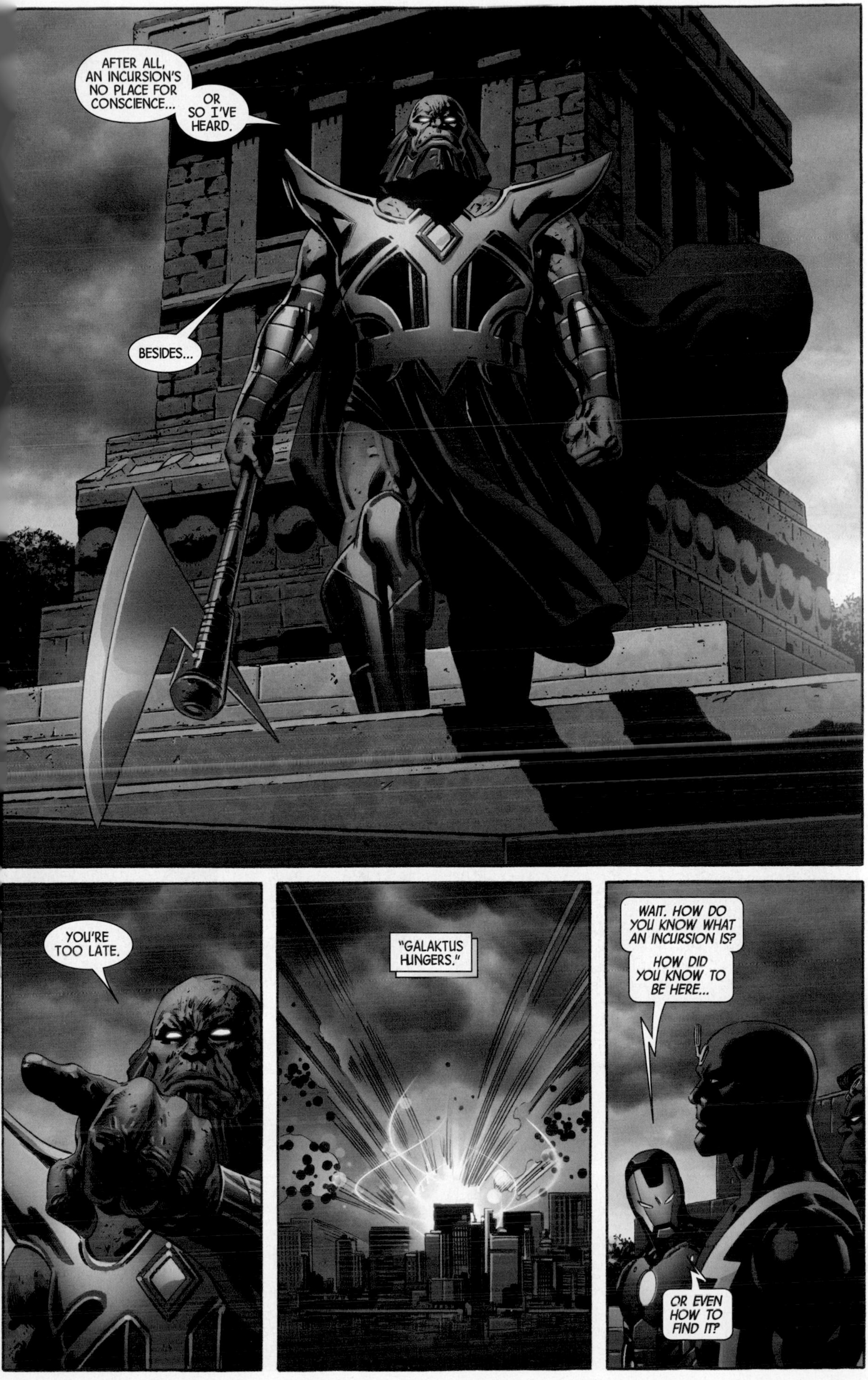
AFTER ALL, AN INCURSION'S NO PLACE FOR CONSCIENCE...
OR SO I'VE HEARD.
BESIDES...
YOU'RE TOO LATE.
"GALAKTUS HUNGERS."
WAIT. HOW DO YOU KNOW WHAT AN INCURSION IS?
HOW DID YOU KNOW TO BE HERE...
OR EVEN HOW TO FIND IT?

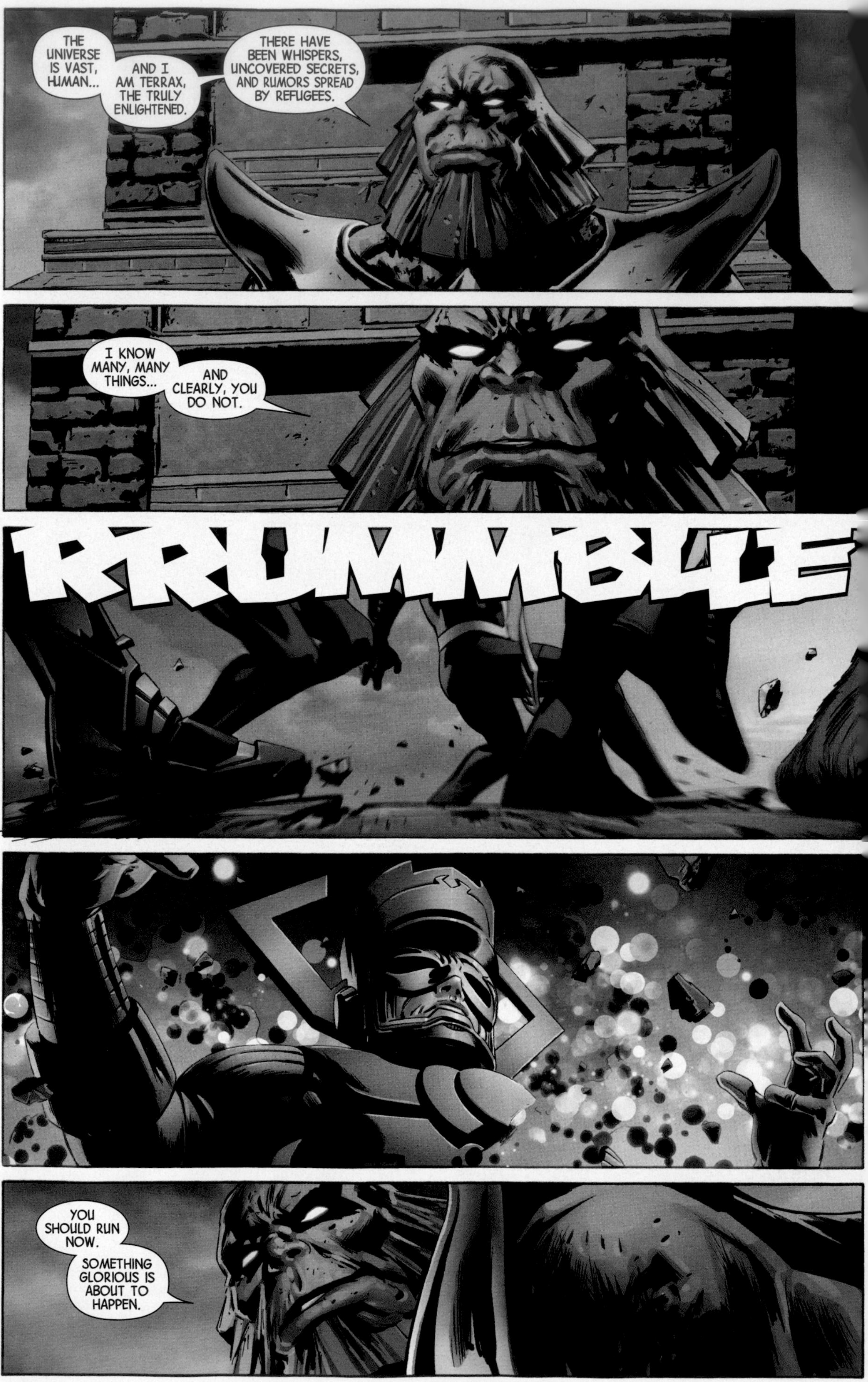
THE UNIVERSE IS VAST, HUMAN...
AND I AM TERRAX, THE TRULY ENLIGHTENED.
THERE HAVE BEEN WHISPERS, UNCOVERED SECRETS, AND RUMORS SPREAD BY REFUGEES.
I KNOW MANY, MANY THINGS...
AND CLEARLY, YOU DO NOT.
RRUMMBLLE
YOU SHOULD RUN NOW.
SOMETHING GLORIOUS IS ABOUT TO HAPPEN.

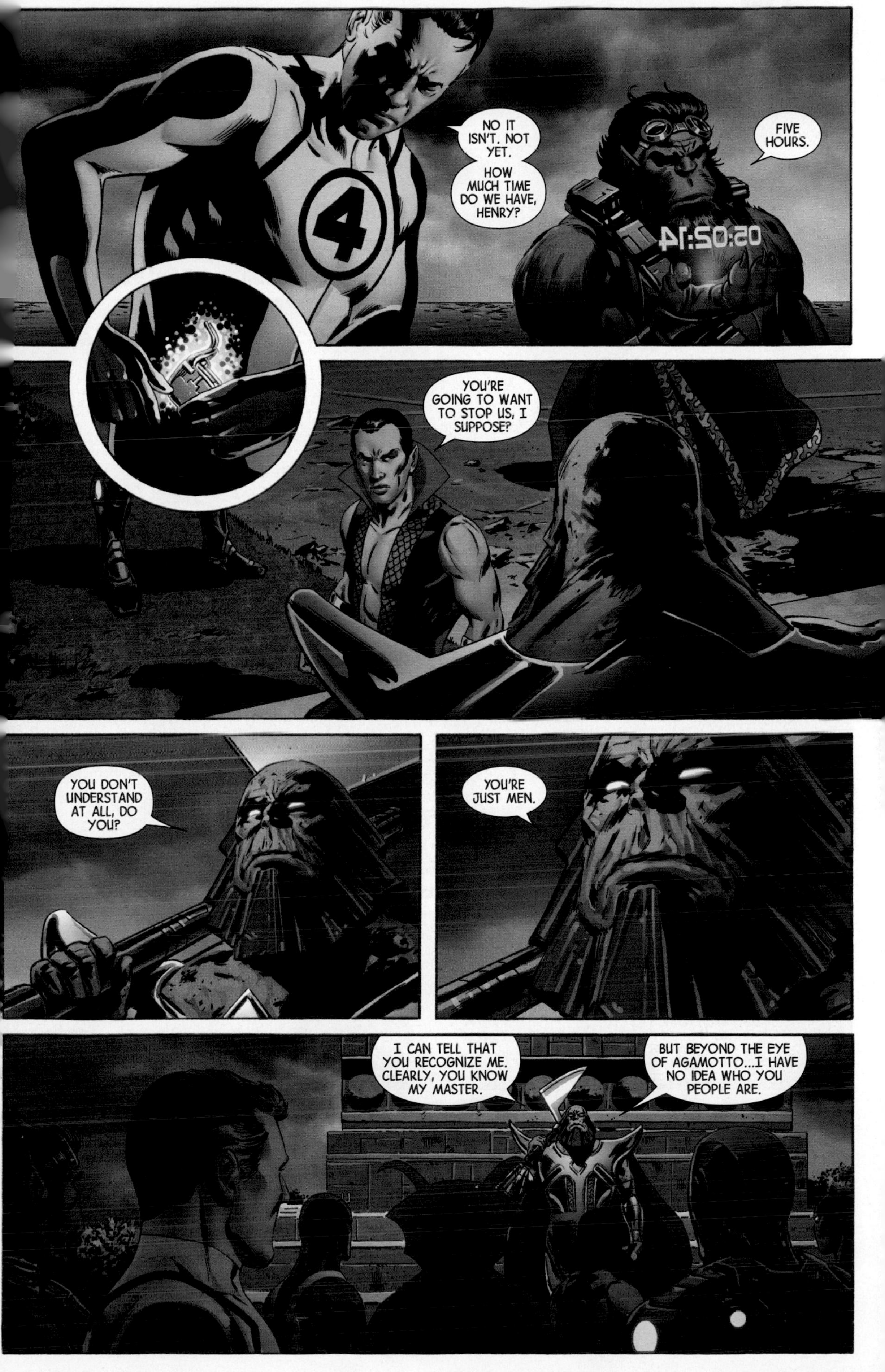
NO IT ISN'T. NOT YET.
HOW MUCH TIME DO WE HAVE, HENRY?
FIVE HOURS.
YOU'RE GOING TO WANT TO STOP US, I SUPPOSE?
YOU DON'T UNDERSTAND AT ALL, DO YOU?
YOU'RE JUST MEN.
I CAN TELL THAT YOU RECOGNIZE ME. CLEARLY, YOU KNOW MY MASTER.
BUT BEYOND THE EYE OF AGAMOTTO...I HAVE NO IDEA WHO YOU PEOPLE ARE.

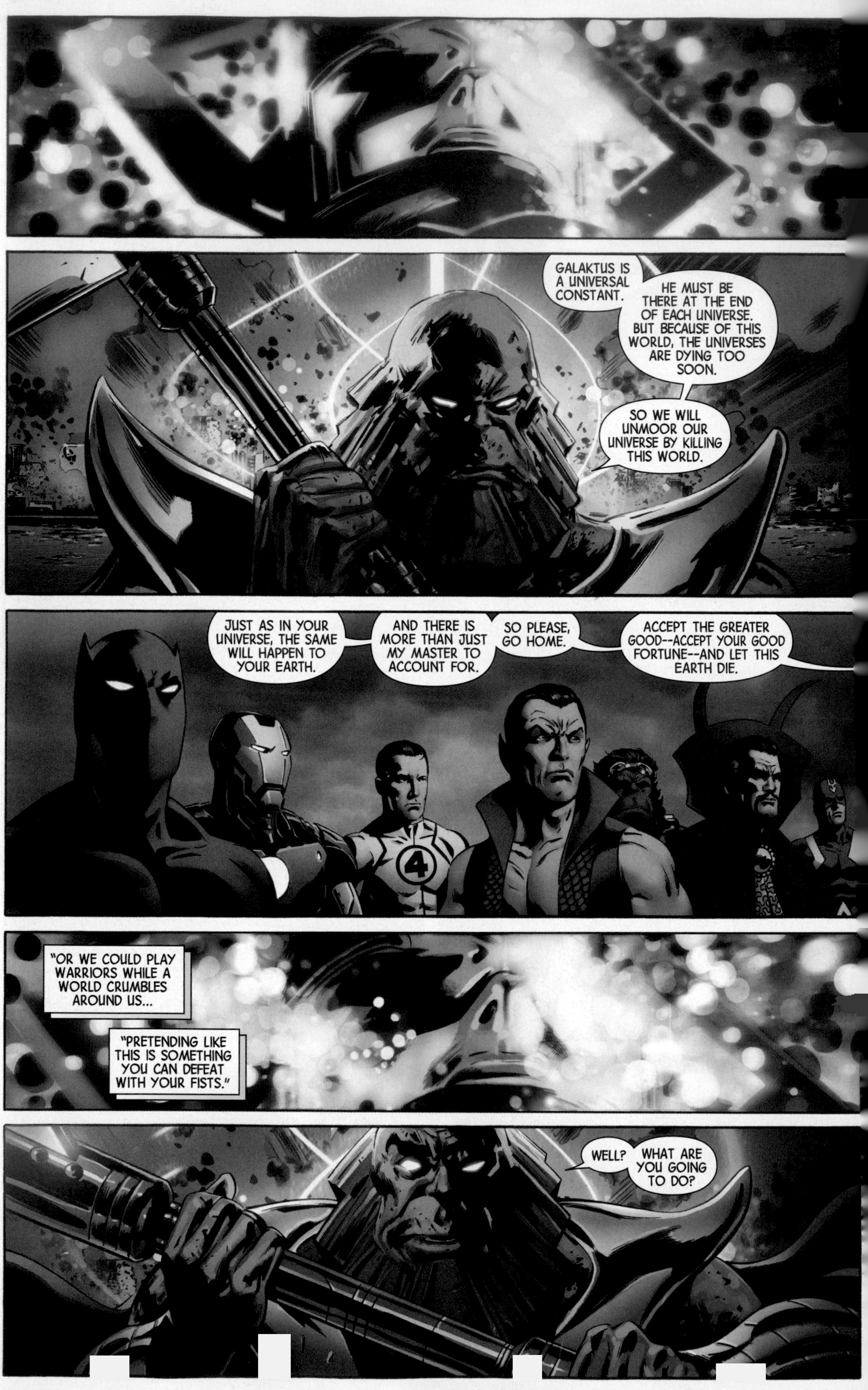
GALAKTUS IS A UNIVERSAL CONSTANT.
HE MUST BE THERE AT THE END OF EACH UNIVERSE. BUT BECAUSE OF THIS WORLD, THE UNIVERSES ARE DYING TOO SOON.
SO WE WILL UNMOOR OUR UNIVERSE BY KILLING THIS WORLD.
JUST AS IN YOUR UNIVERSE, THE SAME WILL HAPPEN TO YOUR EARTH.
AND THERE IS MORE THAN JUST MY MASTER TO ACCOUNT FOR.
SO PLEASE, GO HOME.
ACCEPT THE GREATER GOOD--ACCEPT YOUR GOOD FORTUNE--AND LET THIS EARTH DIE.
"OR WE COULD PLAY WARRIORS WHILE A WORLD CRUMBLES AROUND US...
"PRETENDING LIKE THIS IS SOMETHING YOU CAN DEFEAT WITH YOUR FISTS."
WELL?
WHAT ARE YOU GOING TO DO?

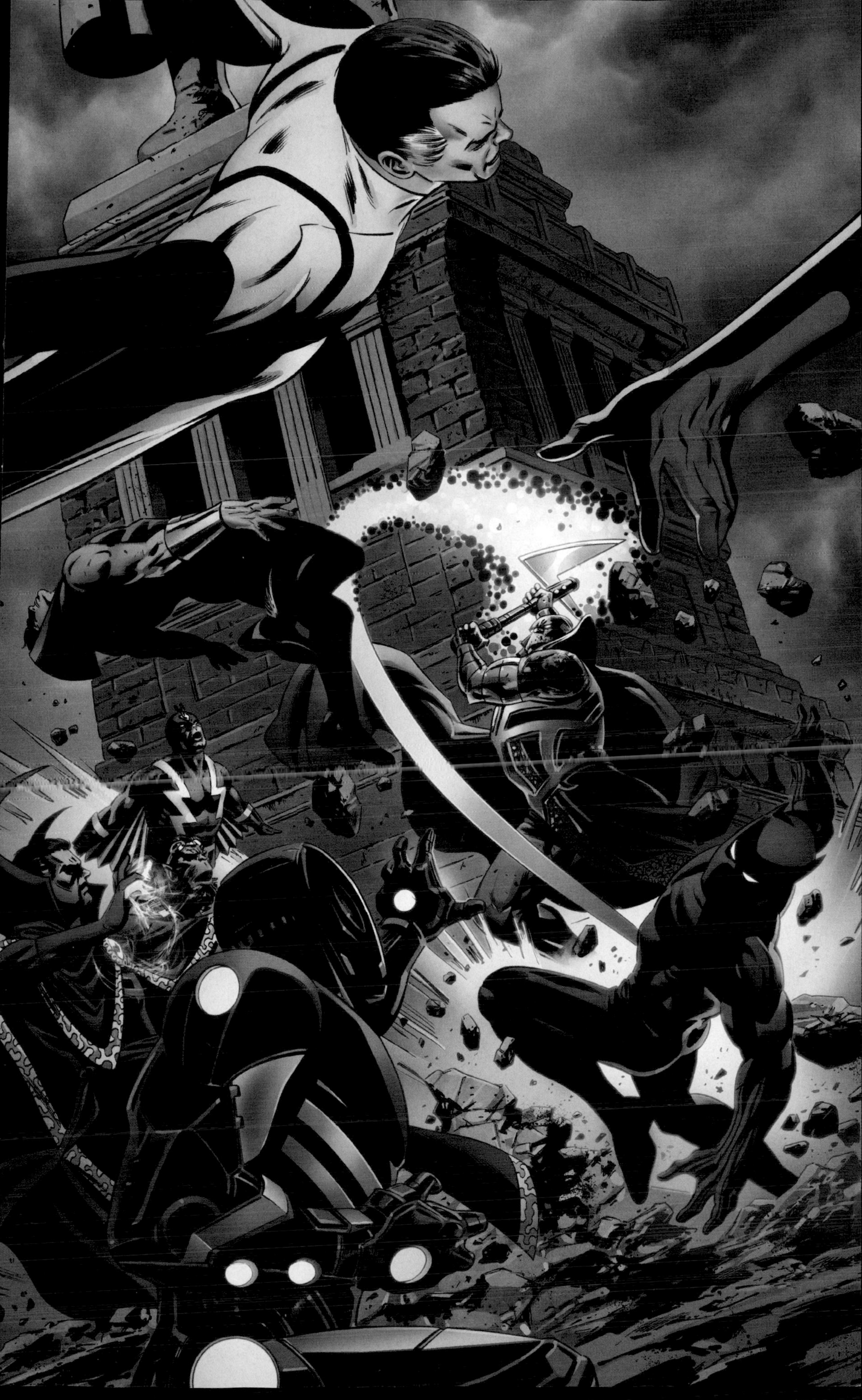

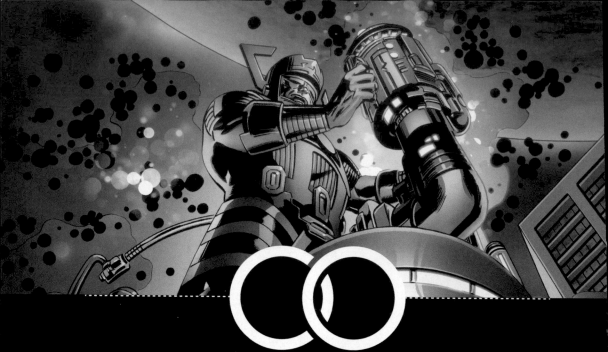

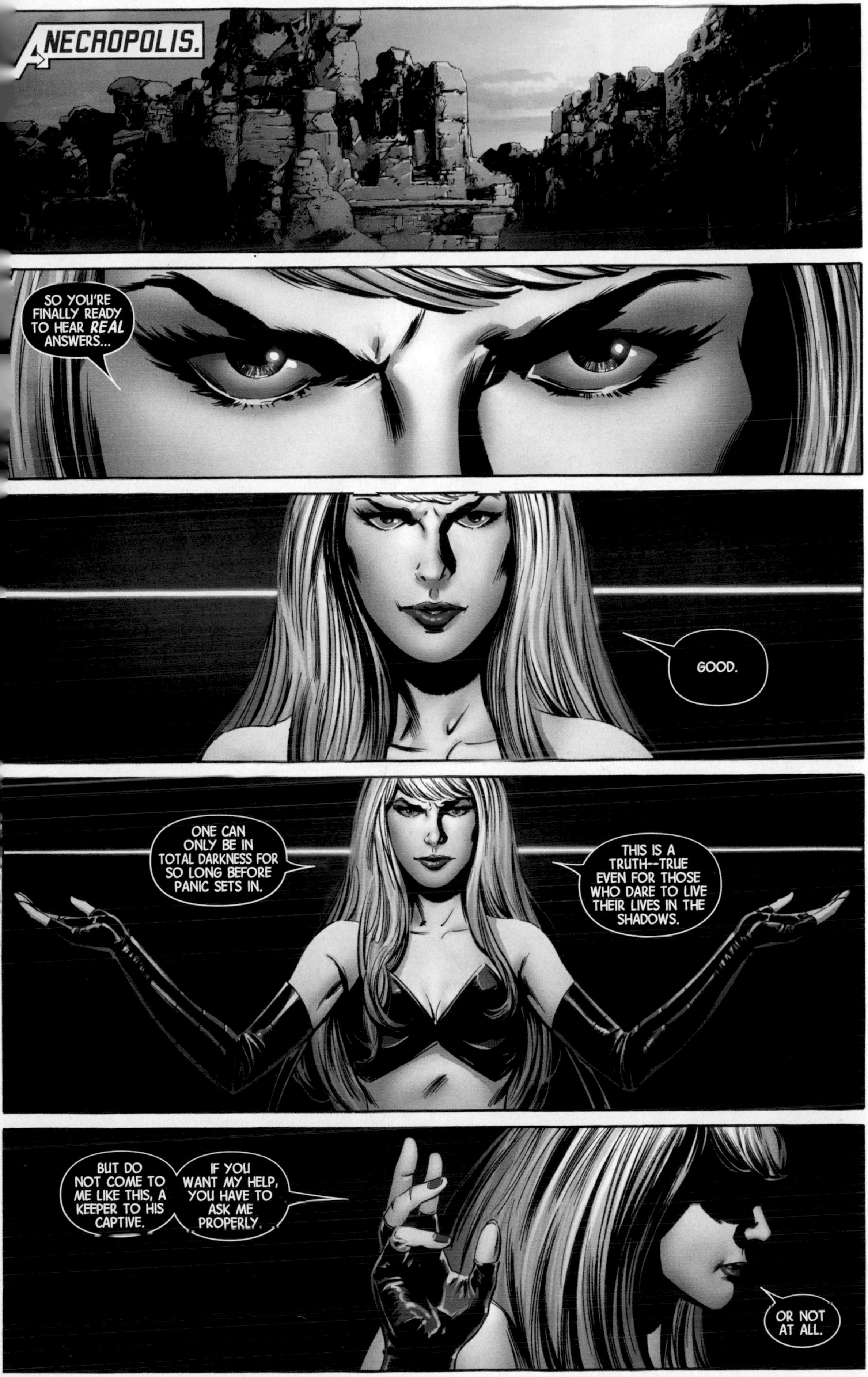
NECROPOLIS.
SO YOU'RE FINALLY READY TO HEAR REAL ANSWERS...
GOOD.
ONE CAN ONLY BE IN TOTAL DARKNESS FOR SO LONG BEFORE PANIC SETS IN.
THIS IS A TRUTH--TRUE EVEN FOR THOSE WHO DARE TO LIVE THEIR LIVES IN THE SHADOWS.
BUT DO NOT COME TO ME LIKE THIS, A KEEPER TO HIS CAPTIVE.
IF YOU WANT MY HELP, YOU HAVE TO ASK ME PROPERLY.
OR NOT AT ALL.

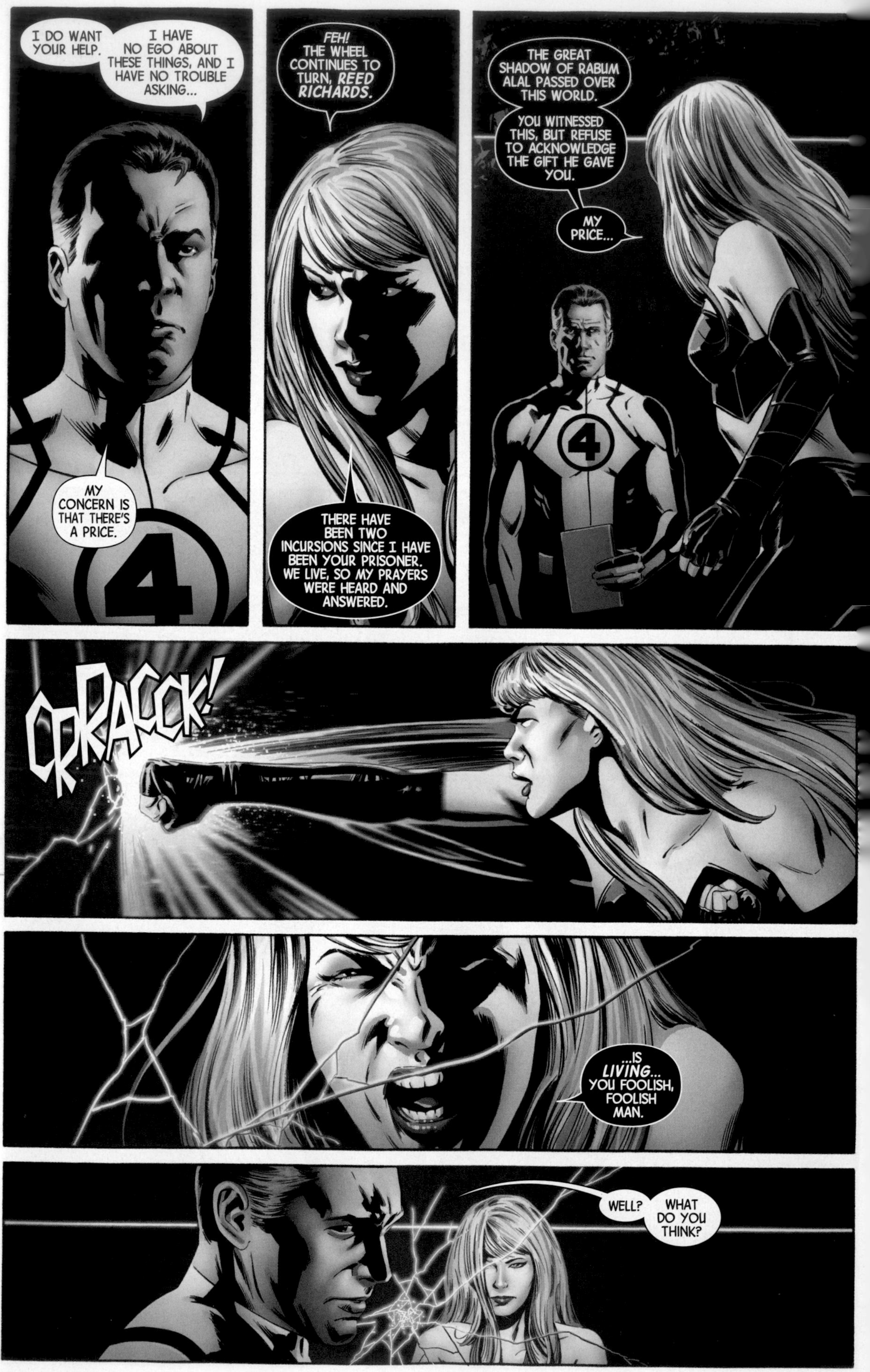
I DO WANT YOUR HELP.
I HAVE NO EGO ABOUT THESE THINGS, AND I HAVE NO TROUBLE ASKING...
MY CONCERN IS THAT THERE'S A PRICE.
FEH! THE WHEEL CONTINUES TO TURN, REED RICHARDS.
THERE HAVE BEEN TWO INCURSIONS SINCE I HAVE BEEN YOUR PRISONER. WE LIVE, SO MY PRAYERS WERE HEARD AND ANSWERED.
THE GREAT SHADOW OF RABUM ALAL PASSED OVER THIS WORLD.
YOU WITNESSED THIS, BUT REFUSE TO ACKNOWLEDGE THE GIFT HE GAVE YOU.
MY PRICE...
CRRACCK!
...IS LIVING... YOU FOOLISH, FOOLISH MAN.
WELL? WHAT DO YOU THINK?

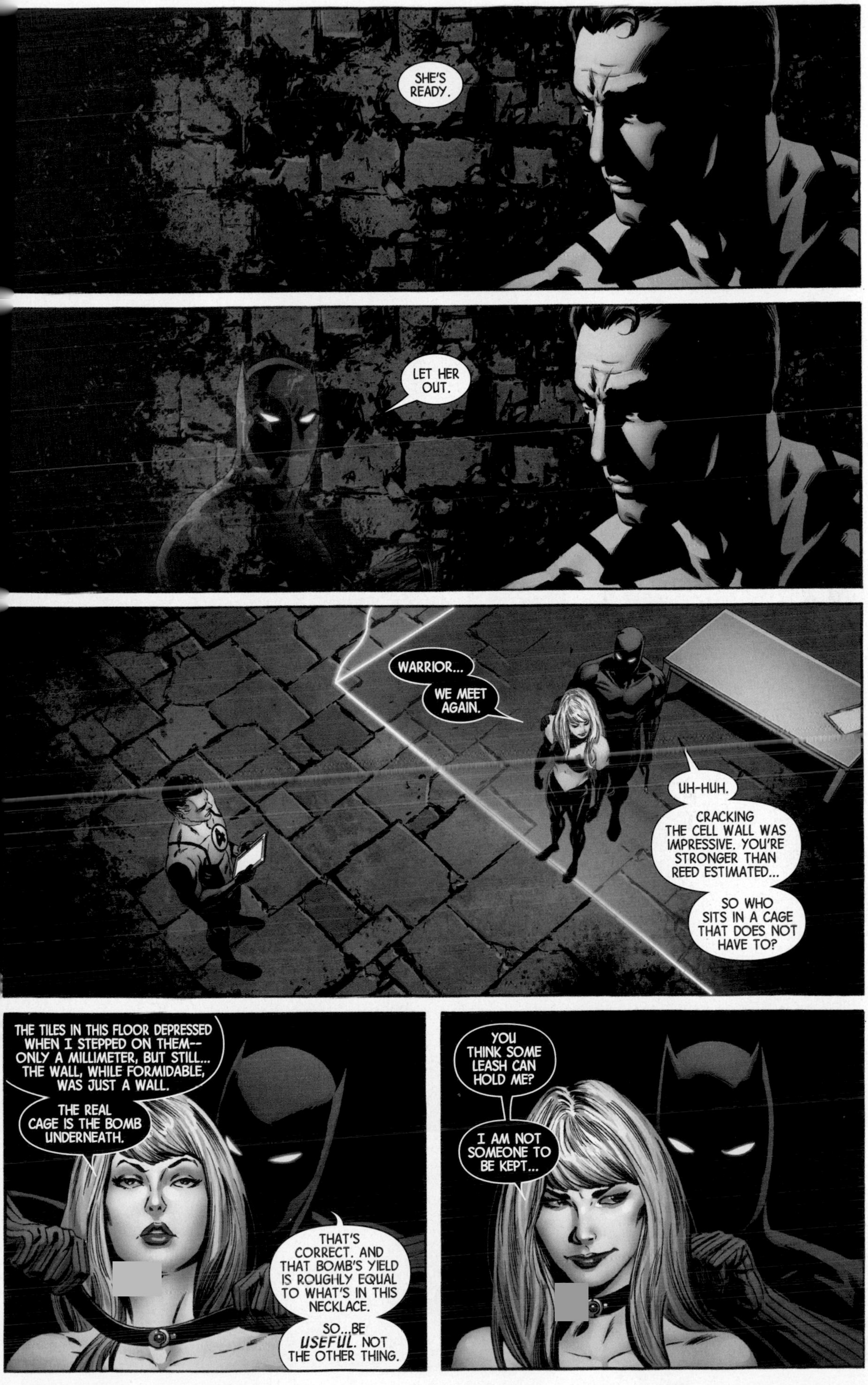
SHE'S READY.
LET HER OUT.
WARRIOR...
WE MEET AGAIN.
UH-HUH.
CRACKING THE CELL WALL WAS IMPRESSIVE. YOU'RE STRONGER THAN REED ESTIMATED...
SO WHO SITS IN A CAGE THAT DOES NOT HAVE TO?
THE TILES IN THIS FLOOR DEPRESSED WHEN I STEPPED ON THEM-- ONLY A MILLIMETER, BUT STILL... THE WALL, WHILE FORMIDABLE, WAS JUST A WALL.
THE REAL CAGE IS THE BOMB UNDERNEATH.
THAT'S CORRECT. AND THAT BOMB'S YIELD IS ROUGHLY EQUAL TO WHAT'S IN THIS NECKLACE.
SO...BE USEFUL. NOT THE OTHER THING.
YOU THINK SOME LEASH CAN HOLD ME?
I AM NOT SOMEONE TO BE KEPT...

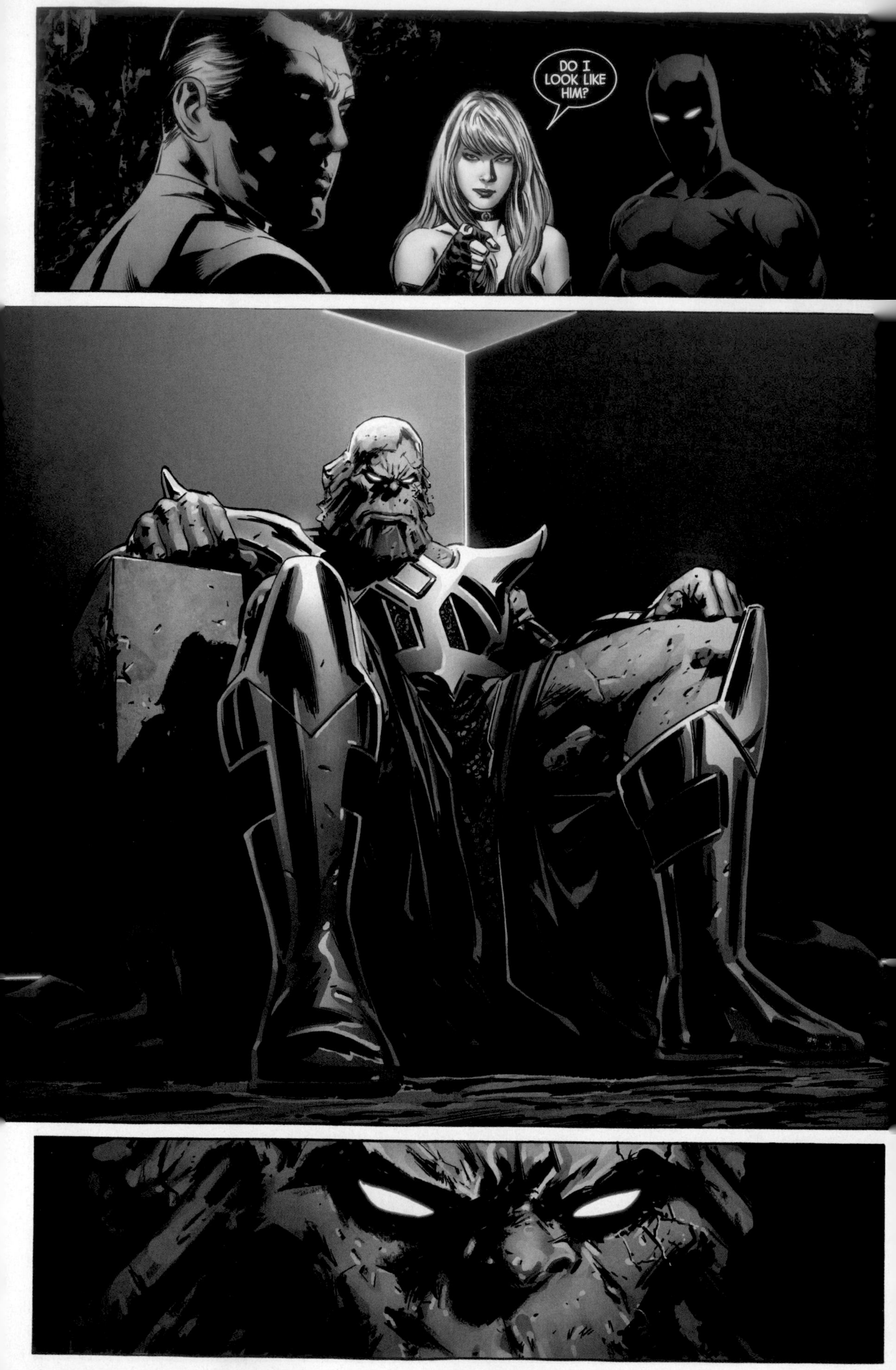
DO I LOOK LIKE HIM?

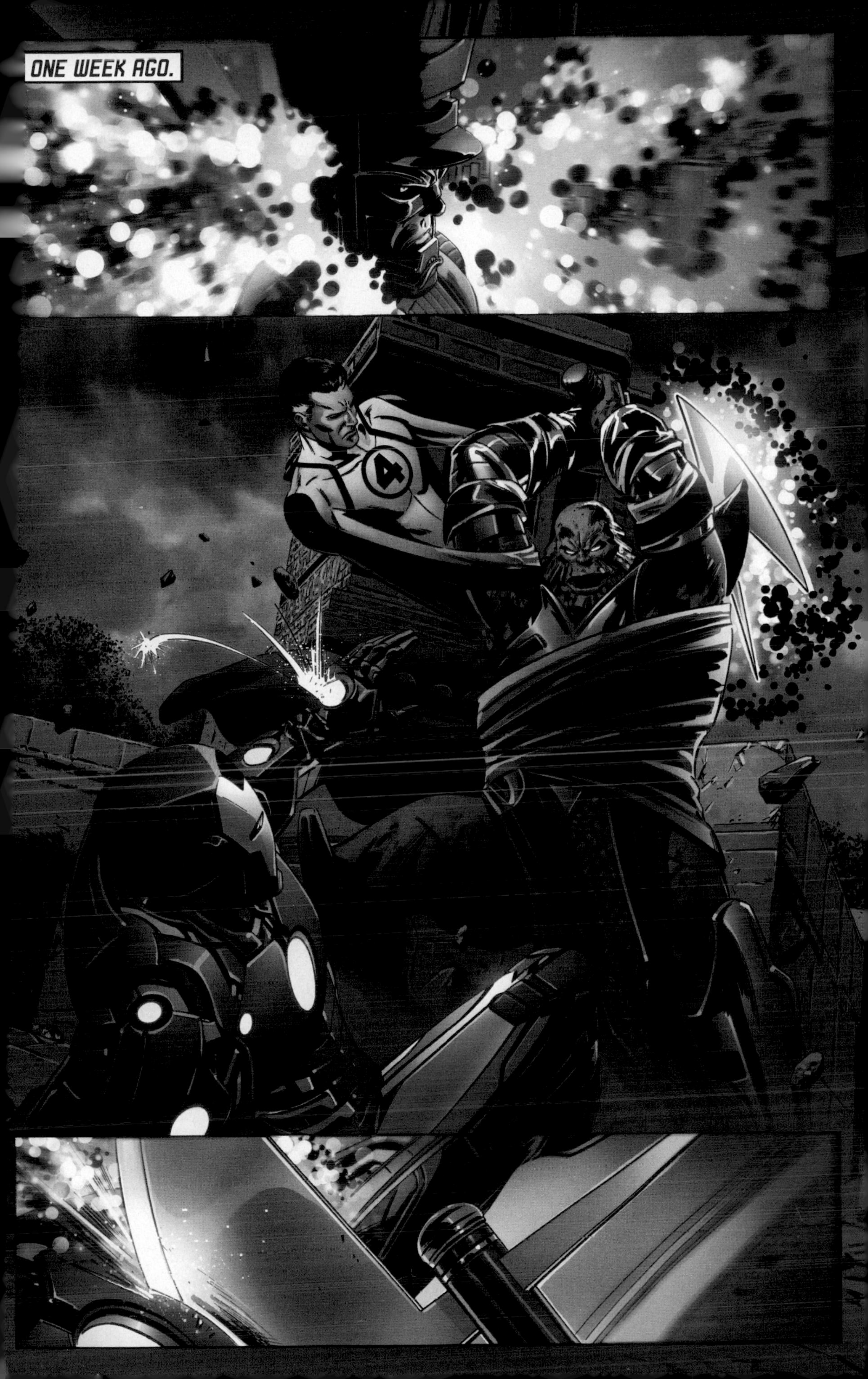
ONE WEEK AGO.

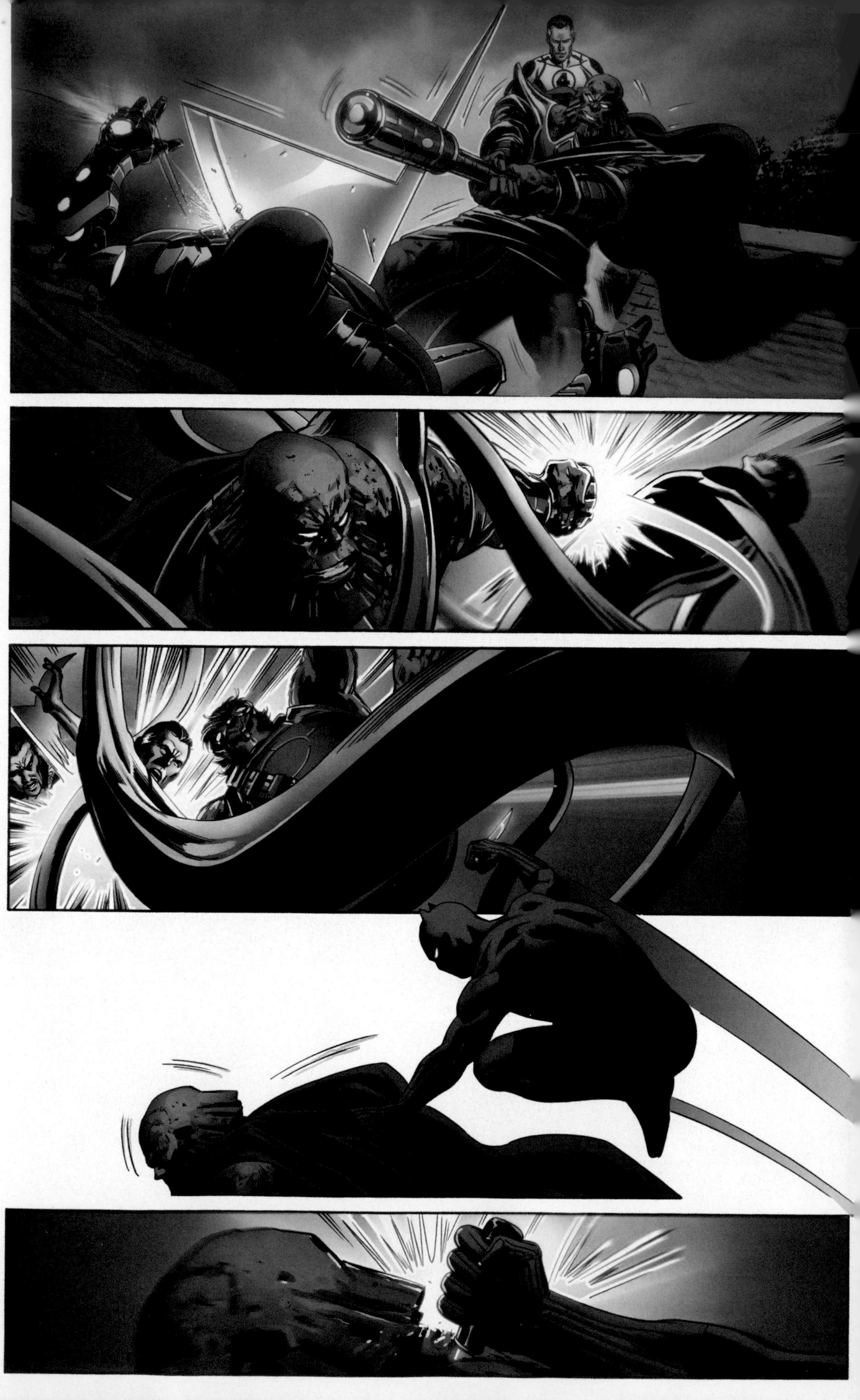

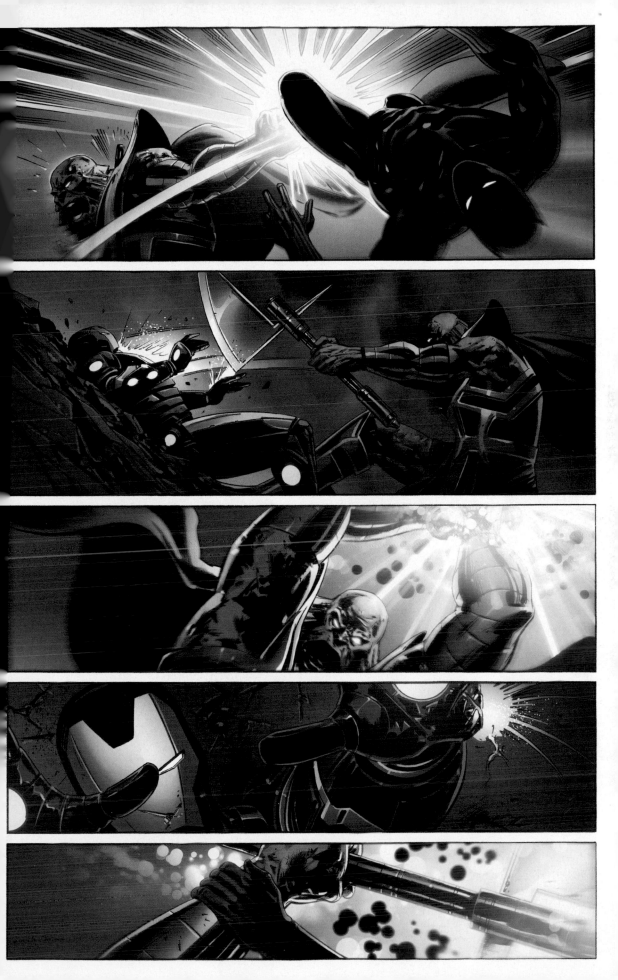

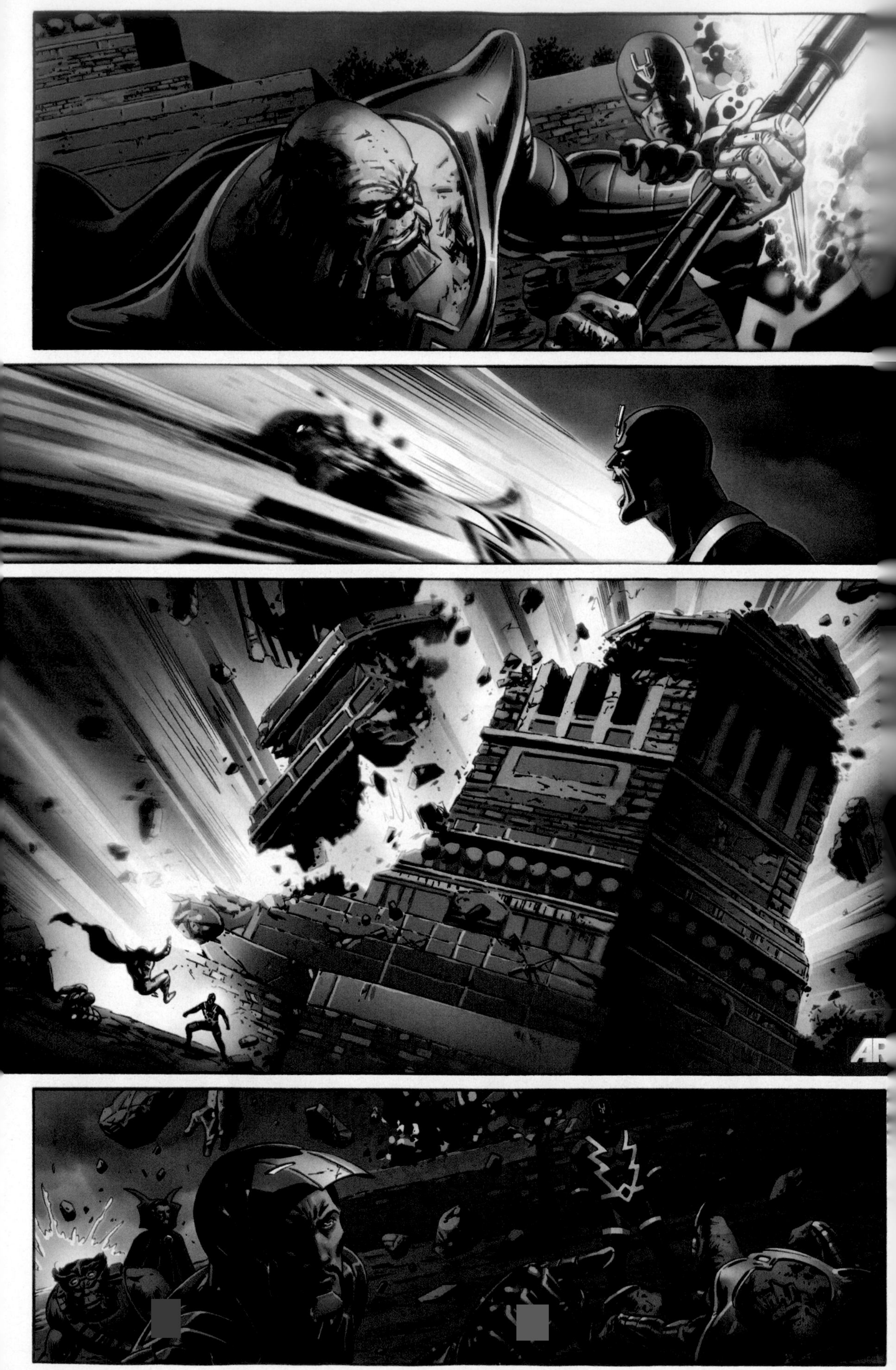

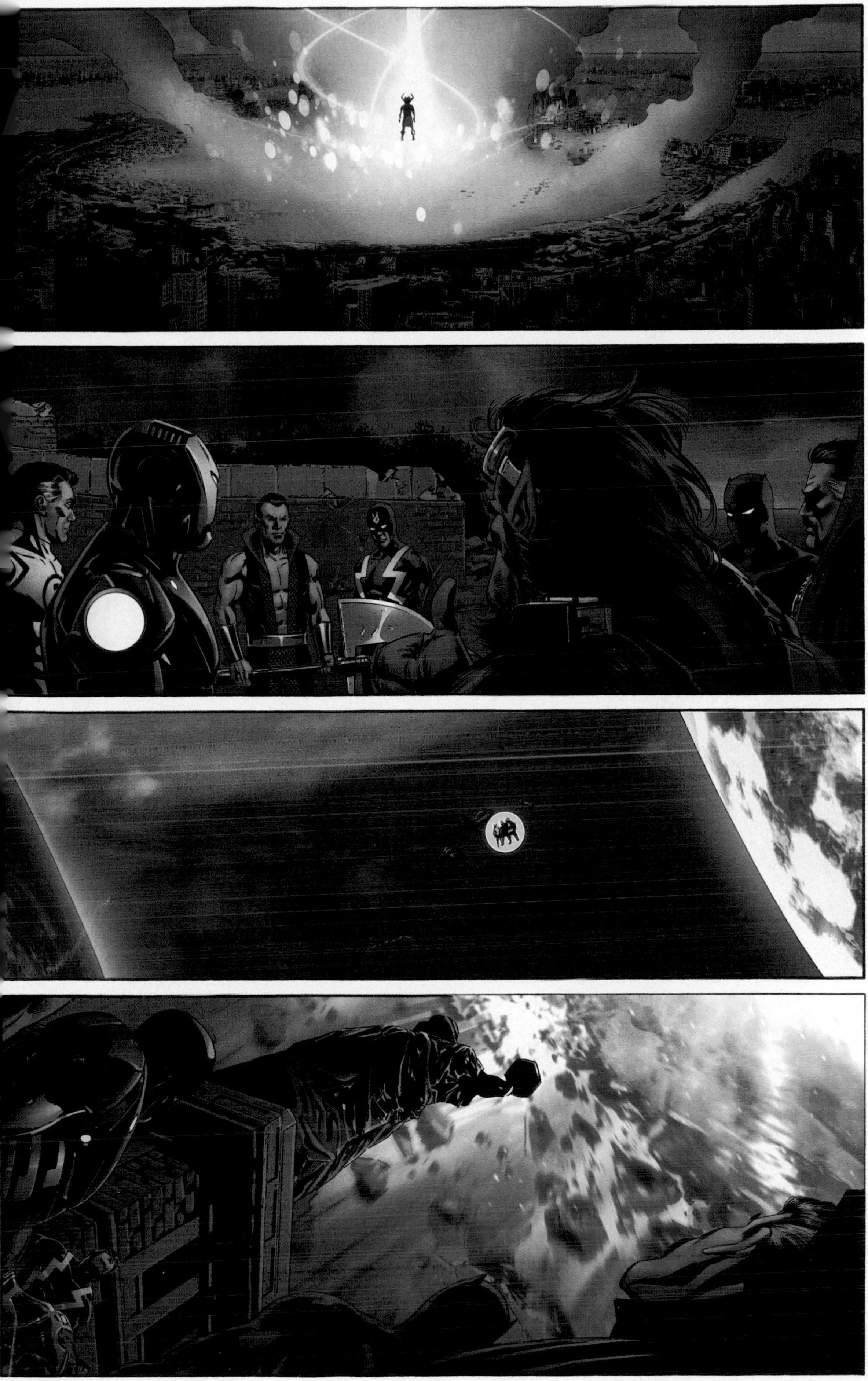

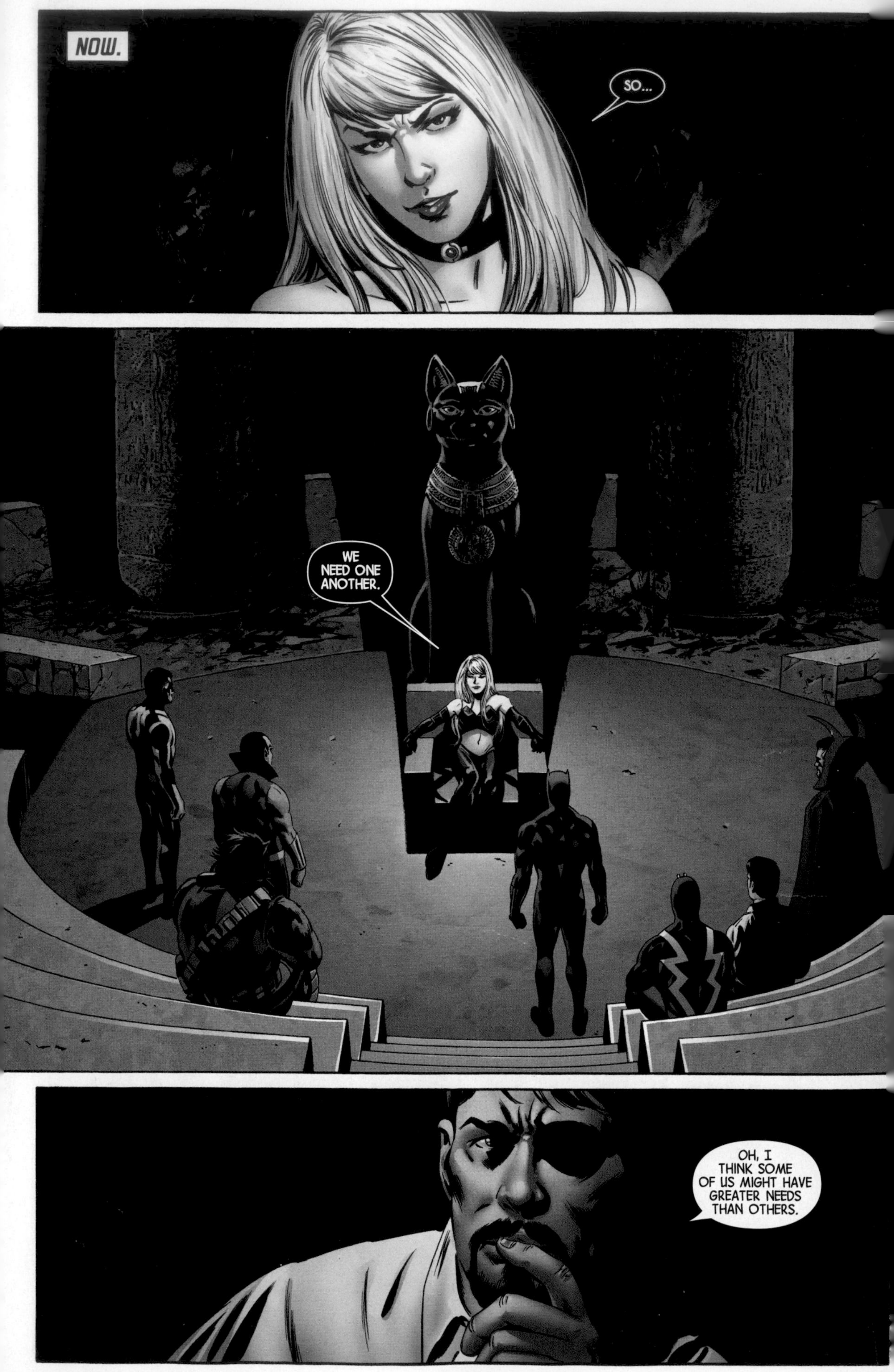
NOW.
SO...
WE NEED ONE ANOTHER.
OH, I THINK SOME OF US MIGHT HAVE GREATER NEEDS THAN OTHERS.

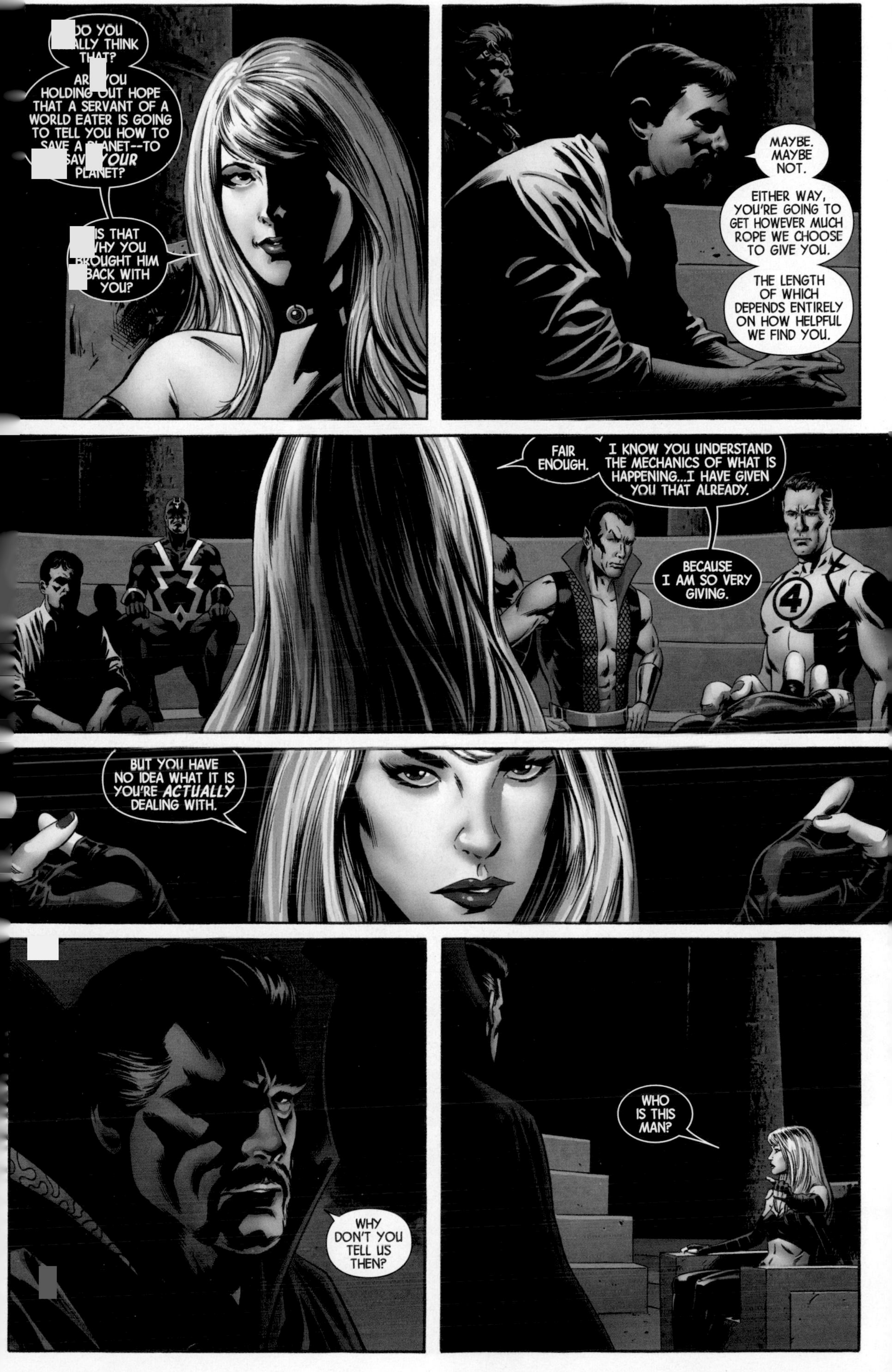
DO YOU REALLY THINK THAT?
ARE YOU HOLDING OUT HOPE THAT A SERVANT OF A WORLD EATER IS GOING TO TELL YOU HOW TO SAVE A PLANET--TO SAVE *YOUR* PLANET?
IS THAT WHY YOU BROUGHT HIM BACK WITH YOU?
MAYBE. MAYBE NOT.
EITHER WAY, YOU'RE GOING TO GET HOWEVER MUCH ROPE WE CHOOSE TO GIVE YOU.
THE LENGTH OF WHICH DEPENDS ENTIRELY ON HOW HELPFUL WE FIND YOU.
FAIR ENOUGH.
I KNOW YOU UNDERSTAND THE MECHANICS OF WHAT IS HAPPENING...I HAVE GIVEN YOU THAT ALREADY.
BECAUSE I AM SO VERY GIVING.
BUT YOU HAVE NO IDEA WHAT IT IS YOU'RE *ACTUALLY* DEALING WITH.
WHY DON'T YOU TELL US THEN?
WHO IS THIS MAN?

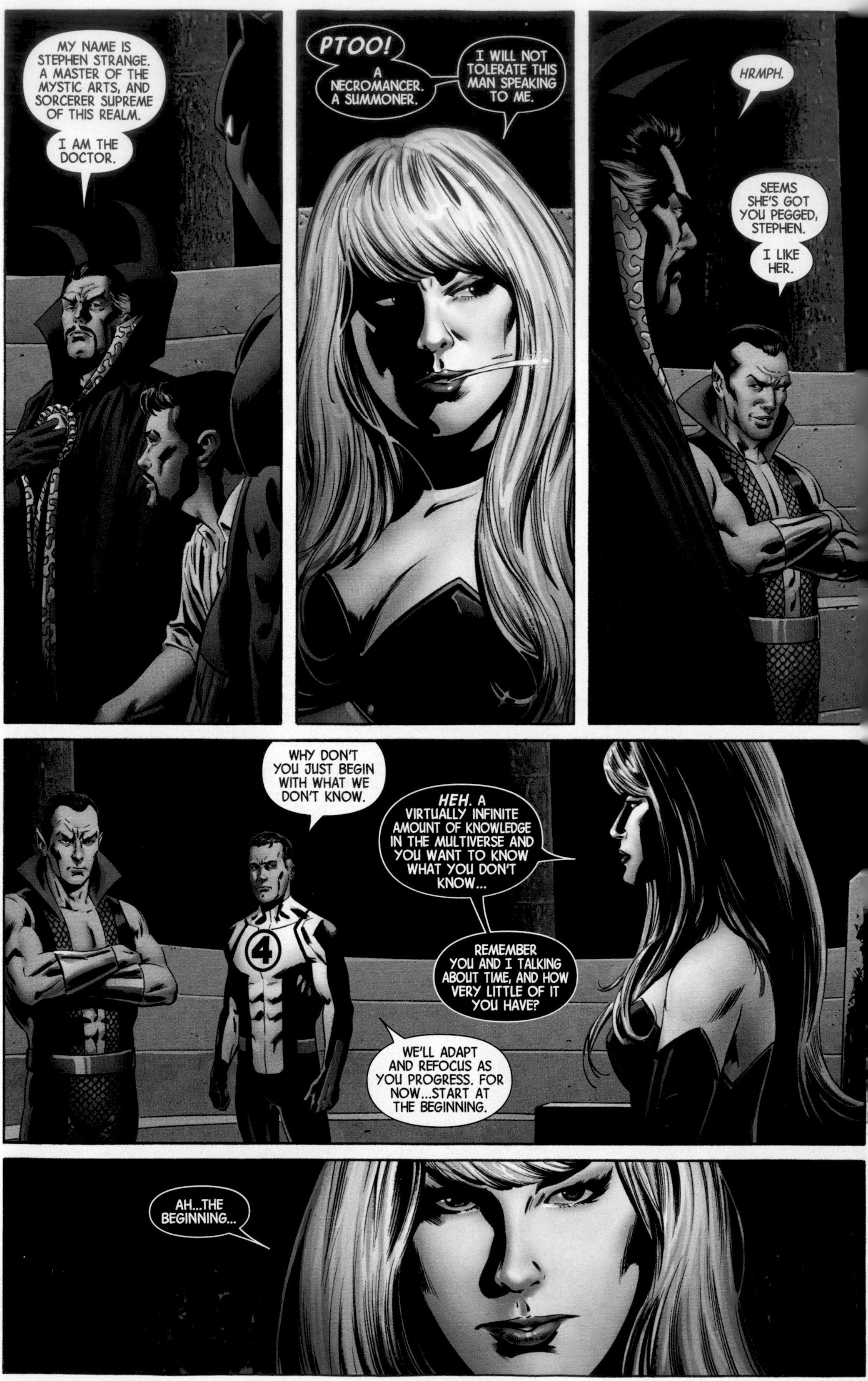
MY NAME IS STEPHEN STRANGE. A MASTER OF THE MYSTIC ARTS, AND SORCERER SUPREME OF THIS REALM.
I AM THE DOCTOR.
PTOO!
A NECROMANCER. A SUMMONER.
I WILL NOT TOLERATE THIS MAN SPEAKING TO ME.
HRMPH.
SEEMS SHE'S GOT YOU PEGGED, STEPHEN.
I LIKE HER.
WHY DON'T YOU JUST BEGIN WITH WHAT WE DON'T KNOW.
HEH. A VIRTUALLY INFINITE AMOUNT OF KNOWLEDGE IN THE MULTIVERSE AND YOU WANT TO KNOW WHAT YOU DON'T KNOW...
REMEMBER YOU AND I TALKING ABOUT TIME, AND HOW VERY LITTLE OF IT YOU HAVE?
WE'LL ADAPT AND REFOCUS AS YOU PROGRESS. FOR NOW...START AT THE BEGINNING.
AH...THE BEGINNING...

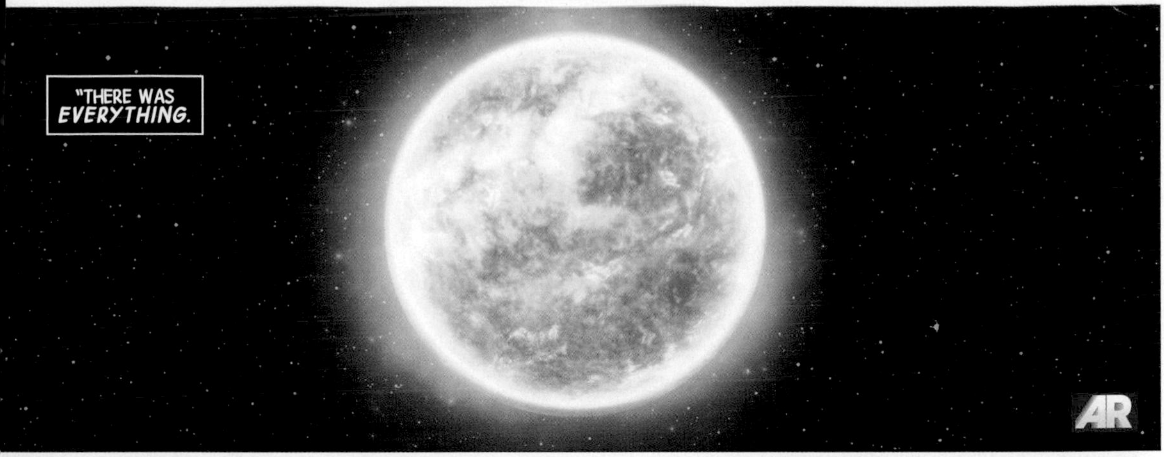
"THERE WAS EVERYTHING.

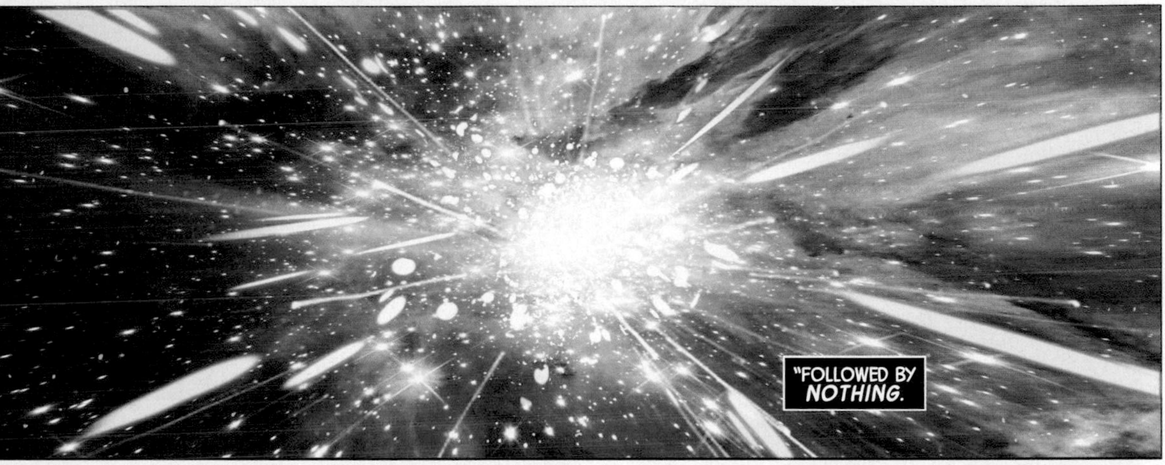
"FOLLOWED BY NOTHING.

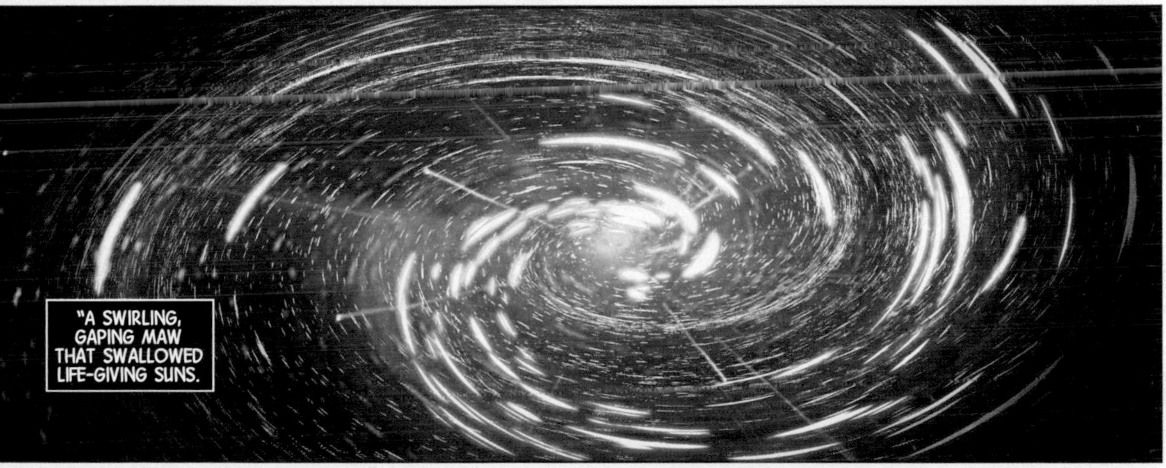
"A SWIRLING, GAPING MAW THAT SWALLOWED LIFE-GIVING SUNS.

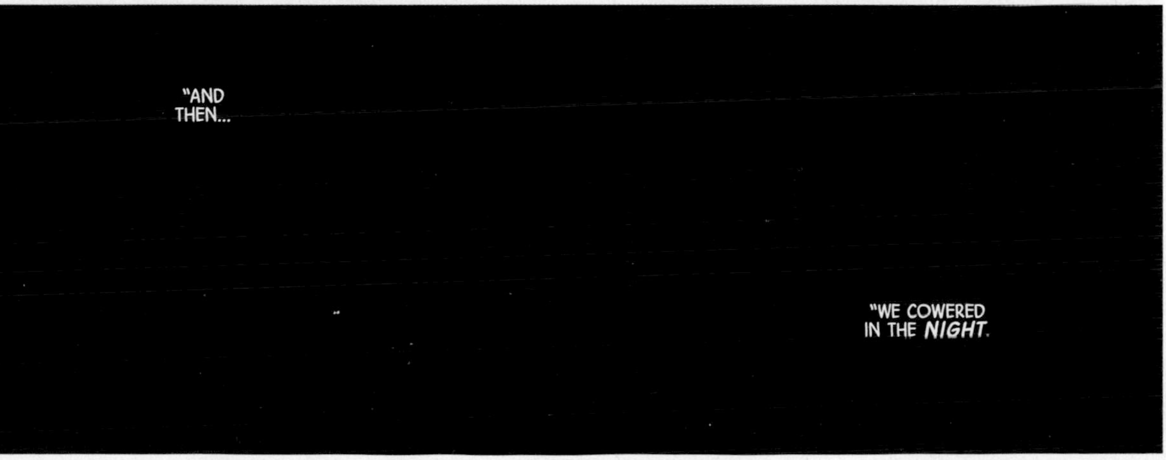
"AND THEN...
"WE COWERED IN THE NIGHT.

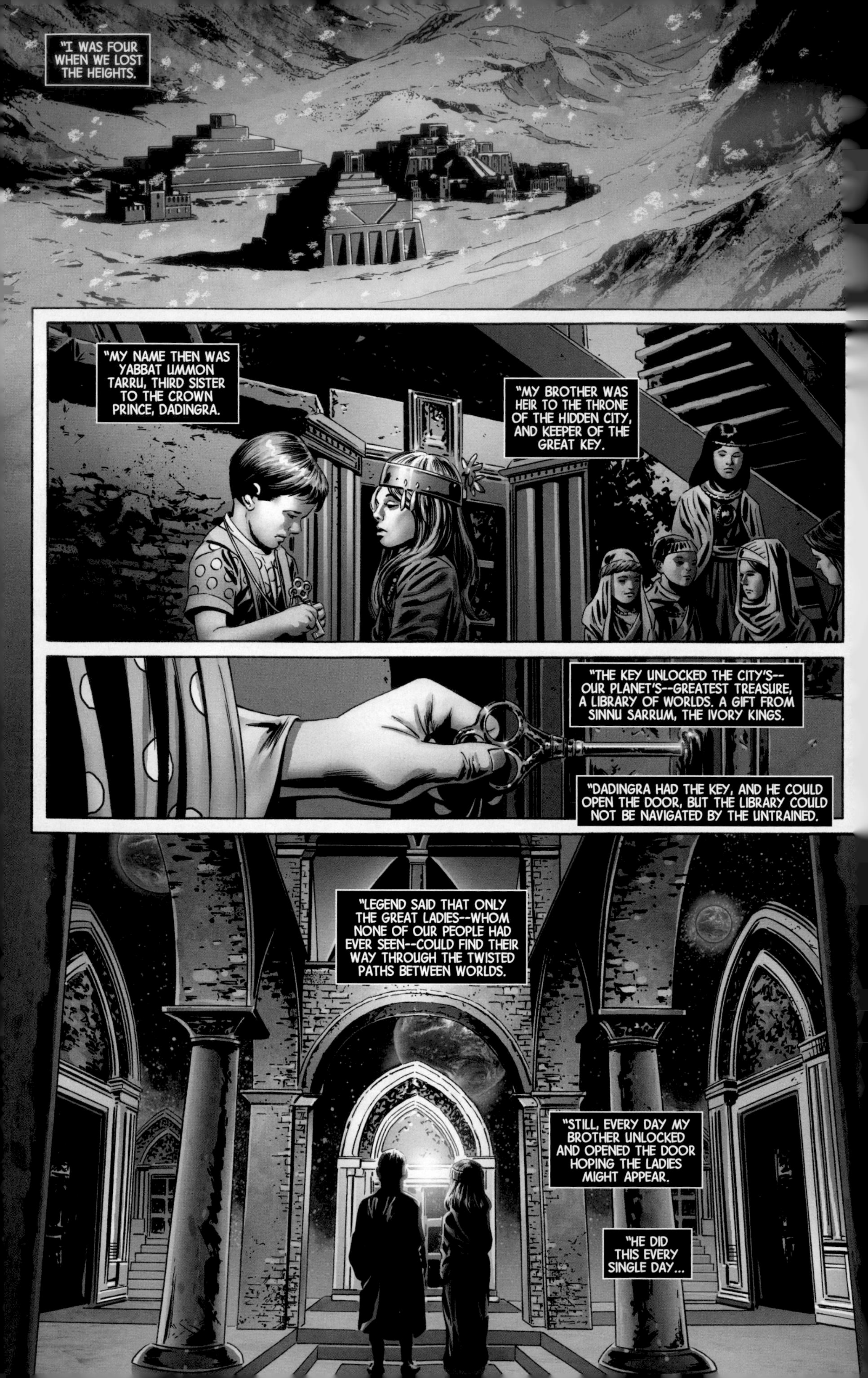
"I WAS FOUR WHEN WE LOST THE HEIGHTS.
"MY NAME THEN WAS YABBAT UMMON TARRU, THIRD SISTER TO THE CROWN PRINCE, DADINGRA.
"MY BROTHER WAS HEIR TO THE THRONE OF THE HIDDEN CITY, AND KEEPER OF THE GREAT KEY.
"THE KEY UNLOCKED THE CITY'S--OUR PLANET'S--GREATEST TREASURE, A LIBRARY OF WORLDS. A GIFT FROM SINNU SARRUM, THE IVORY KINGS.
"DADINGRA HAD THE KEY, AND HE COULD OPEN THE DOOR, BUT THE LIBRARY COULD NOT BE NAVIGATED BY THE UNTRAINED.
"LEGEND SAID THAT ONLY THE GREAT LADIES--WHOM NONE OF OUR PEOPLE HAD EVER SEEN--COULD FIND THEIR WAY THROUGH THE TWISTED PATHS BETWEEN WORLDS.
"STILL, EVERY DAY MY BROTHER UNLOCKED AND OPENED THE DOOR HOPING THE LADIES MIGHT APPEAR.
"HE DID THIS EVERY SINGLE DAY...

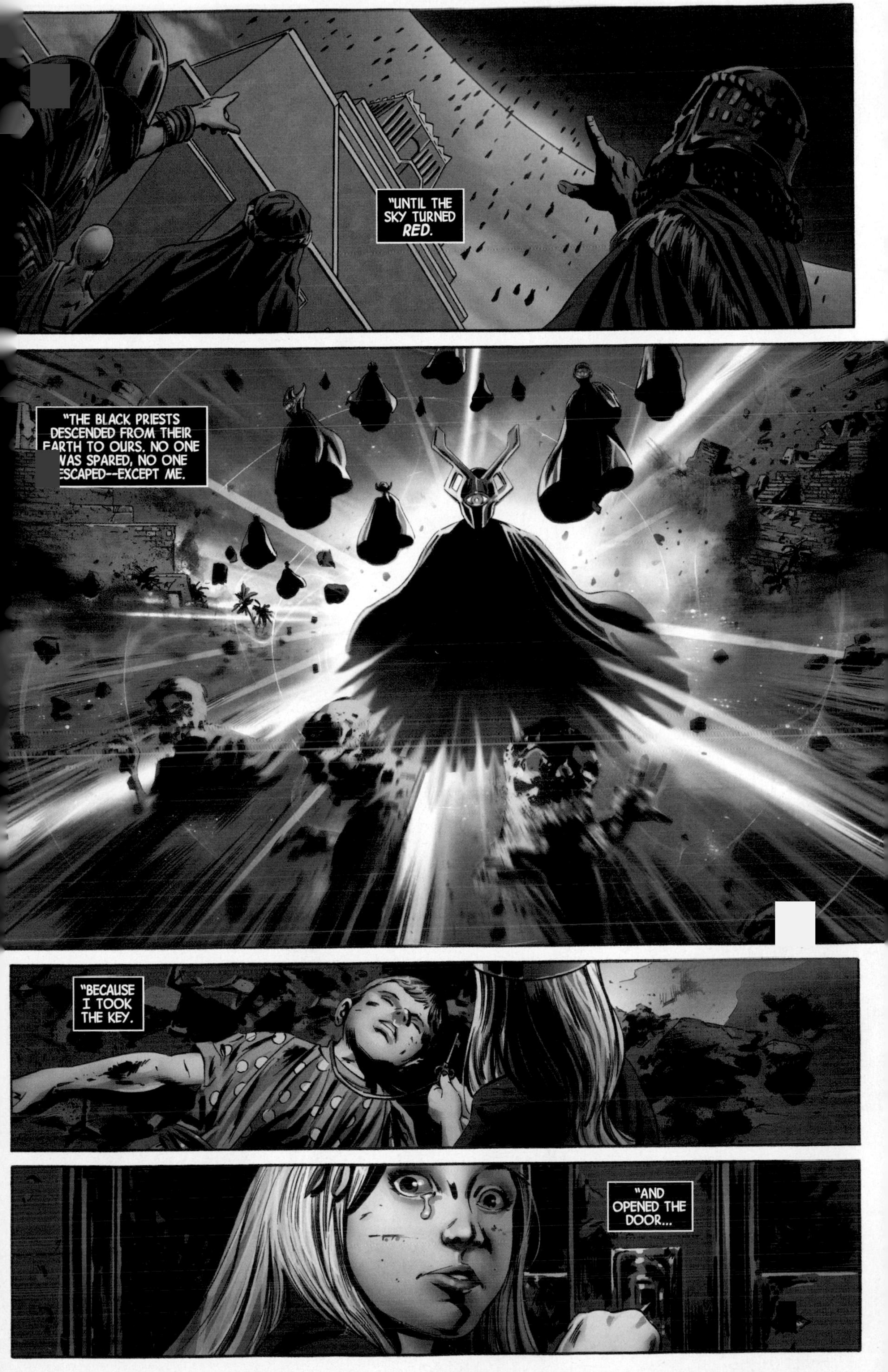
"UNTIL THE SKY TURNED RED.
"THE BLACK PRIESTS DESCENDED FROM THEIR EARTH TO OURS. NO ONE WAS SPARED, NO ONE ESCAPED--EXCEPT ME.
"BECAUSE I TOOK THE KEY.
"AND OPENED THE DOOR...

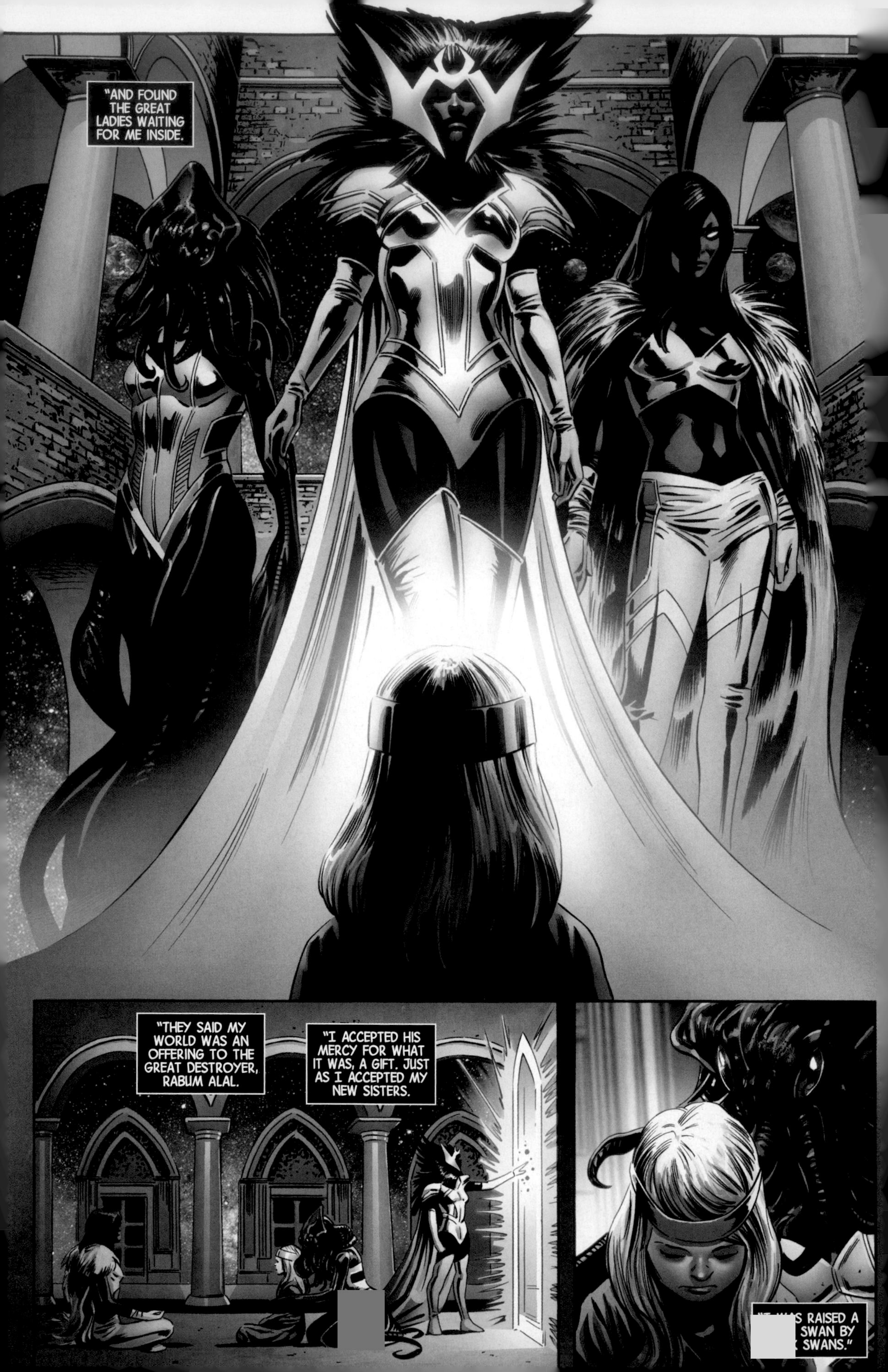
"AND FOUND THE GREAT LADIES WAITING FOR ME INSIDE.
"THEY SAID MY WORLD WAS AN OFFERING TO THE GREAT DESTROYER, RABUM ALAL.
"I ACCEPTED HIS MERCY FOR WHAT IT WAS, A GIFT. JUST AS I ACCEPTED MY NEW SISTERS.
RAISED A SWAN BY SWANS."

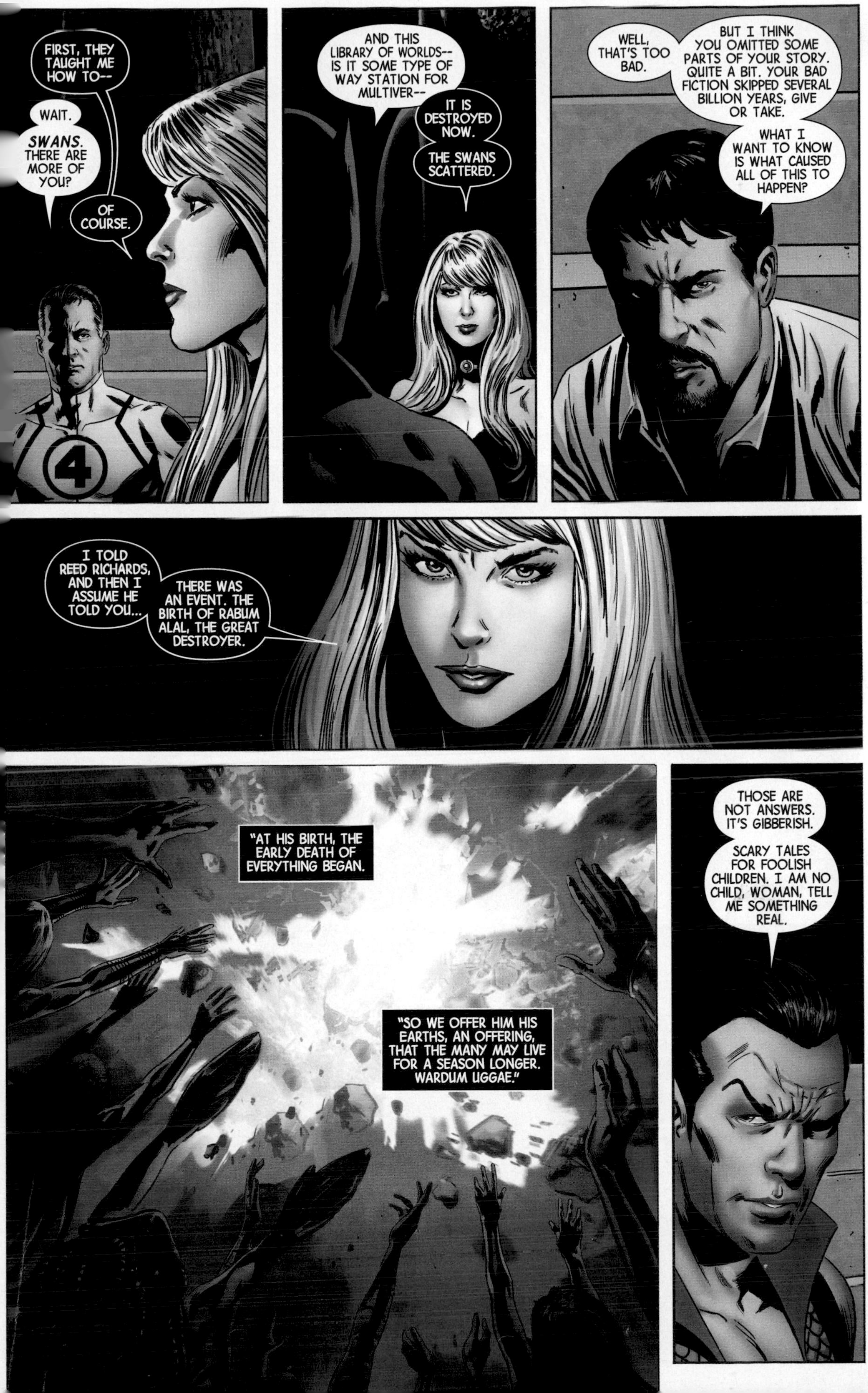
FIRST, THEY TAUGHT ME HOW TO--
WAIT.
SWANS. THERE ARE MORE OF YOU?
OF COURSE.
AND THIS LIBRARY OF WORLDS-- IS IT SOME TYPE OF WAY STATION FOR MULTIVER--
IT IS DESTROYED NOW.
THE SWANS SCATTERED.
WELL, THAT'S TOO BAD.
BUT I THINK YOU OMITTED SOME PARTS OF YOUR STORY. QUITE A BIT. YOUR BAD FICTION SKIPPED SEVERAL BILLION YEARS, GIVE OR TAKE.
WHAT I WANT TO KNOW IS WHAT CAUSED ALL OF THIS TO HAPPEN?
I TOLD REED RICHARDS, AND THEN I ASSUME HE TOLD YOU...
THERE WAS AN EVENT. THE BIRTH OF RABUM ALAL, THE GREAT DESTROYER.
"AT HIS BIRTH, THE EARLY DEATH OF EVERYTHING BEGAN.
"SO WE OFFER HIM HIS EARTHS, AN OFFERING, THAT THE MANY MAY LIVE FOR A SEASON LONGER. WARDUM UGGAE."
THOSE ARE NOT ANSWERS. IT'S GIBBERISH.
SCARY TALES FOR FOOLISH CHILDREN. I AM NO CHILD, WOMAN, TELL ME SOMETHING REAL.

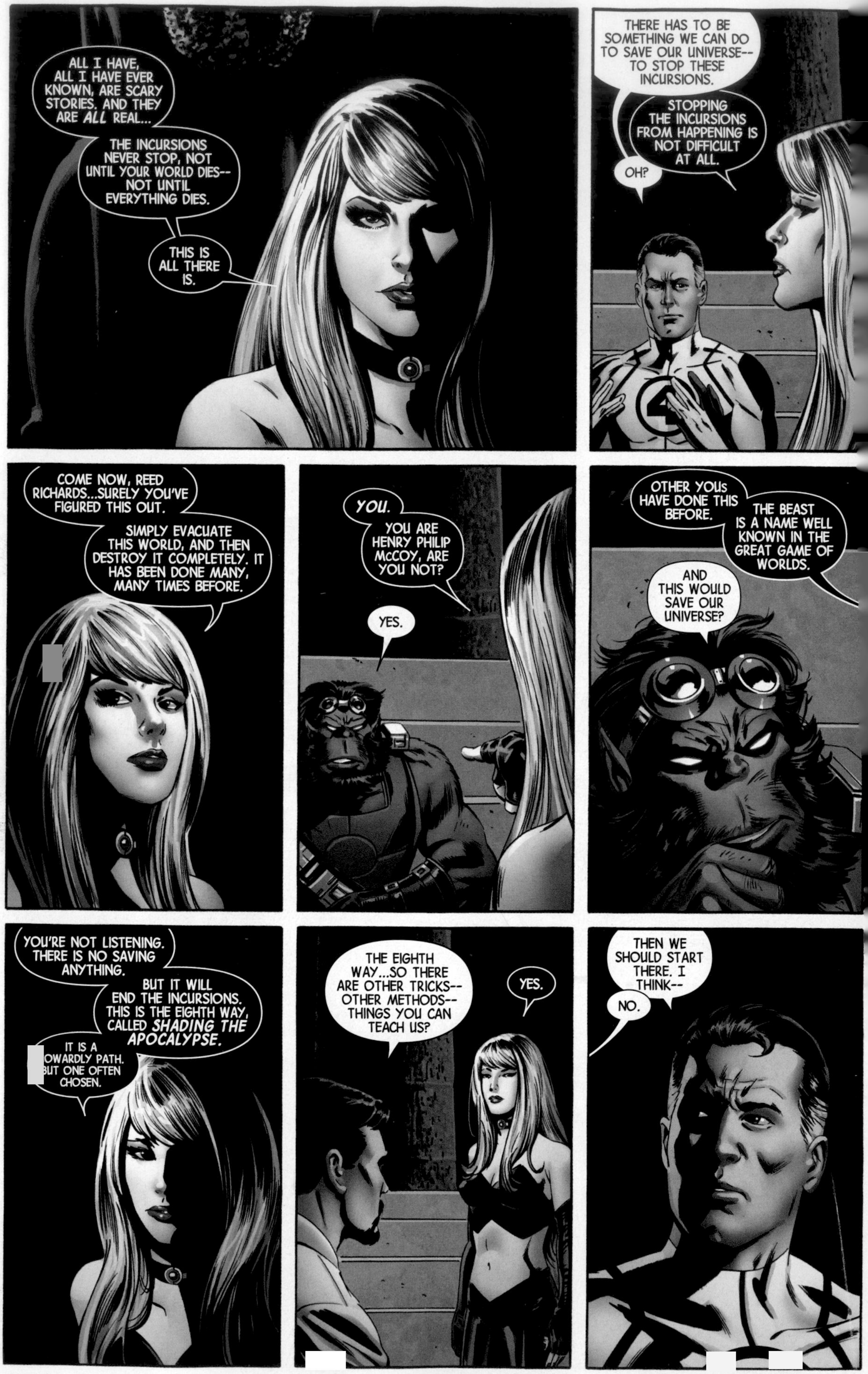
ALL I HAVE, ALL I HAVE EVER KNOWN, ARE SCARY STORIES. AND THEY ARE *ALL* REAL...
THE INCURSIONS NEVER STOP, NOT UNTIL YOUR WORLD DIES-- NOT UNTIL EVERYTHING DIES.
THIS IS ALL THERE IS.
THERE HAS TO BE SOMETHING WE CAN DO TO SAVE OUR UNIVERSE-- TO STOP THESE INCURSIONS.
STOPPING THE INCURSIONS FROM HAPPENING IS NOT DIFFICULT AT ALL.
OH?
COME NOW, REED RICHARDS...SURELY YOU'VE FIGURED THIS OUT.
SIMPLY EVACUATE THIS WORLD, AND THEN DESTROY IT COMPLETELY. IT HAS BEEN DONE MANY, MANY TIMES BEFORE.
YOU.
YOU ARE HENRY PHILIP McCOY, ARE YOU NOT?
YES.
OTHER YOUs HAVE DONE THIS BEFORE.
THE BEAST IS A NAME WELL KNOWN IN THE GREAT GAME OF WORLDS.
AND THIS WOULD SAVE OUR UNIVERSE?
YOU'RE NOT LISTENING. THERE IS NO SAVING ANYTHING.
BUT IT WILL END THE INCURSIONS. THIS IS THE EIGHTH WAY, CALLED ***SHADING THE APOCALYPSE.***
IT IS A OWARDLY PATH. BUT ONE OFTEN CHOSEN.
THE EIGHTH WAY...SO THERE ARE OTHER TRICKS-- OTHER METHODS-- THINGS YOU CAN TEACH US?
YES.
THEN WE SHOULD START THERE. I THINK--
NO.

I STILL HAVE A PROBLEM WITH THIS.

WITH HER.

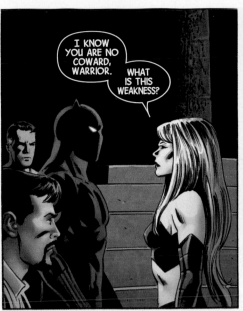

I KNOW YOU ARE NO COWARD, WARRIOR.

WHAT IS THIS WEAKNESS?

I WATCHED YOU KILL A WORLD.

I HAVE DONE WORSE.

YOU WILL ALL DO WORSE.

PERHAPS SOMETHING IN GOOD FAITH... SOMETHING TIMELY.

THE DEVICES YOU HAVE IMPLANTED IN YOUR PALMS--THEY ARE A GOOD START, BUT YOU WILL NEED SOMETHING MORE ACCURATE GOING FORWARD.

A DEVICE SLIGHTLY OUT OF PHASE WITH YOUR NATIVE UNIVERSE WILL ALLOW YOU TO FORECAST COMING INCURSIONS.

MINE ARE IN MY EYES.

AND YOU CAN PREDICT WHEN AN INCURSION WILL OCCUR?

I CAN.

THEN HOW LONG UNTIL THE NEXT ONE?

MINUTES.

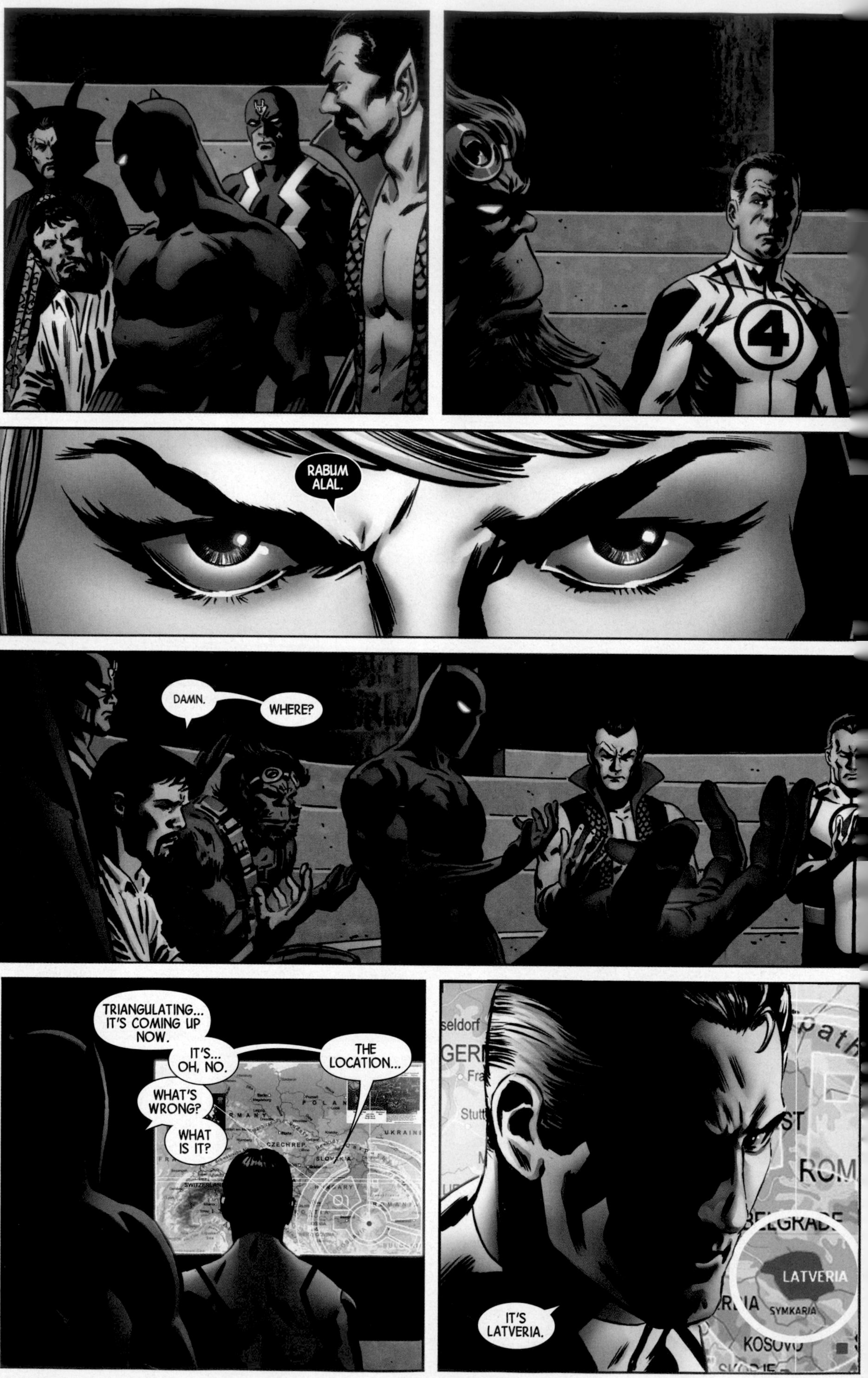
RABUM ALAL.
DAMN.
WHERE?
TRIANGULATING... IT'S COMING UP NOW.
THE LOCATION...
IT'S... OH, NO.
WHAT'S WRONG?
WHAT IS IT?
IT'S LATVERIA.
LATVERIA
SYMKARIA
BELGRADE
KOSOVO

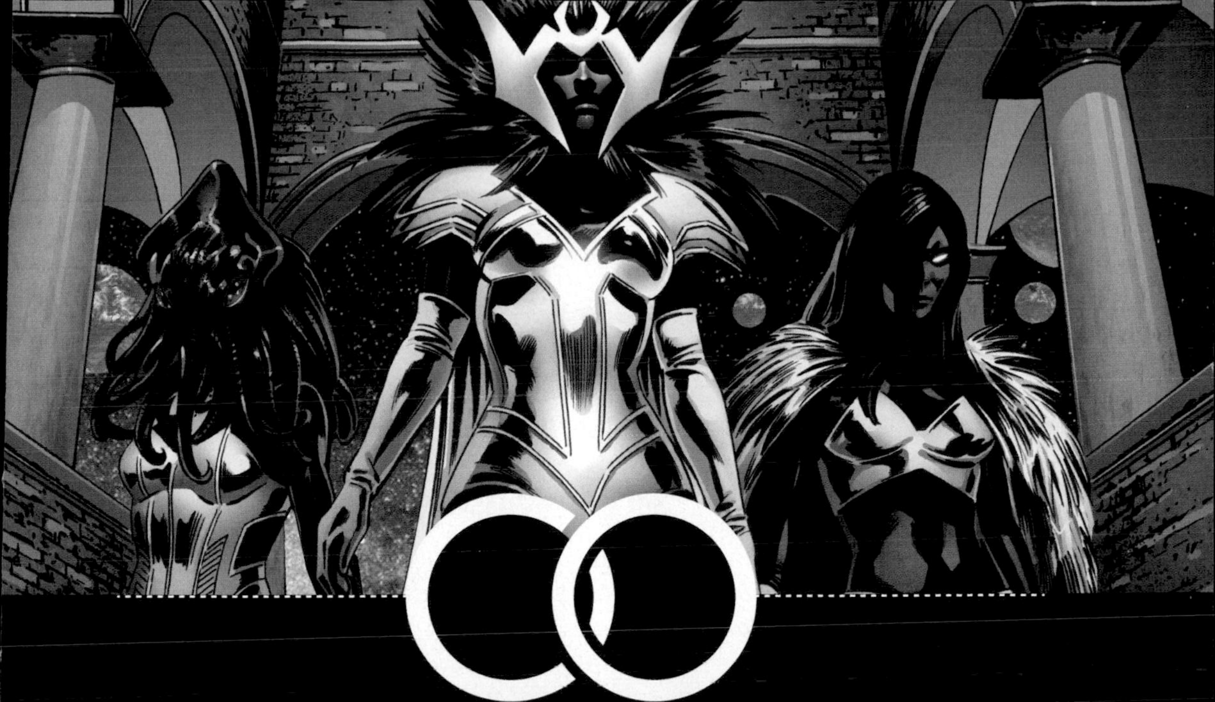

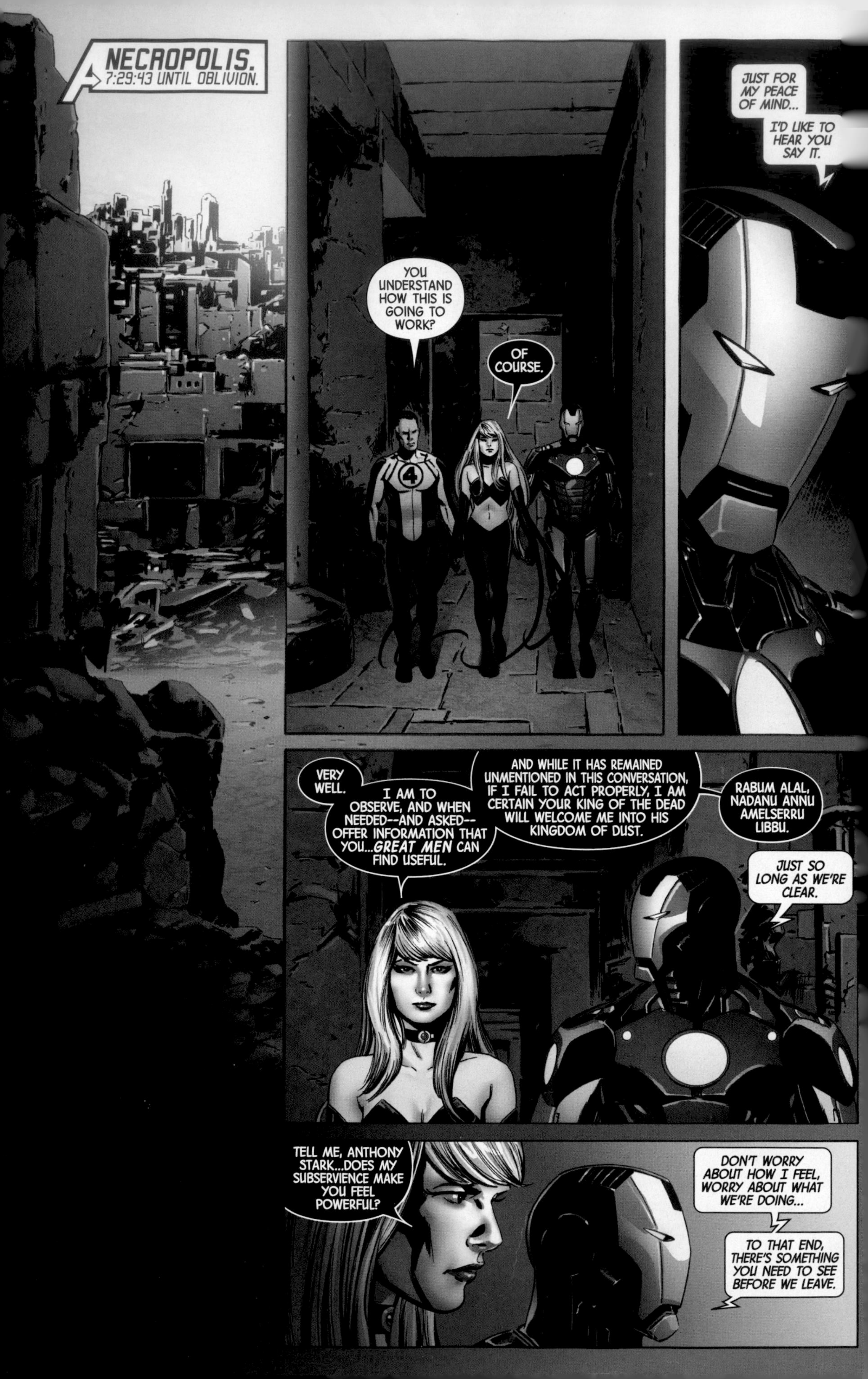
NECROPOLIS.
7:29:43 UNTIL OBLIVION.
YOU UNDERSTAND HOW THIS IS GOING TO WORK?
OF COURSE.
JUST FOR MY PEACE OF MIND...
I'D LIKE TO HEAR YOU SAY IT.
VERY WELL.
I AM TO OBSERVE, AND WHEN NEEDED--AND ASKED--OFFER INFORMATION THAT YOU...GREAT MEN CAN FIND USEFUL.
AND WHILE IT HAS REMAINED UNMENTIONED IN THIS CONVERSATION, IF I FAIL TO ACT PROPERLY, I AM CERTAIN YOUR KING OF THE DEAD WILL WELCOME ME INTO HIS KINGDOM OF DUST.
RABUM ALAL, NADANU ANNU AMELSERRU LIBBU.
JUST SO LONG AS WE'RE CLEAR.
TELL ME, ANTHONY STARK...DOES MY SUBSERVIENCE MAKE YOU FEEL POWERFUL?
DON'T WORRY ABOUT HOW I FEEL, WORRY ABOUT WHAT WE'RE DOING...
TO THAT END, THERE'S SOMETHING YOU NEED TO SEE BEFORE WE LEAVE.

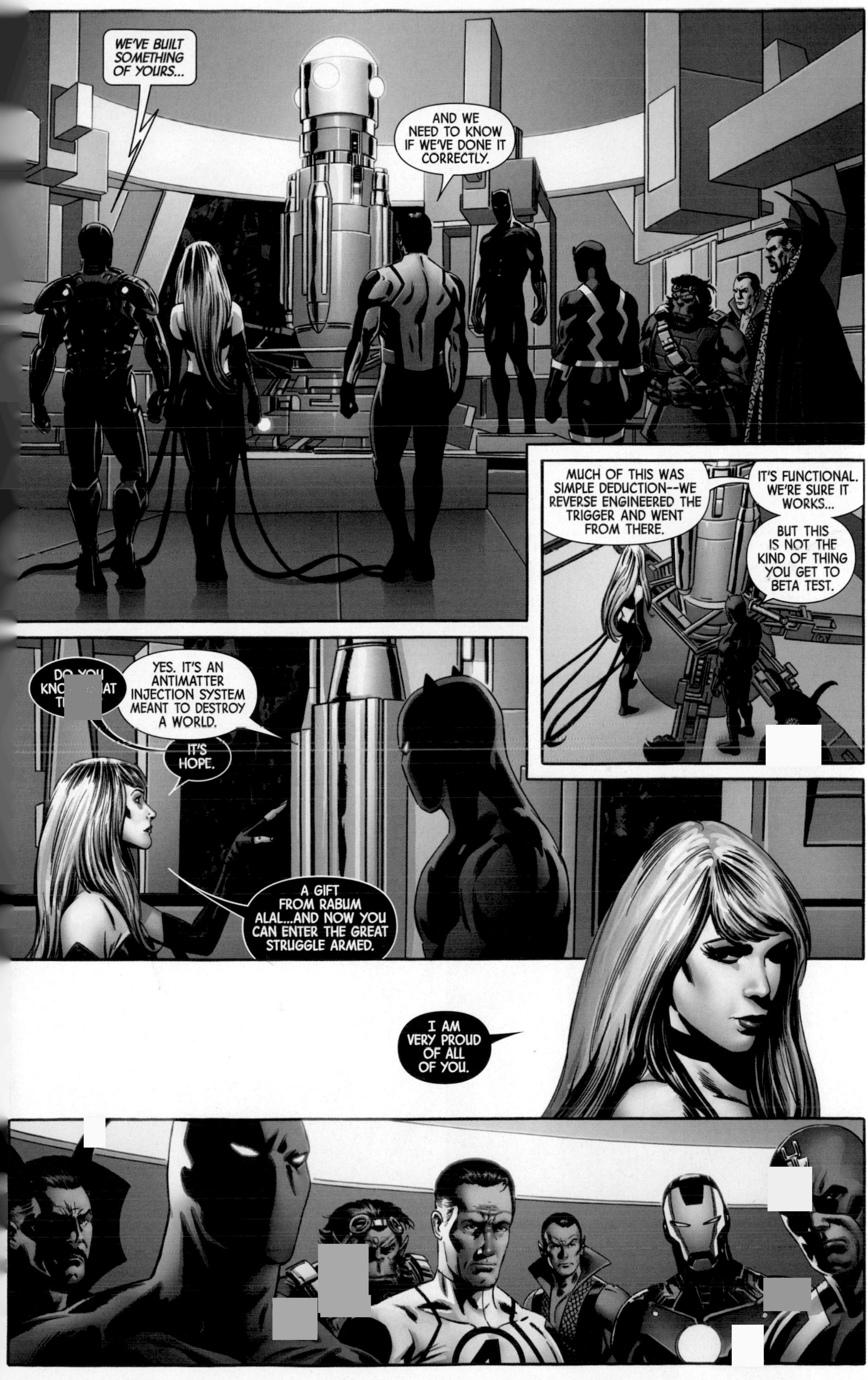
WE'VE BUILT SOMETHING OF YOURS...
AND WE NEED TO KNOW IF WE'VE DONE IT CORRECTLY.
MUCH OF THIS WAS SIMPLE DEDUCTION--WE REVERSE ENGINEERED THE TRIGGER AND WENT FROM THERE.
IT'S FUNCTIONAL. WE'RE SURE IT WORKS...
BUT THIS IS NOT THE KIND OF THING YOU GET TO BETA TEST.
DO YOU
YES. IT'S AN ANTIMATTER INJECTION SYSTEM MEANT TO DESTROY A WORLD.
IT'S HOPE.
A GIFT FROM RABUM ALAL...AND NOW YOU CAN ENTER THE GREAT STRUGGLE ARMED.
I AM VERY PROUD OF ALL OF YOU.

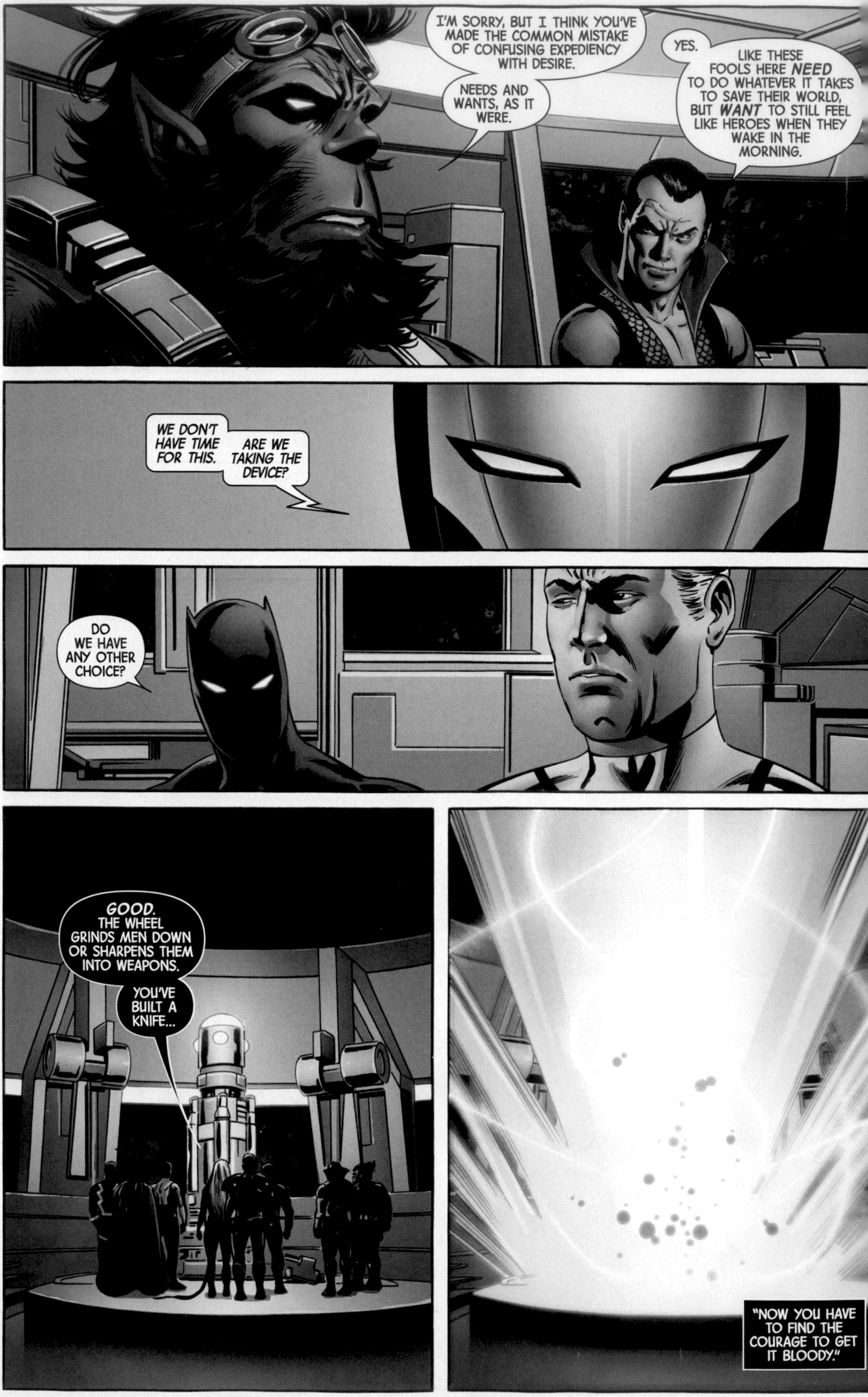
I'M SORRY, BUT I THINK YOU'VE MADE THE COMMON MISTAKE OF CONFUSING EXPEDIENCY WITH DESIRE.
NEEDS AND WANTS, AS IT WERE.
YES.
LIKE THESE FOOLS HERE NEED TO DO WHATEVER IT TAKES TO SAVE THEIR WORLD, BUT WANT TO STILL FEEL LIKE HEROES WHEN THEY WAKE IN THE MORNING.
WE DON'T HAVE TIME FOR THIS.
ARE WE TAKING THE DEVICE?
DO WE HAVE ANY OTHER CHOICE?
GOOD. THE WHEEL GRINDS MEN DOWN OR SHARPENS THEM INTO WEAPONS.
YOU'VE BUILT A KNIFE...
"NOW YOU HAVE TO FIND THE COURAGE TO GET IT BLOODY."

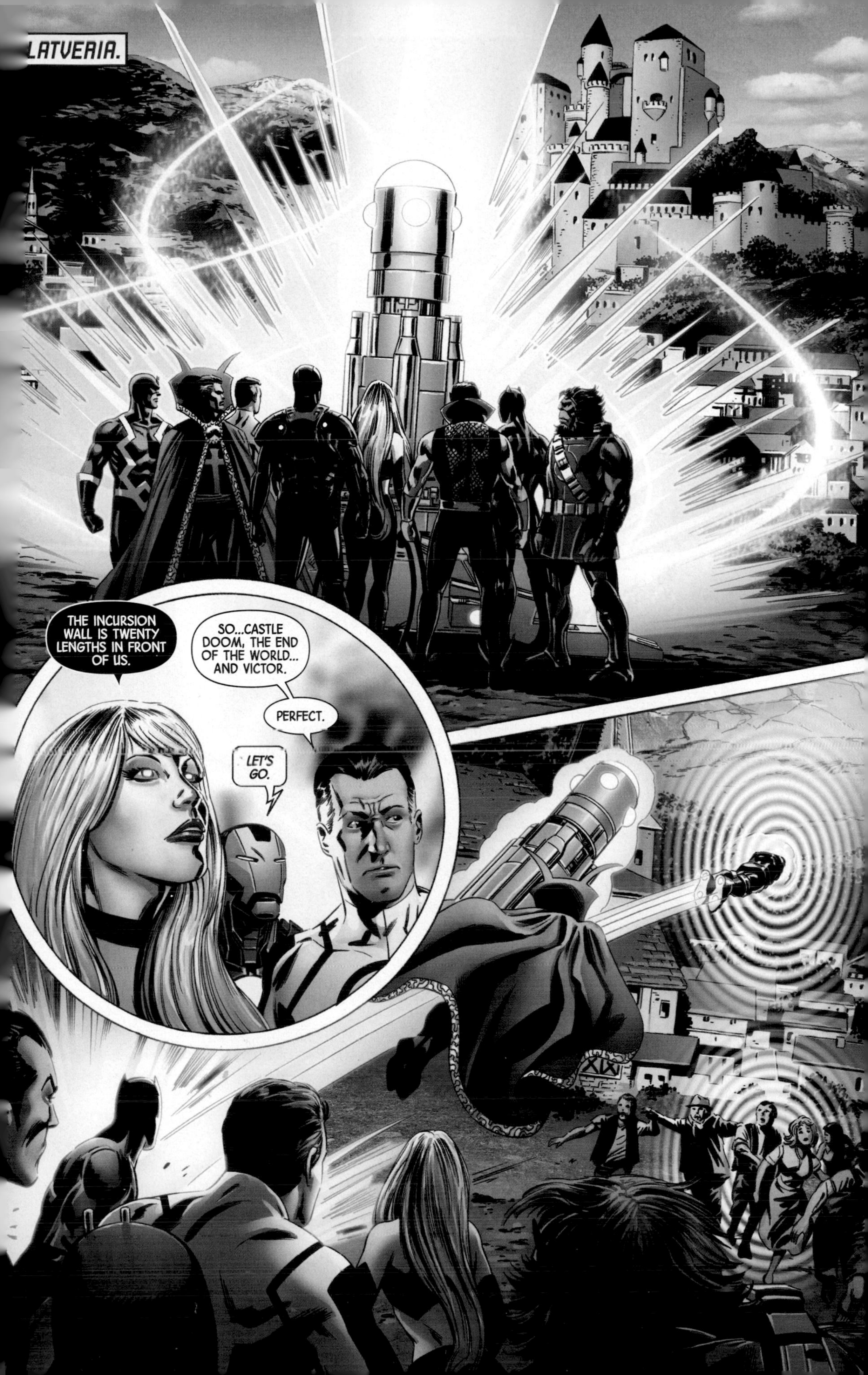
LATVERIA.
THE INCURSION WALL IS TWENTY LENGTHS IN FRONT OF US.
SO...CASTLE DOOM, THE END OF THE WORLD... AND VICTOR.
PERFECT.
LET'S GO.

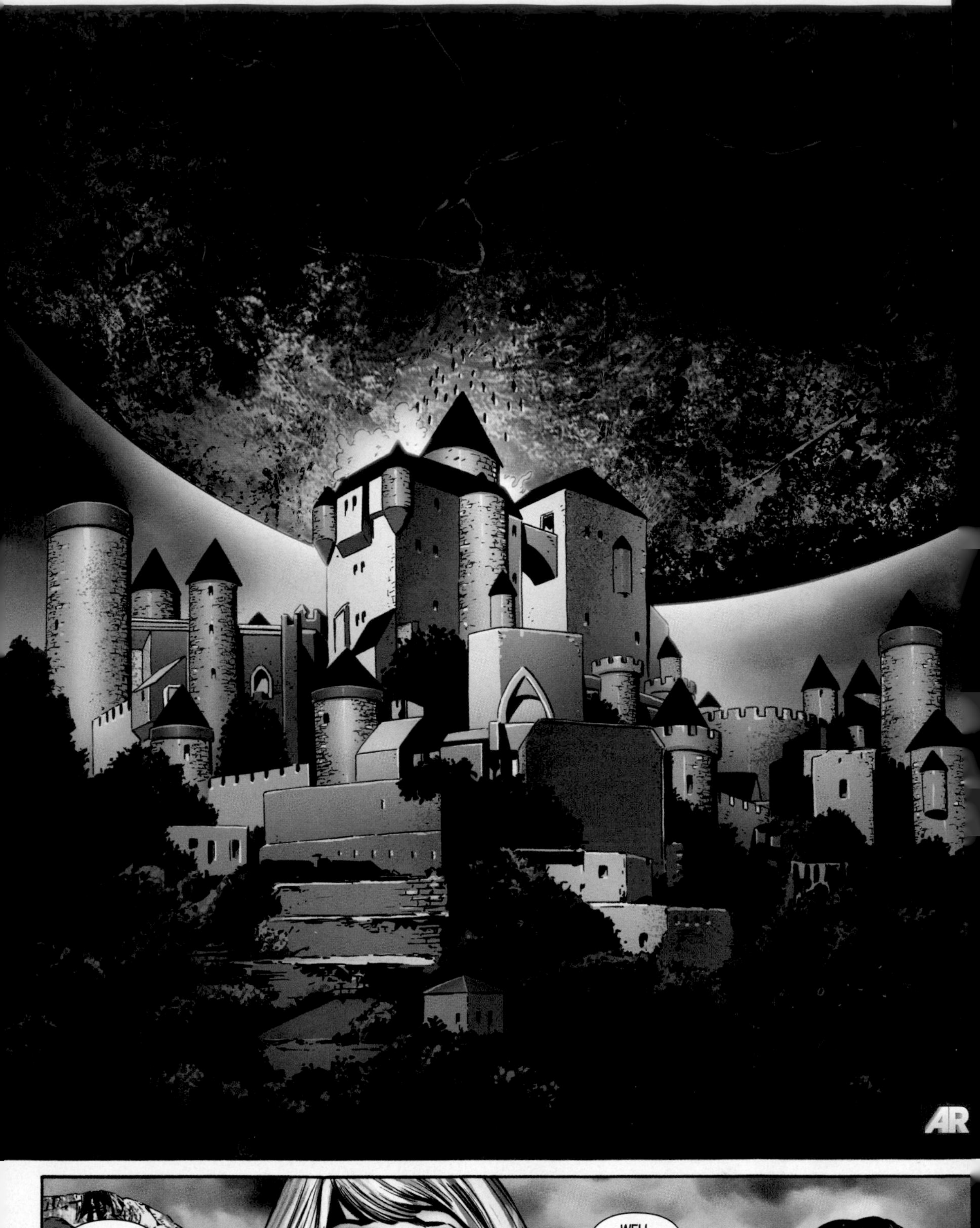

AR

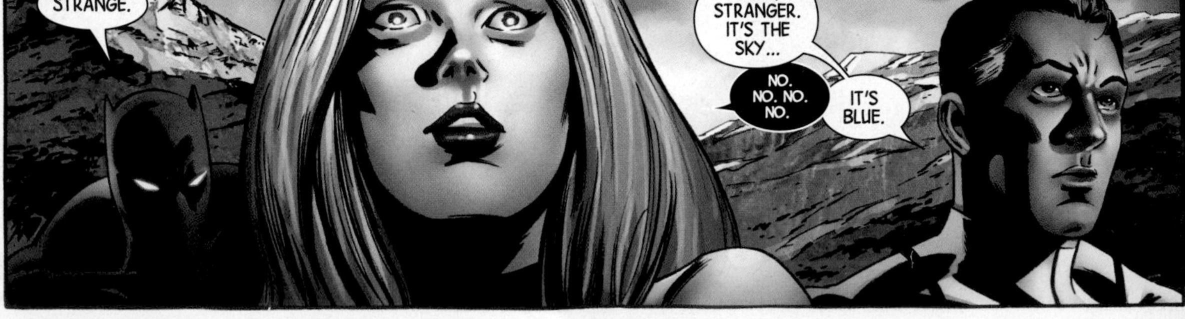

STRANGE.
WELL, STRANGER. IT'S THE SKY...
NO. NO. NO. NO.
IT'S BLUE.

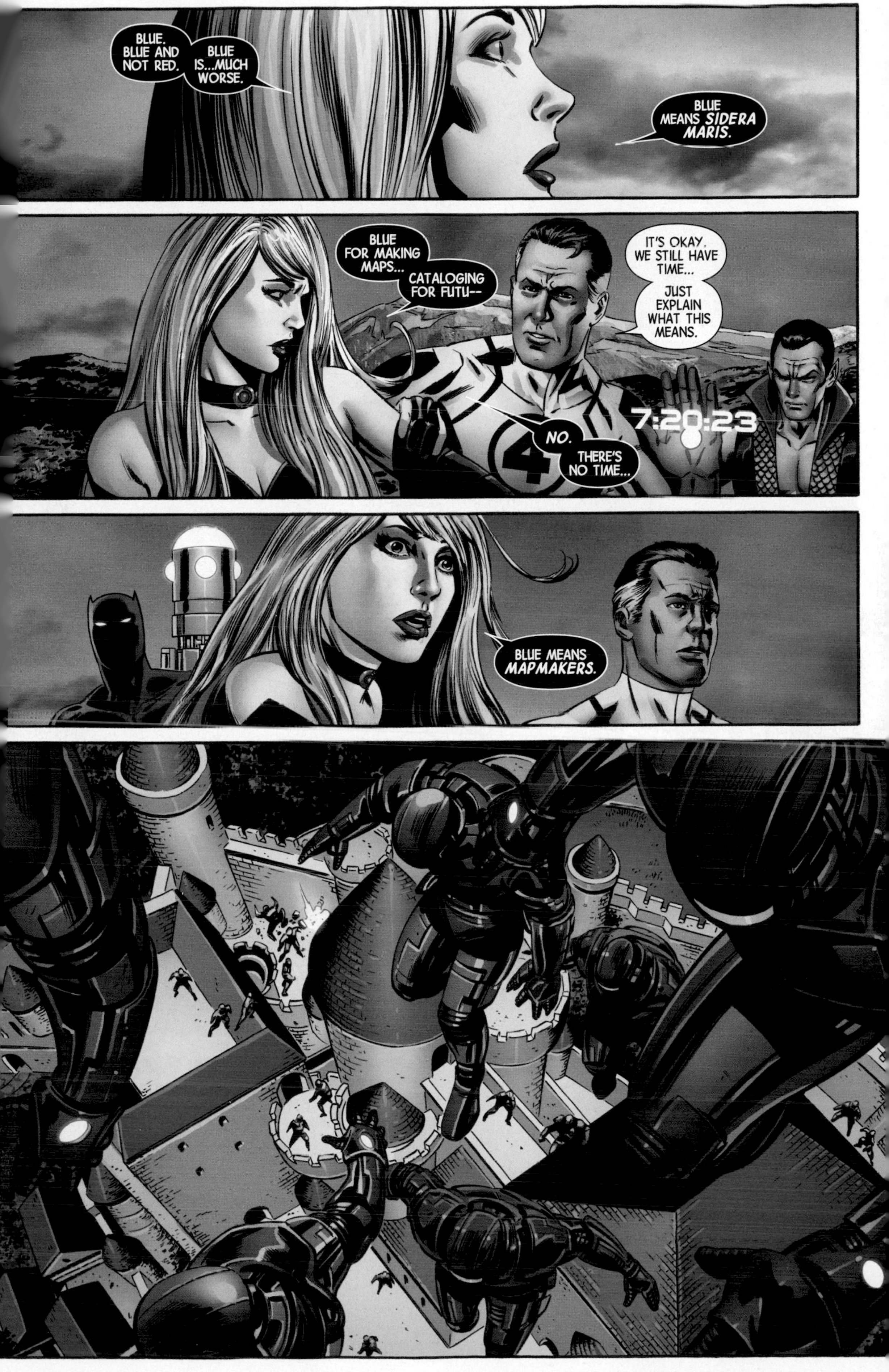
BLUE. BLUE AND NOT RED.
BLUE IS...MUCH WORSE.
BLUE MEANS SIDERA MARIS.
BLUE FOR MAKING MAPS...
CATALOGING FOR FUTU--
IT'S OKAY. WE STILL HAVE TIME...
JUST EXPLAIN WHAT THIS MEANS.
7:20:23
NO.
THERE'S NO TIME...
BLUE MEANS MAPMAKERS.

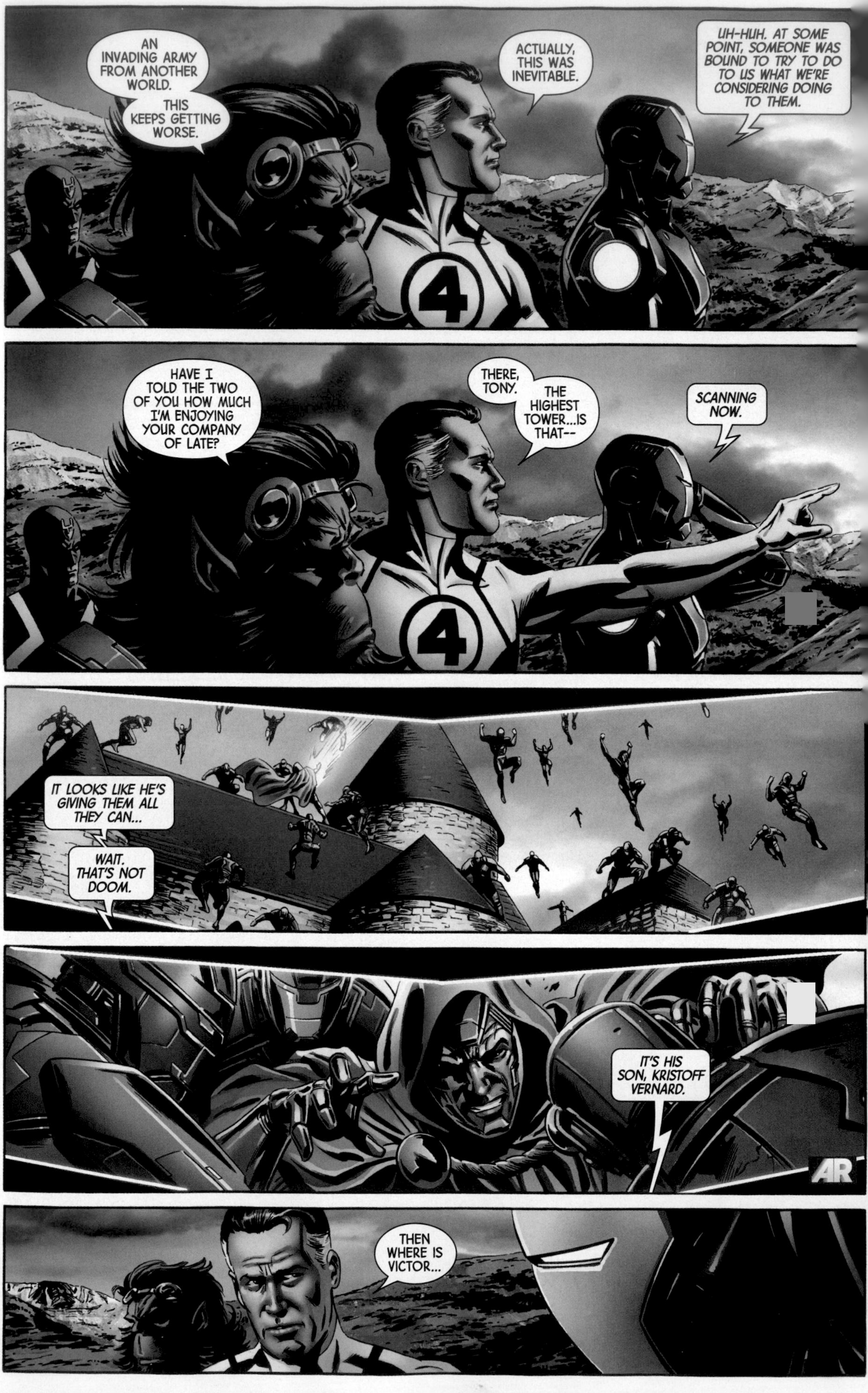
AN INVADING ARMY FROM ANOTHER WORLD.
THIS KEEPS GETTING WORSE.
ACTUALLY, THIS WAS INEVITABLE.
UH-HUH. AT SOME POINT, SOMEONE WAS BOUND TO TRY TO DO TO US WHAT WE'RE CONSIDERING DOING TO THEM.
HAVE I TOLD THE TWO OF YOU HOW MUCH I'M ENJOYING YOUR COMPANY OF LATE?
THERE, TONY.
THE HIGHEST TOWER...IS THAT--
SCANNING NOW.
IT LOOKS LIKE HE'S GIVING THEM ALL THEY CAN...
WAIT. THAT'S NOT DOOM.
IT'S HIS SON, KRISTOFF VERNARD.
AR
THEN WHERE IS VICTOR...

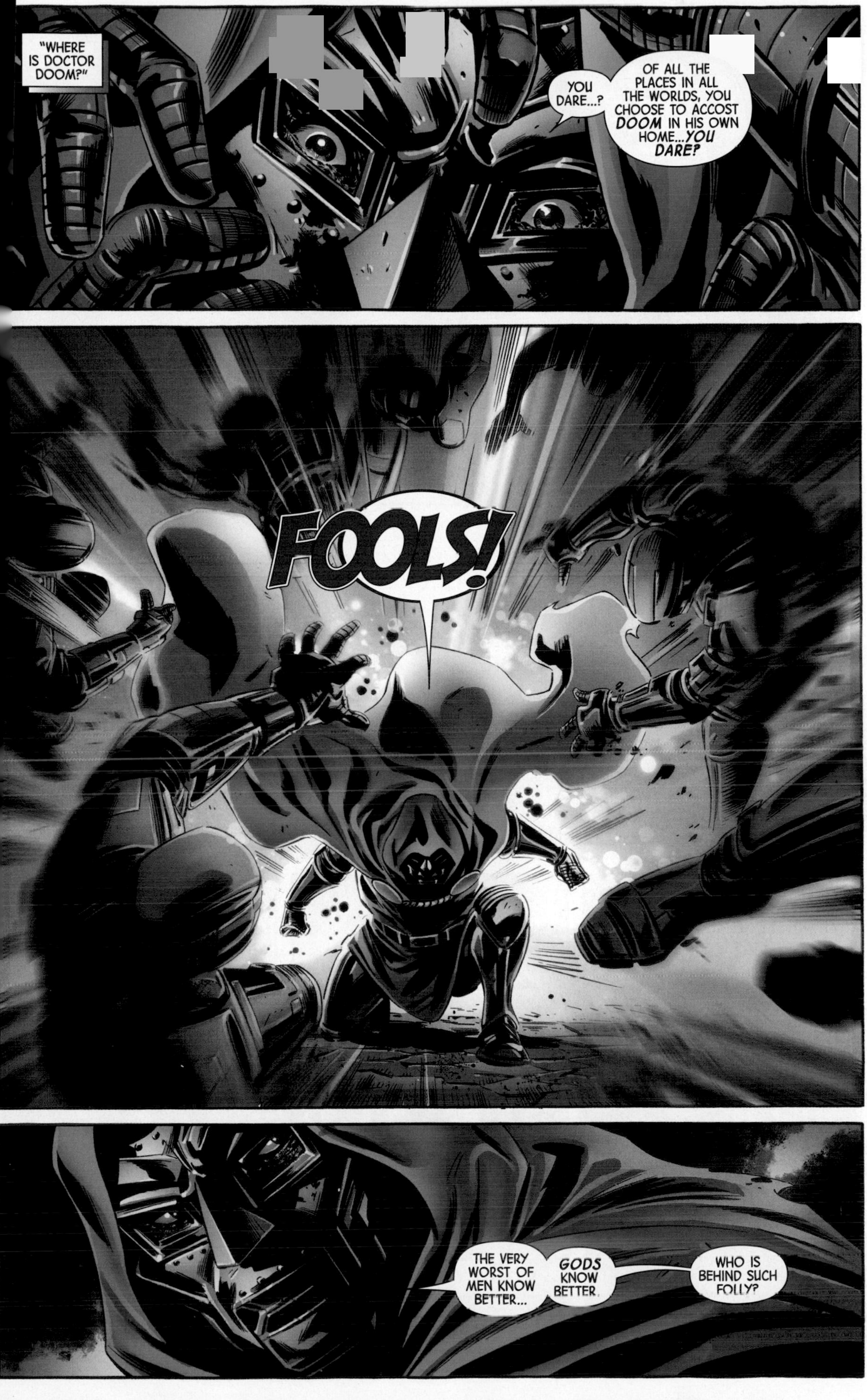
"WHERE IS DOCTOR DOOM?"
YOU DARE...?
OF ALL THE PLACES IN ALL THE WORLDS, YOU CHOOSE TO ACCOST DOOM IN HIS OWN HOME...YOU DARE?
FOOLS!
THE VERY WORST OF MEN KNOW BETTER...
GODS KNOW BETTER.
WHO IS BEHIND SUCH FOLLY?

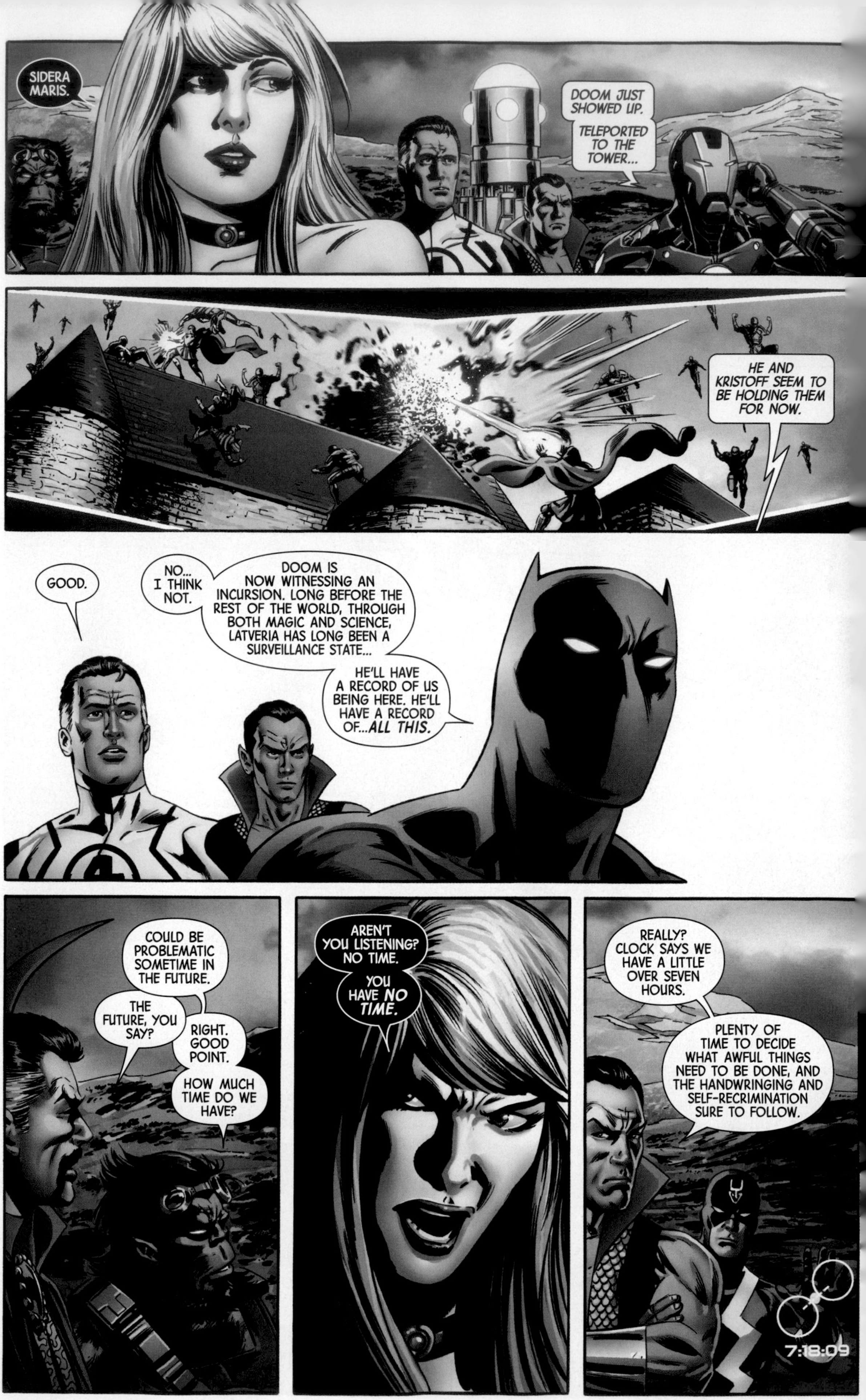

SIDERA MARIS.
DOOM JUST SHOWED UP.
TELEPORTED TO THE TOWER...
HE AND KRISTOFF SEEM TO BE HOLDING THEM FOR NOW.
GOOD.
NO... I THINK NOT.
DOOM IS NOW WITNESSING AN INCURSION. LONG BEFORE THE REST OF THE WORLD, THROUGH BOTH MAGIC AND SCIENCE, LATVERIA HAS LONG BEEN A SURVEILLANCE STATE...
HE'LL HAVE A RECORD OF US BEING HERE. HE'LL HAVE A RECORD OF...ALL THIS.
COULD BE PROBLEMATIC SOMETIME IN THE FUTURE.
THE FUTURE, YOU SAY?
RIGHT. GOOD POINT.
HOW MUCH TIME DO WE HAVE?
AREN'T YOU LISTENING? NO TIME.
YOU HAVE NO TIME.
REALLY? CLOCK SAYS WE HAVE A LITTLE OVER SEVEN HOURS.
PLENTY OF TIME TO DECIDE WHAT AWFUL THINGS NEED TO BE DONE, AND THE HANDWRINGING AND SELF-RECRIMINATION SURE TO FOLLOW.
7:18:09

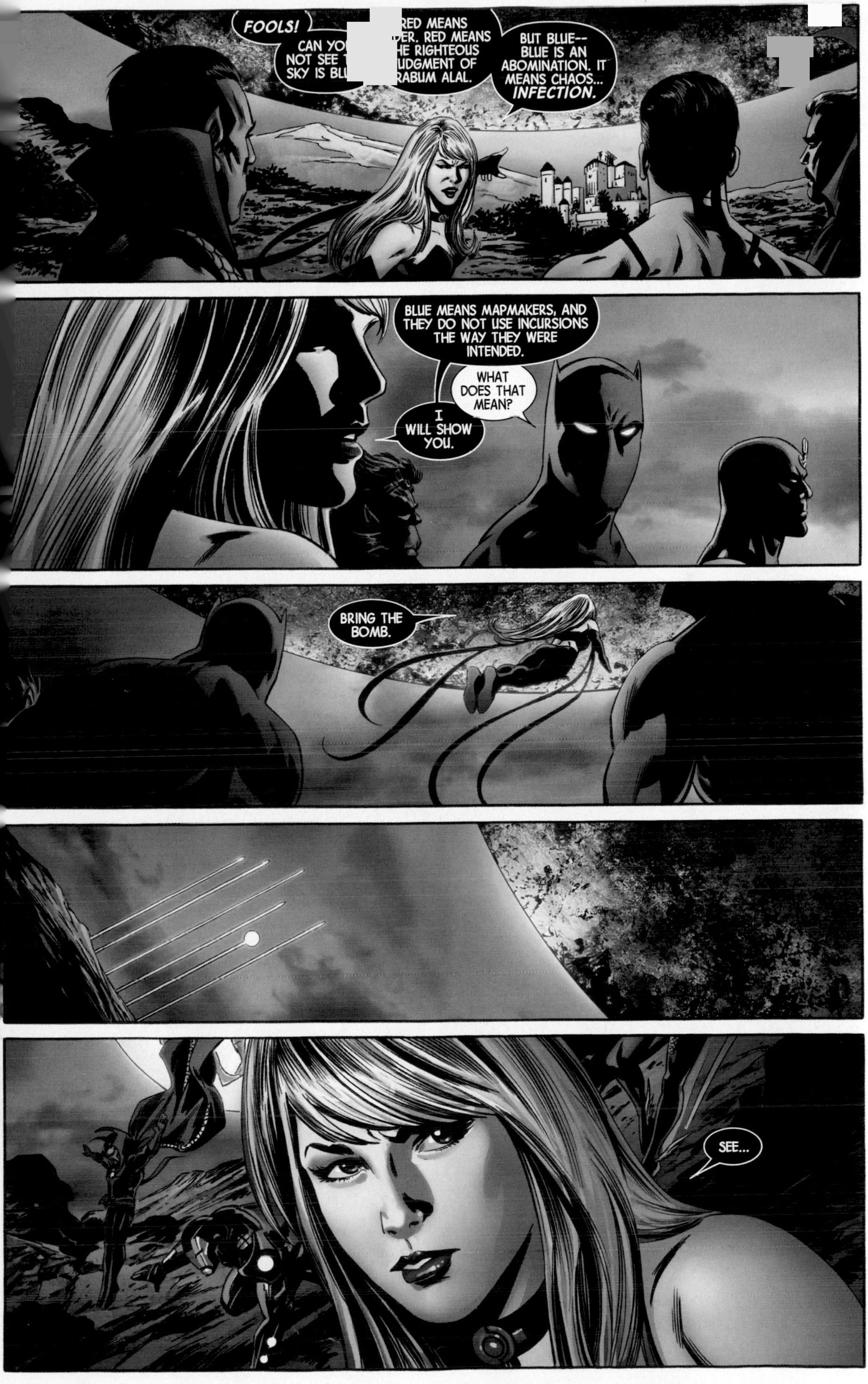
FOOLS!
CAN YO NOT SEE T SKY IS BL
RED MEANS DER. RED MEANS HE RIGHTEOUS UDGMENT OF RABUM ALAL.
BUT BLUE-- BLUE IS AN ABOMINATION. IT MEANS CHAOS... INFECTION.
BLUE MEANS MAPMAKERS, AND THEY DO NOT USE INCURSIONS THE WAY THEY WERE INTENDED.
WHAT DOES THAT MEAN?
I WILL SHOW YOU.
BRING THE BOMB.
SEE...

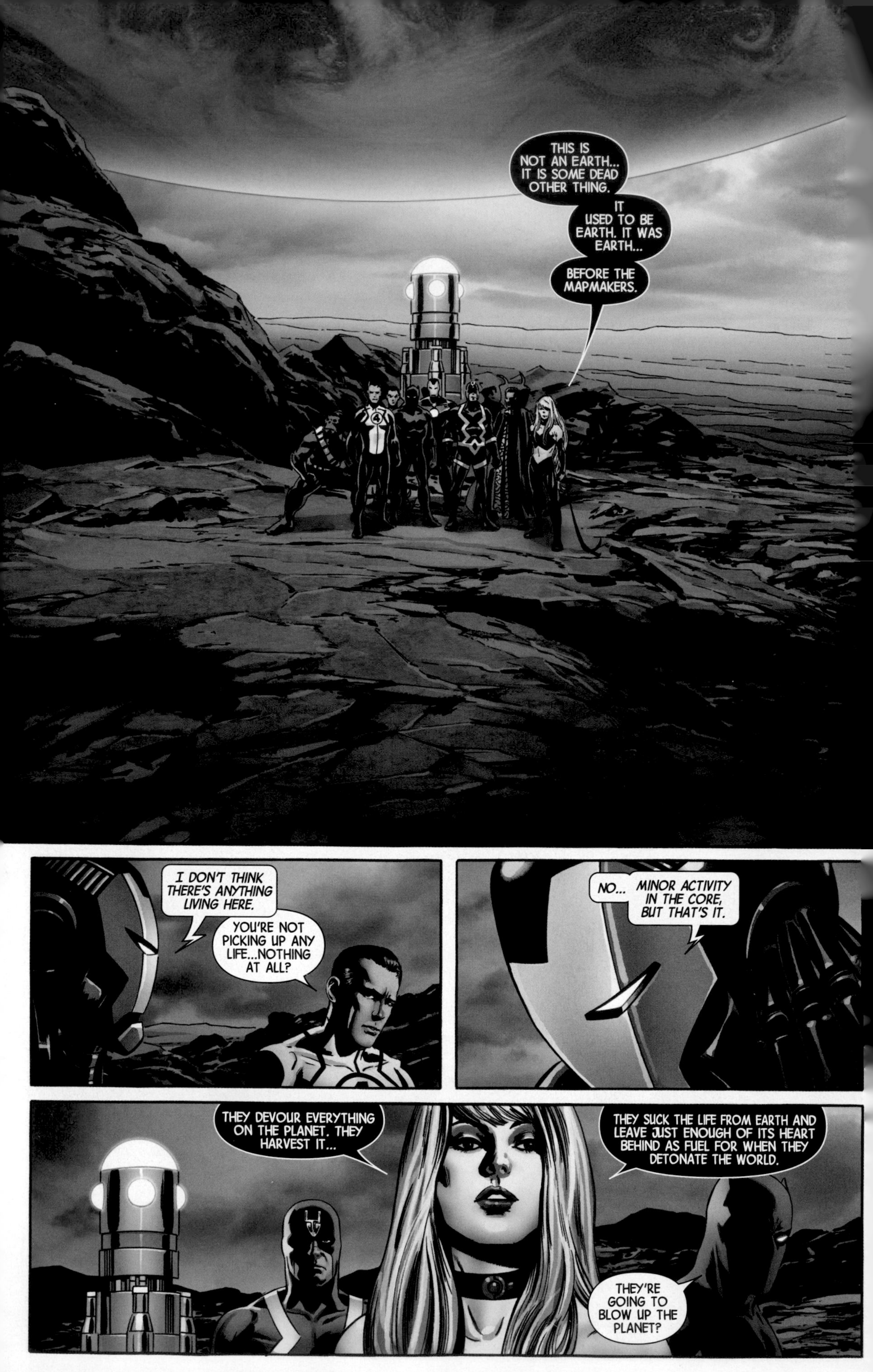
THIS IS NOT AN EARTH... IT IS SOME DEAD OTHER THING.
IT USED TO BE EARTH. IT WAS EARTH...
BEFORE THE MAPMAKERS.
I DON'T THINK THERE'S ANYTHING LIVING HERE.
YOU'RE NOT PICKING UP ANY LIFE...NOTHING AT ALL?
NO...
MINOR ACTIVITY IN THE CORE, BUT THAT'S IT.
THEY DEVOUR EVERYTHING ON THE PLANET. THEY HARVEST IT...
THEY SUCK THE LIFE FROM EARTH AND LEAVE JUST ENOUGH OF ITS HEART BEHIND AS FUEL FOR WHEN THEY DETONATE THE WORLD.
THEY'RE GOING TO BLOW UP THE PLANET?

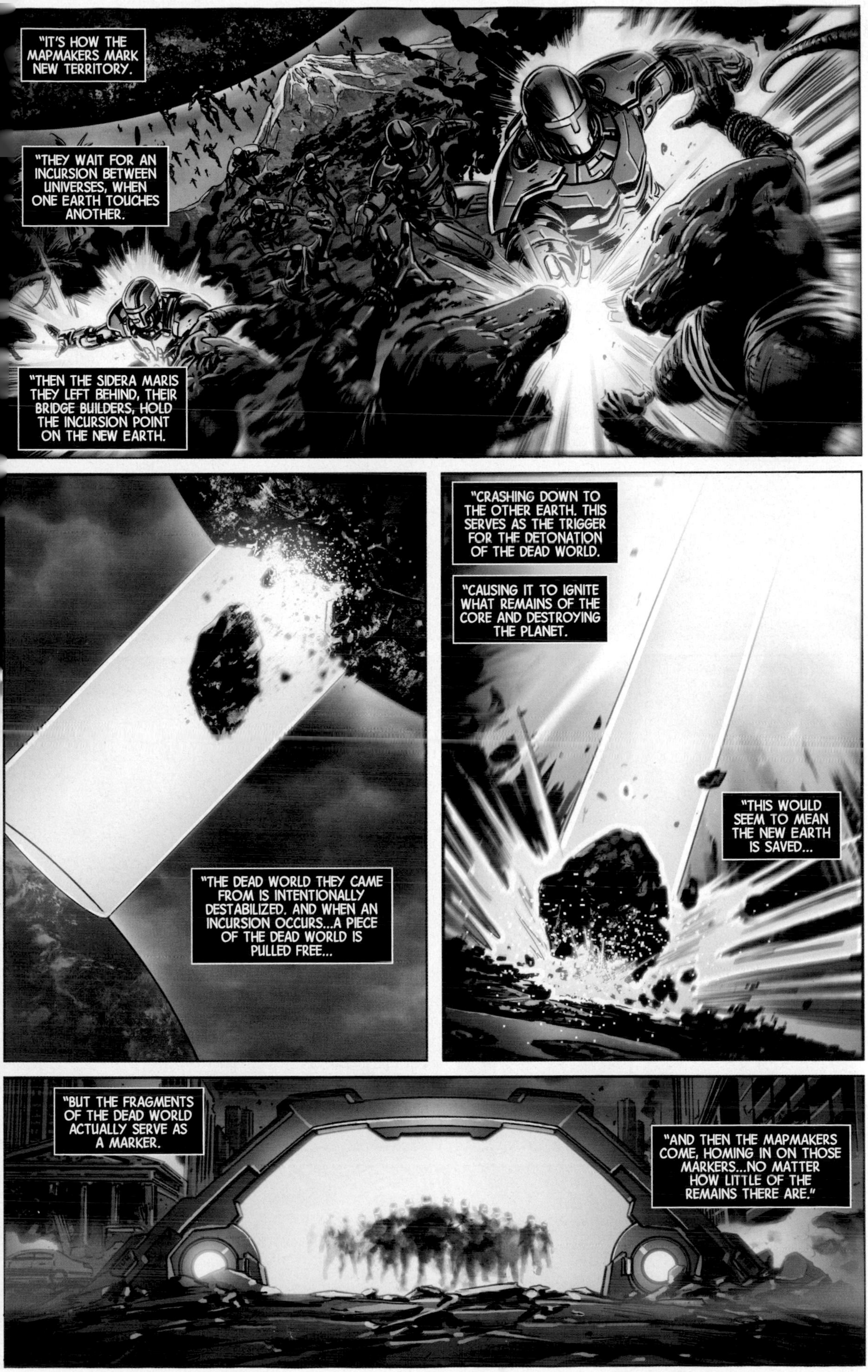
"IT'S HOW THE MAPMAKERS MARK NEW TERRITORY.
"THEY WAIT FOR AN INCURSION BETWEEN UNIVERSES, WHEN ONE EARTH TOUCHES ANOTHER.
"THEN THE SIDERA MARIS THEY LEFT BEHIND, THEIR BRIDGE BUILDERS, HOLD THE INCURSION POINT ON THE NEW EARTH.
"THE DEAD WORLD THEY CAME FROM IS INTENTIONALLY DESTABILIZED. AND WHEN AN INCURSION OCCURS...A PIECE OF THE DEAD WORLD IS PULLED FREE...
"CRASHING DOWN TO THE OTHER EARTH. THIS SERVES AS THE TRIGGER FOR THE DETONATION OF THE DEAD WORLD.
"CAUSING IT TO IGNITE WHAT REMAINS OF THE CORE AND DESTROYING THE PLANET.
"THIS WOULD SEEM TO MEAN THE NEW EARTH IS SAVED...
"BUT THE FRAGMENTS OF THE DEAD WORLD ACTUALLY SERVE AS A MARKER.
"AND THEN THE MAPMAKERS COME, HOMING IN ON THOSE MARKERS...NO MATTER HOW LITTLE OF THE REMAINS THERE ARE."

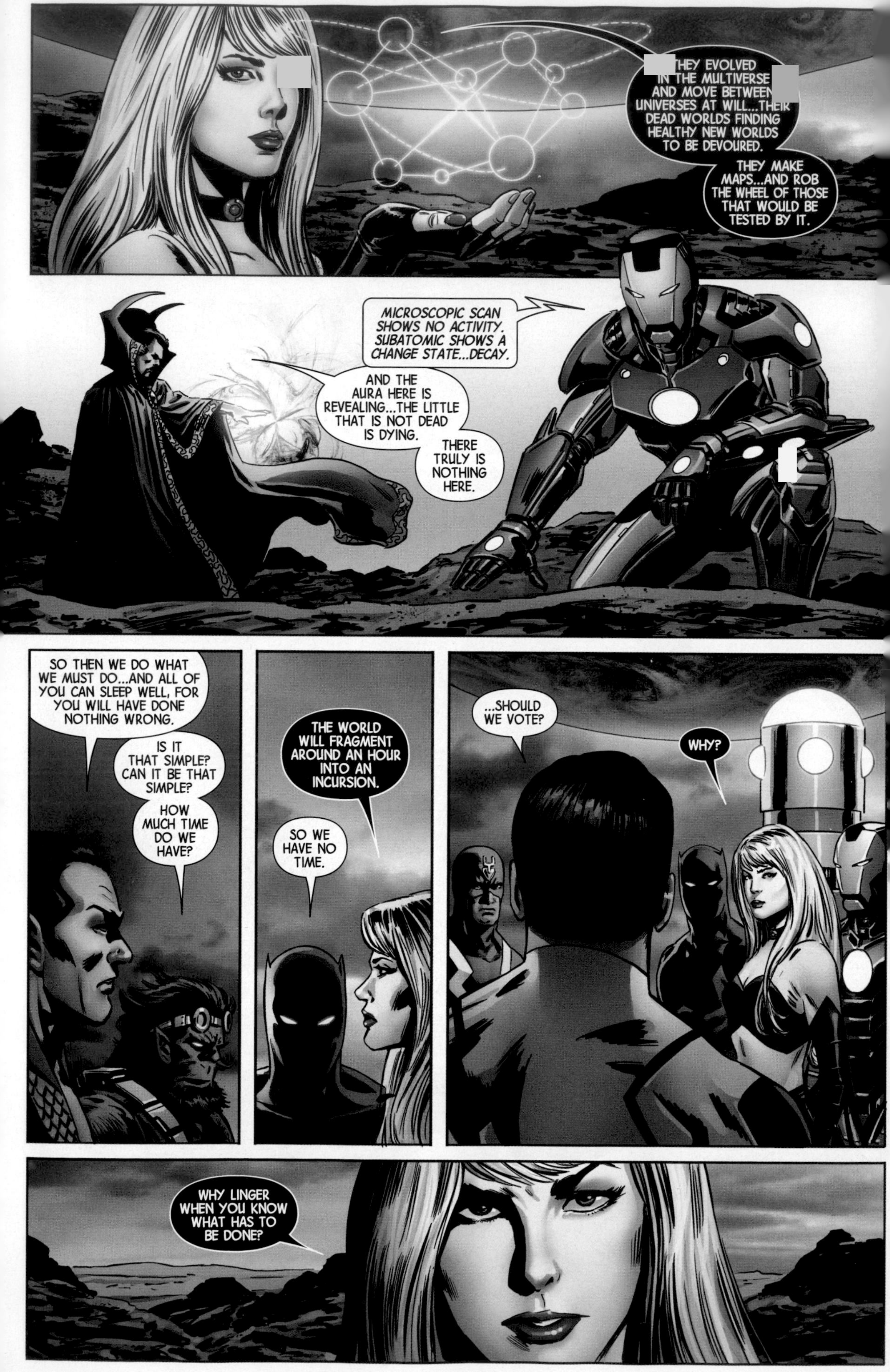
THEY EVOLVED IN THE MULTIVERSE AND MOVE BETWEEN UNIVERSES AT WILL...THEIR DEAD WORLDS FINDING HEALTHY NEW WORLDS TO BE DEVOURED.
THEY MAKE MAPS...AND ROB THE WHEEL OF THOSE THAT WOULD BE TESTED BY IT.
MICROSCOPIC SCAN SHOWS NO ACTIVITY. SUBATOMIC SHOWS A CHANGE STATE...DECAY.
AND THE AURA HERE IS REVEALING...THE LITTLE THAT IS NOT DEAD IS DYING.
THERE TRULY IS NOTHING HERE.
SO THEN WE DO WHAT WE MUST DO...AND ALL OF YOU CAN SLEEP WELL, FOR YOU WILL HAVE DONE NOTHING WRONG.
IS IT THAT SIMPLE? CAN IT BE THAT SIMPLE?
HOW MUCH TIME DO WE HAVE?
THE WORLD WILL FRAGMENT AROUND AN HOUR INTO AN INCURSION.
SO WE HAVE NO TIME.
...SHOULD WE VOTE?
WHY?
WHY LINGER WHEN YOU KNOW WHAT HAS TO BE DONE?

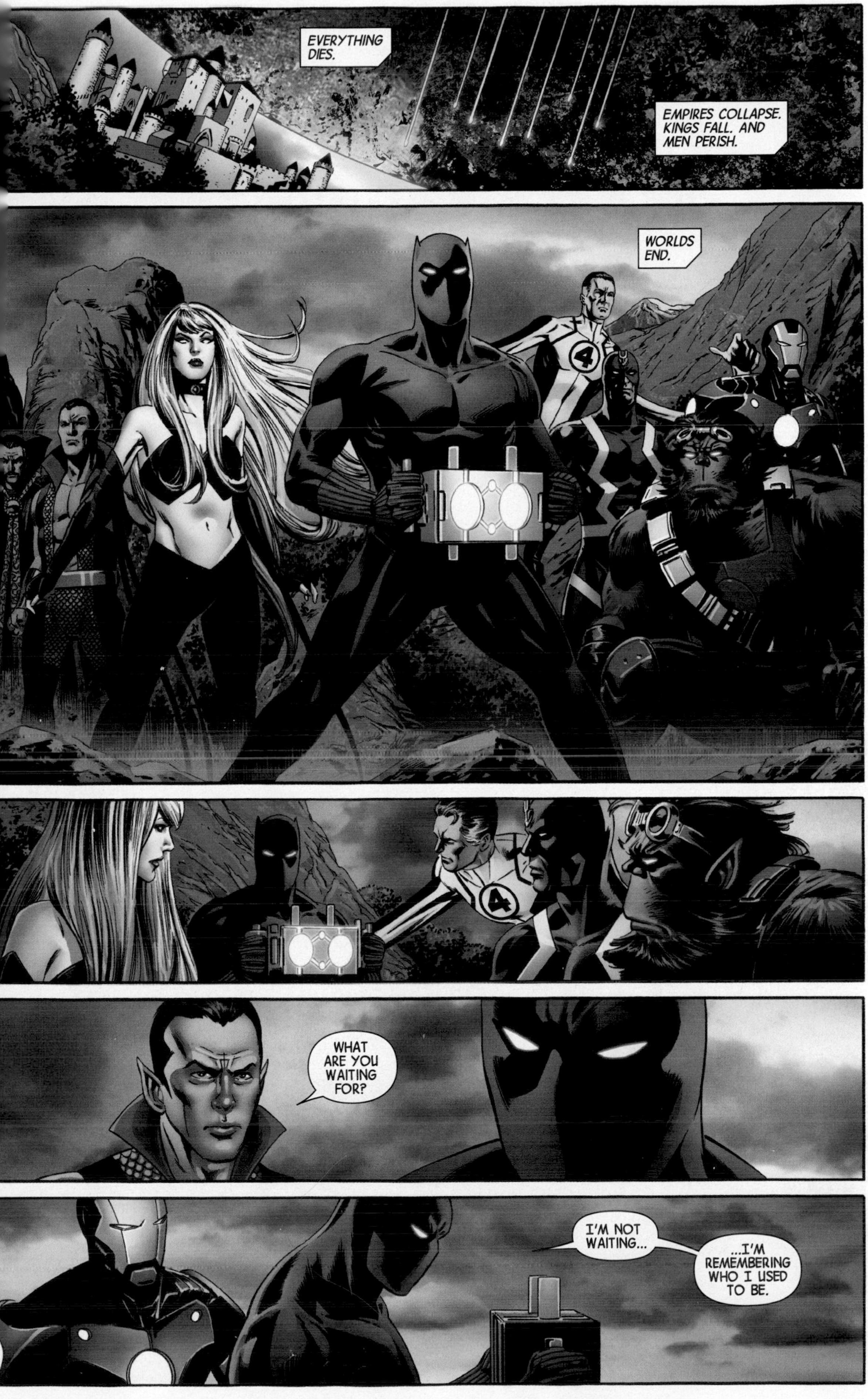
EVERYTHING DIES.
EMPIRES COLLAPSE. KINGS FALL. AND MEN PERISH.
WORLDS END.
WHAT ARE YOU WAITING FOR?
I'M NOT WAITING...
...I'M REMEMBERING WHO I USED TO BE.

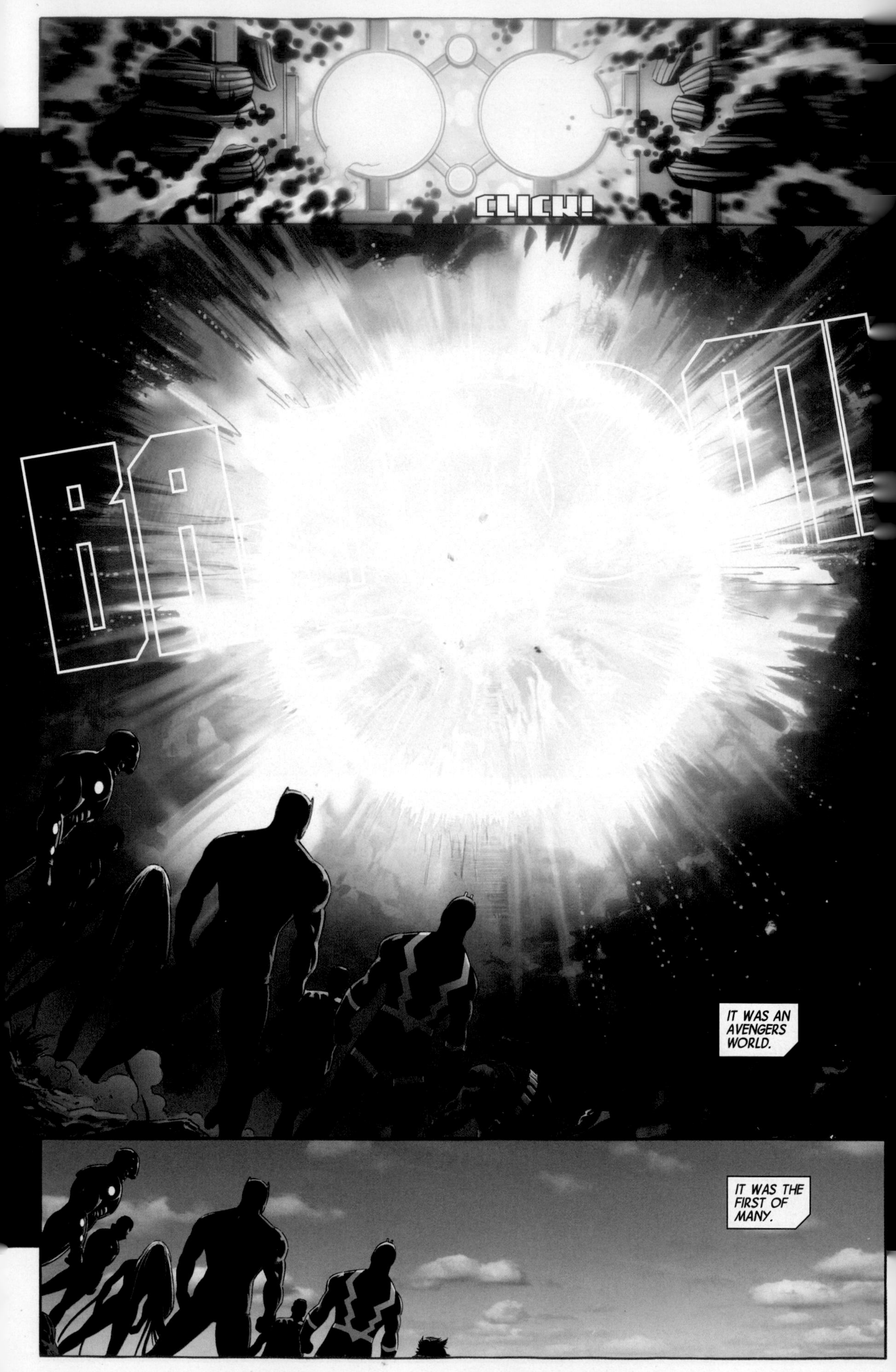
CLICK!
IT WAS AN AVENGERS WORLD.
IT WAS THE FIRST OF MANY.

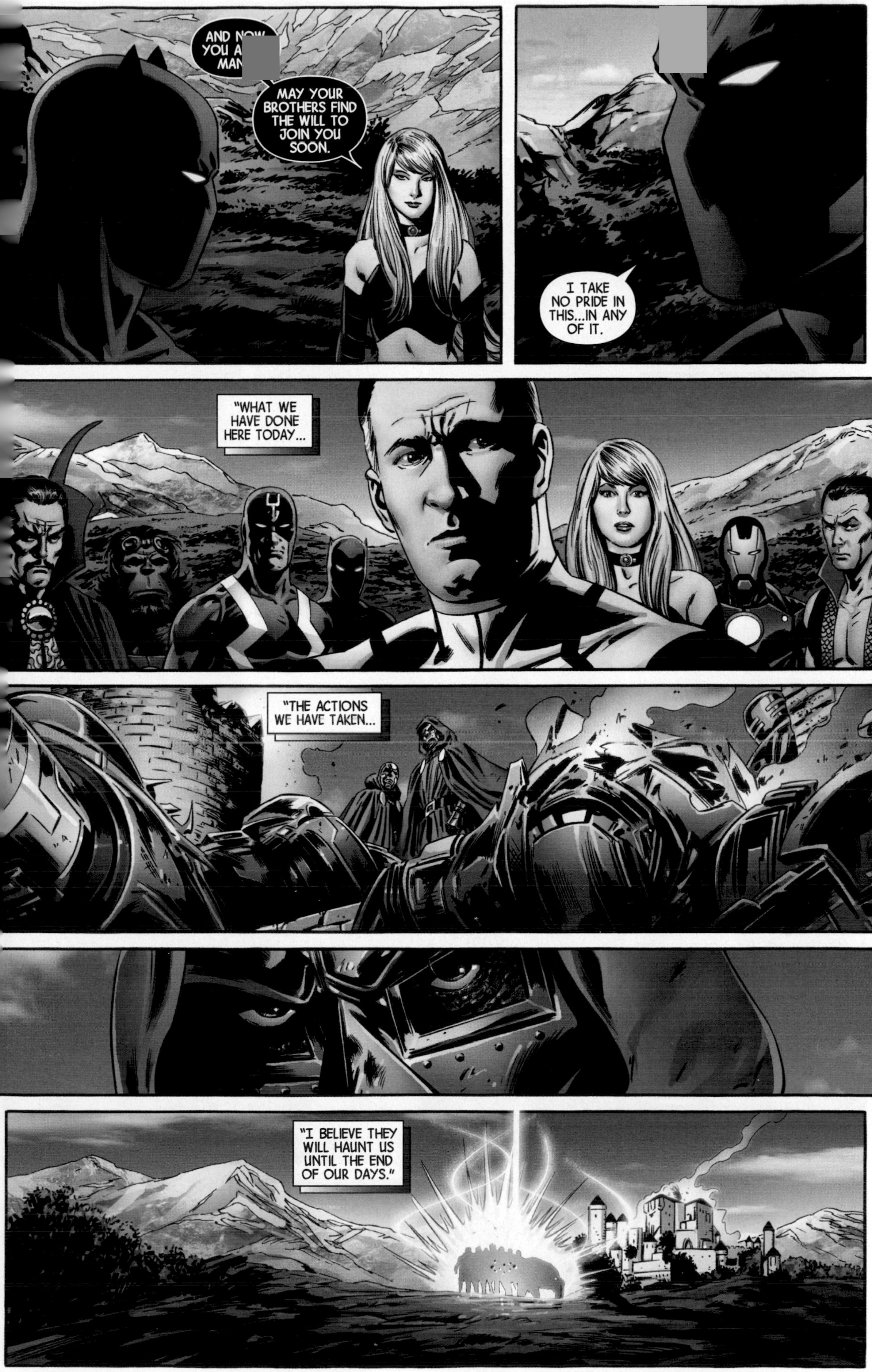
AND NOW YOU A MAN
MAY YOUR BROTHERS FIND THE WILL TO JOIN YOU SOON.
I TAKE NO PRIDE IN THIS...IN ANY OF IT.
"WHAT WE HAVE DONE HERE TODAY...
"THE ACTIONS WE HAVE TAKEN...
"I BELIEVE THEY WILL HAUNT US UNTIL THE END OF OUR DAYS."

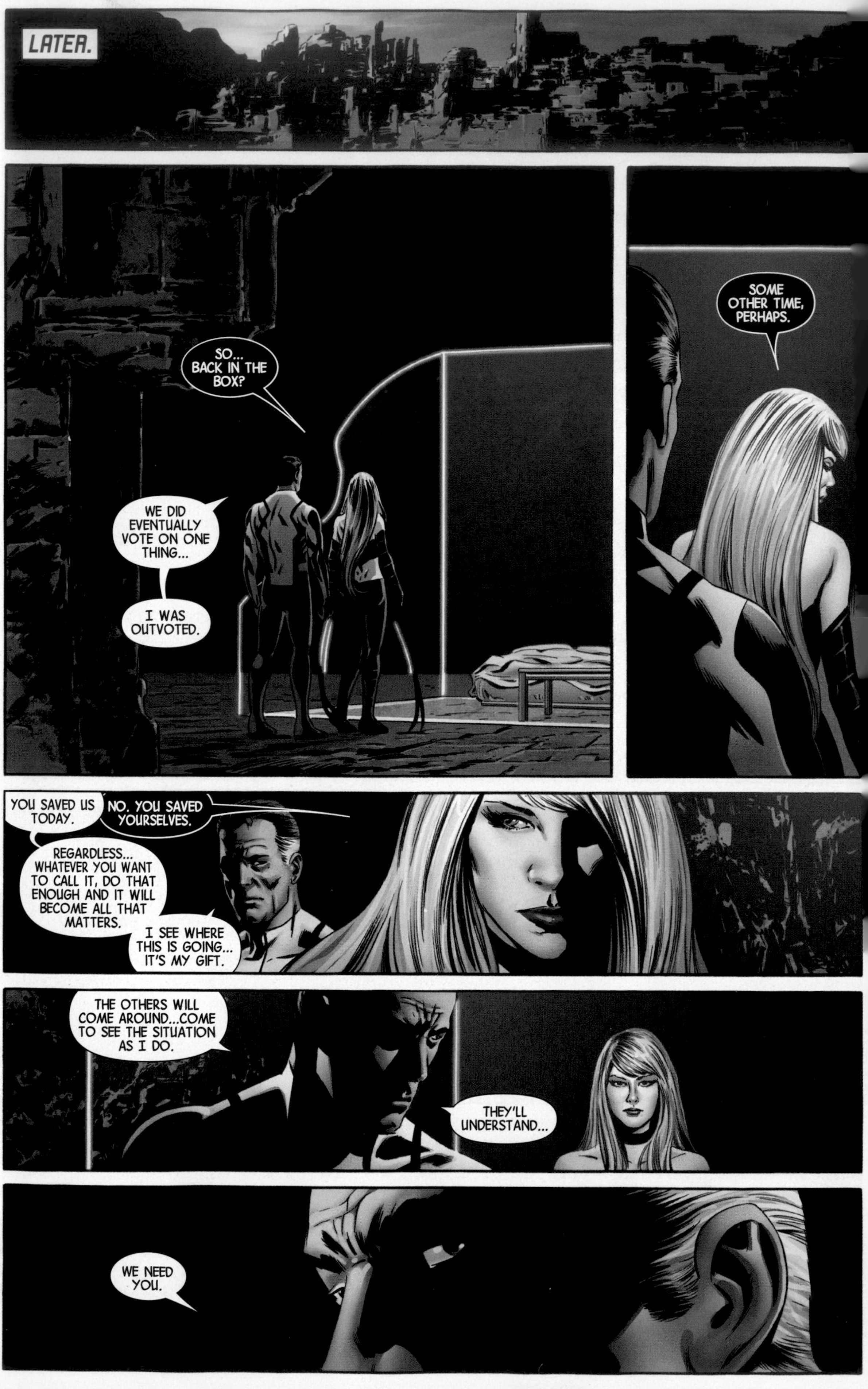
LATER.
SO... BACK IN THE BOX?
WE DID EVENTUALLY VOTE ON ONE THING...
I WAS OUTVOTED.
SOME OTHER TIME, PERHAPS.
YOU SAVED US TODAY.
NO. YOU SAVED YOURSELVES.
REGARDLESS... WHATEVER YOU WANT TO CALL IT, DO THAT ENOUGH AND IT WILL BECOME ALL THAT MATTERS.
I SEE WHERE THIS IS GOING... IT'S MY GIFT.
THE OTHERS WILL COME AROUND...COME TO SEE THE SITUATION AS I DO.
THEY'LL UNDERSTAND...
WE NEED YOU.

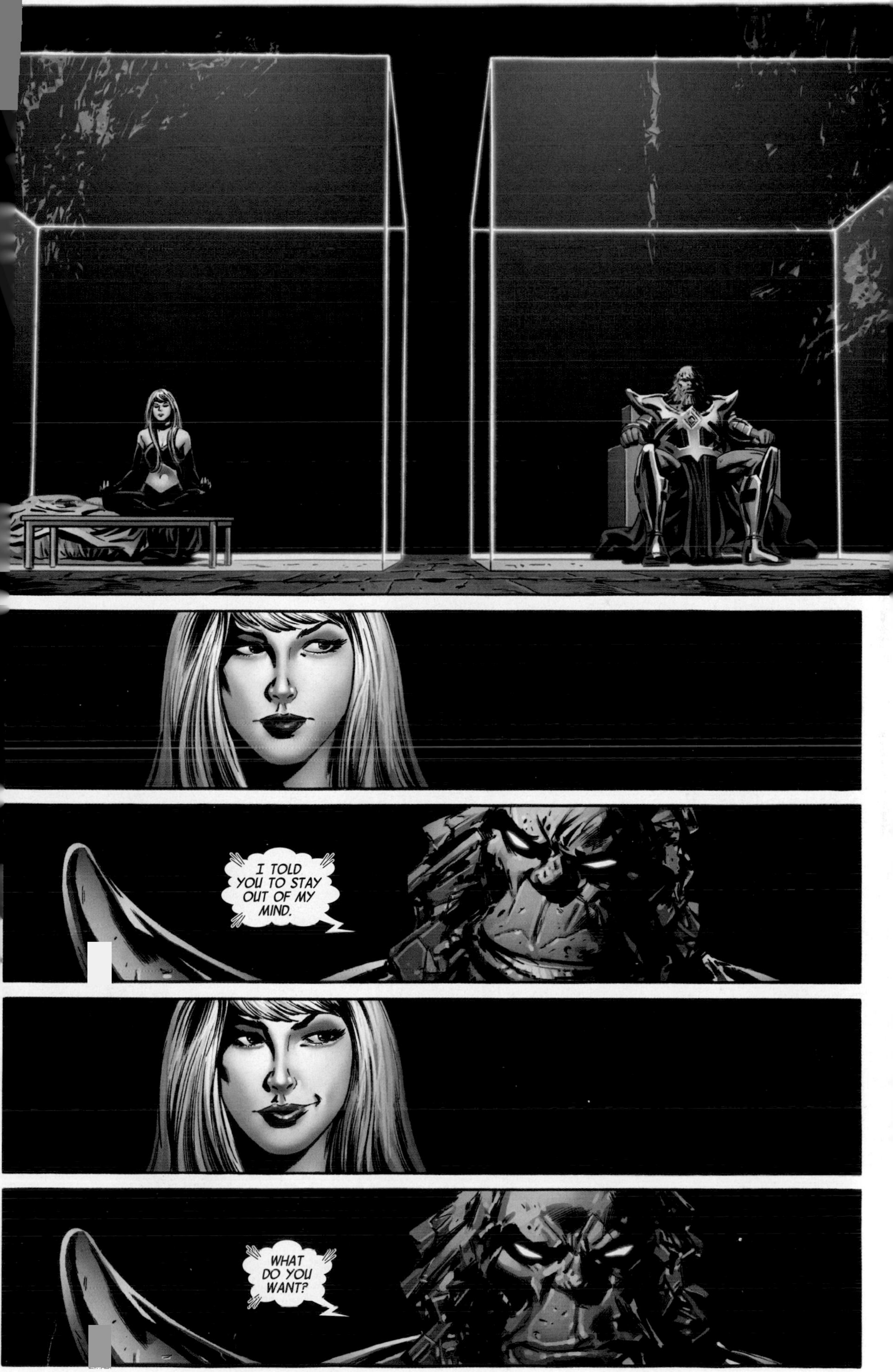
I TOLD YOU TO STAY OUT OF MY MIND.
WHAT DO YOU WANT?

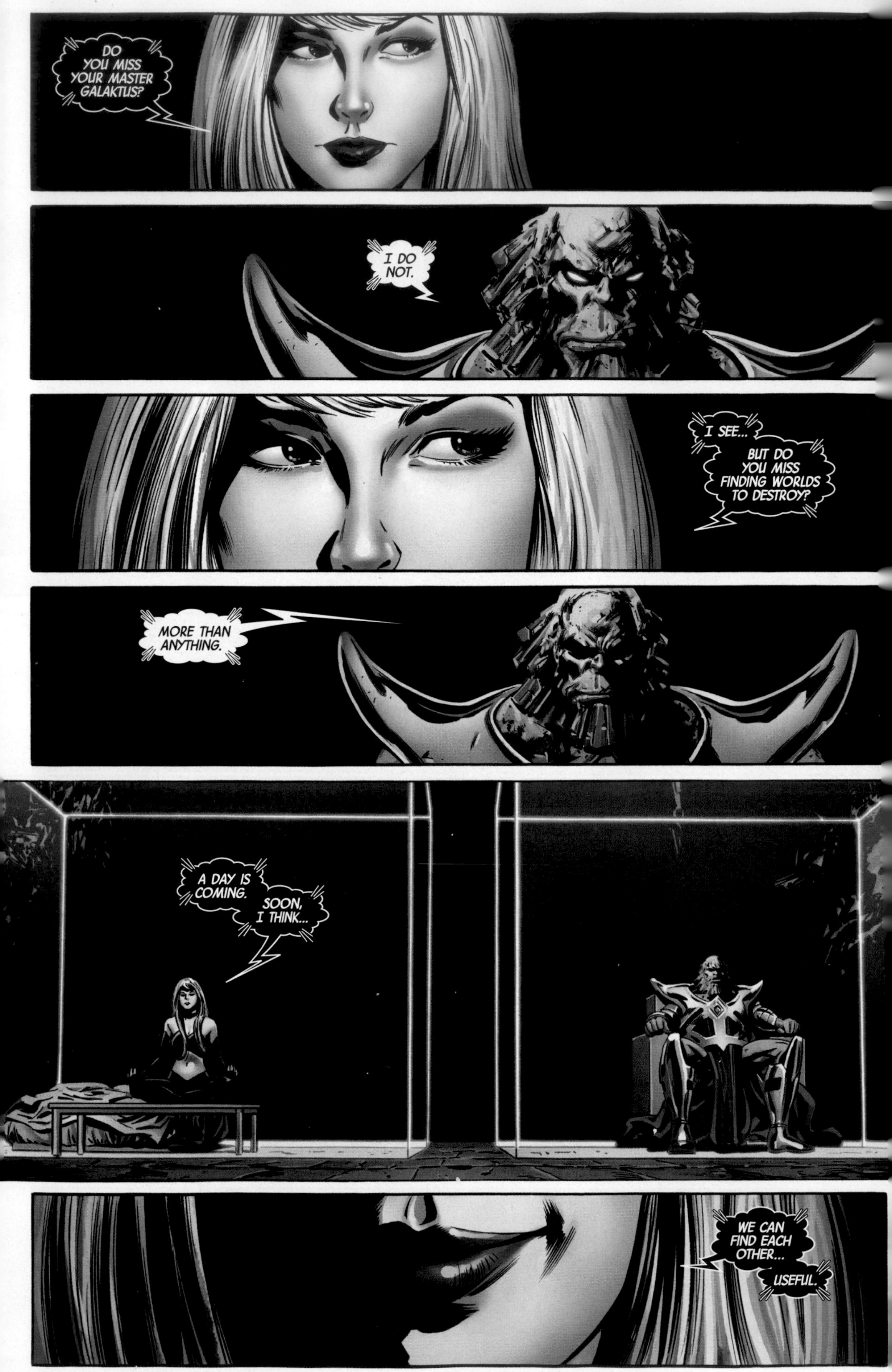
DO YOU MISS YOUR MASTER GALAKTUS?
I DO NOT.
I SEE...
BUT DO YOU MISS FINDING WORLDS TO DESTROY?
MORE THAN ANYTHING.
A DAY IS COMING.
SOON, I THINK...
WE CAN FIND EACH OTHER...
USEFUL.

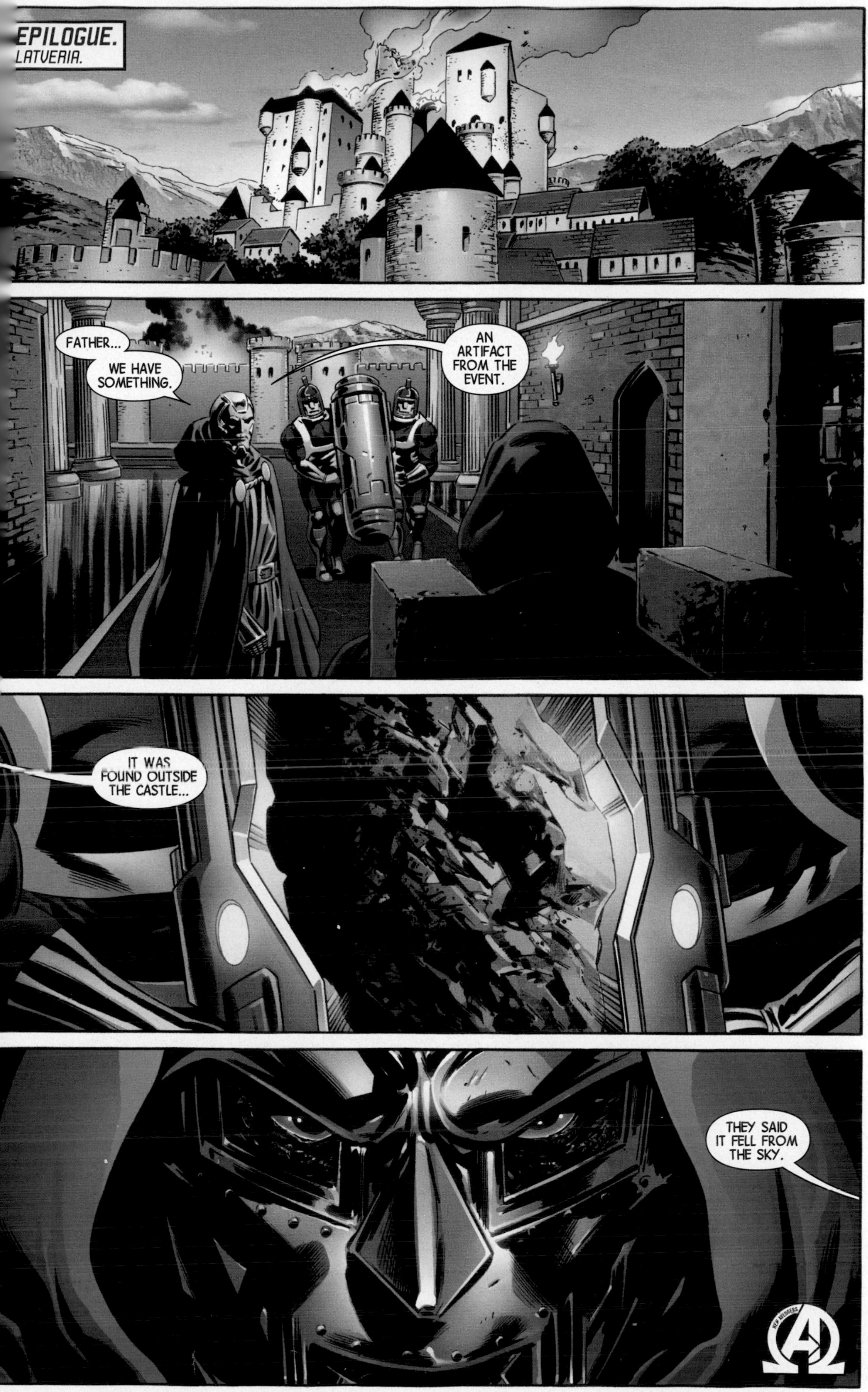
EPILOGUE.
LATVERIA.
FATHER...
WE HAVE SOMETHING.
AN ARTIFACT FROM THE EVENT.
IT WAS FOUND OUTSIDE THE CASTLE...
THEY SAID IT FELL FROM THE SKY.

#1

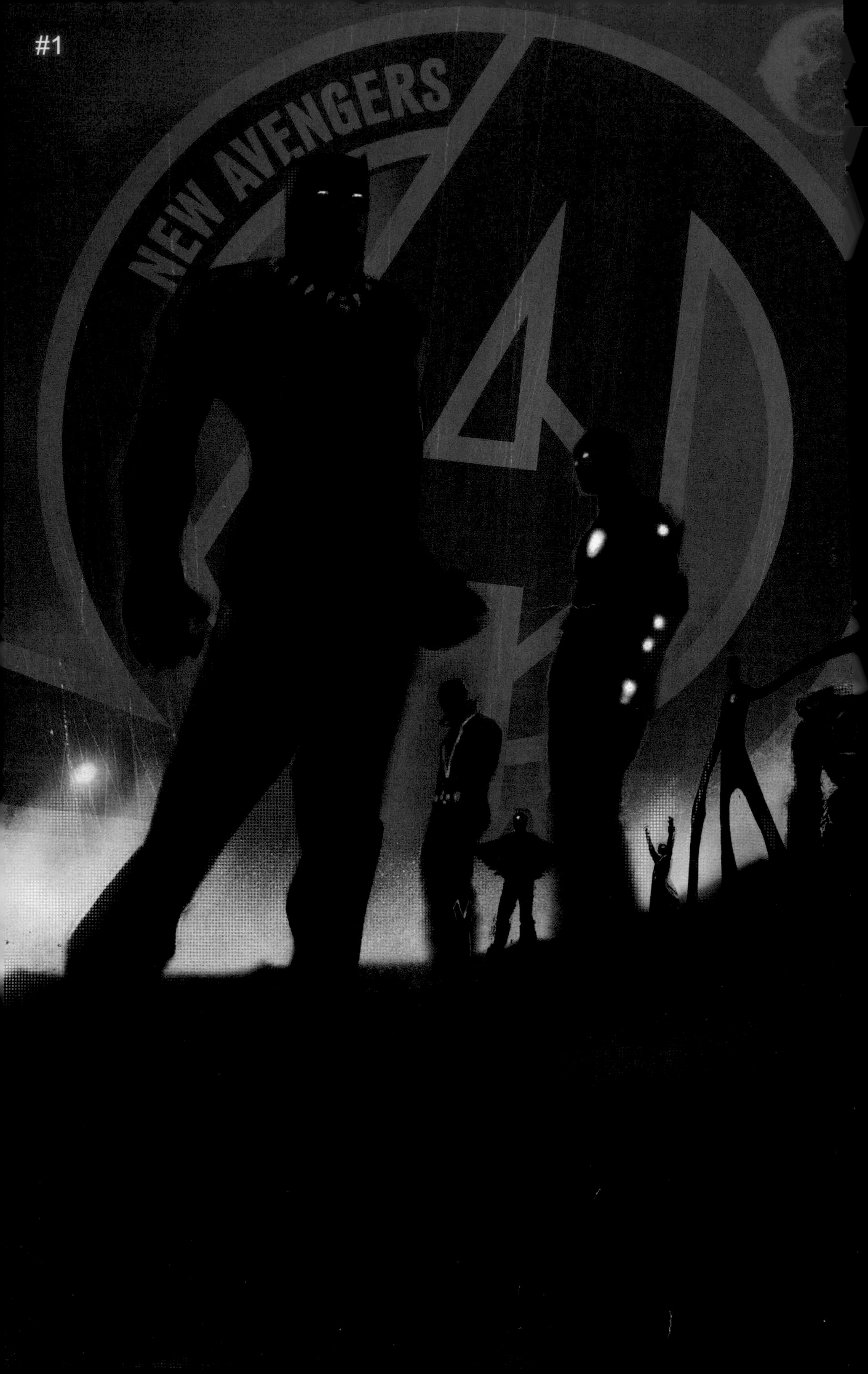
NEW AVENGERS

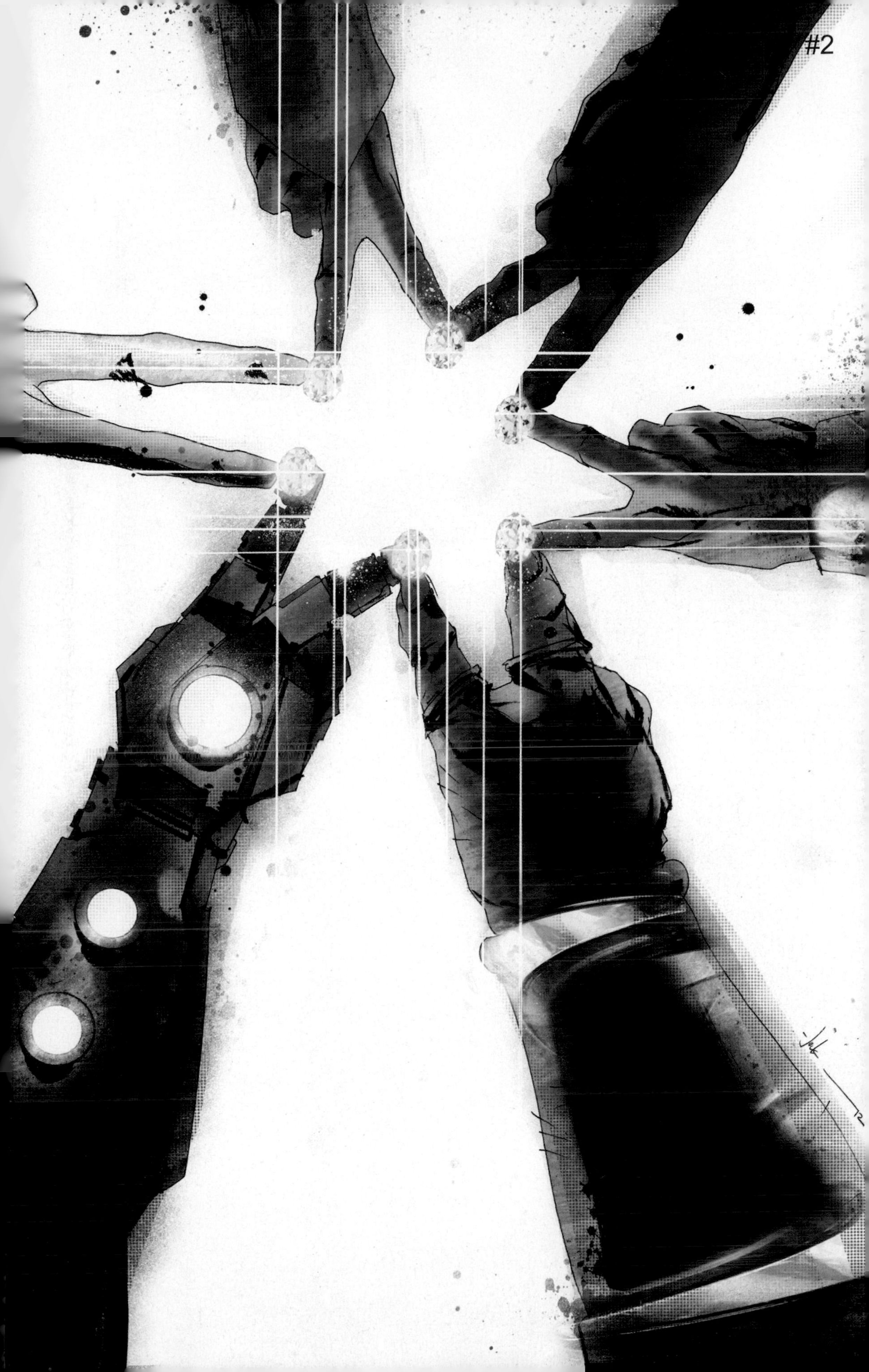
#2

#3

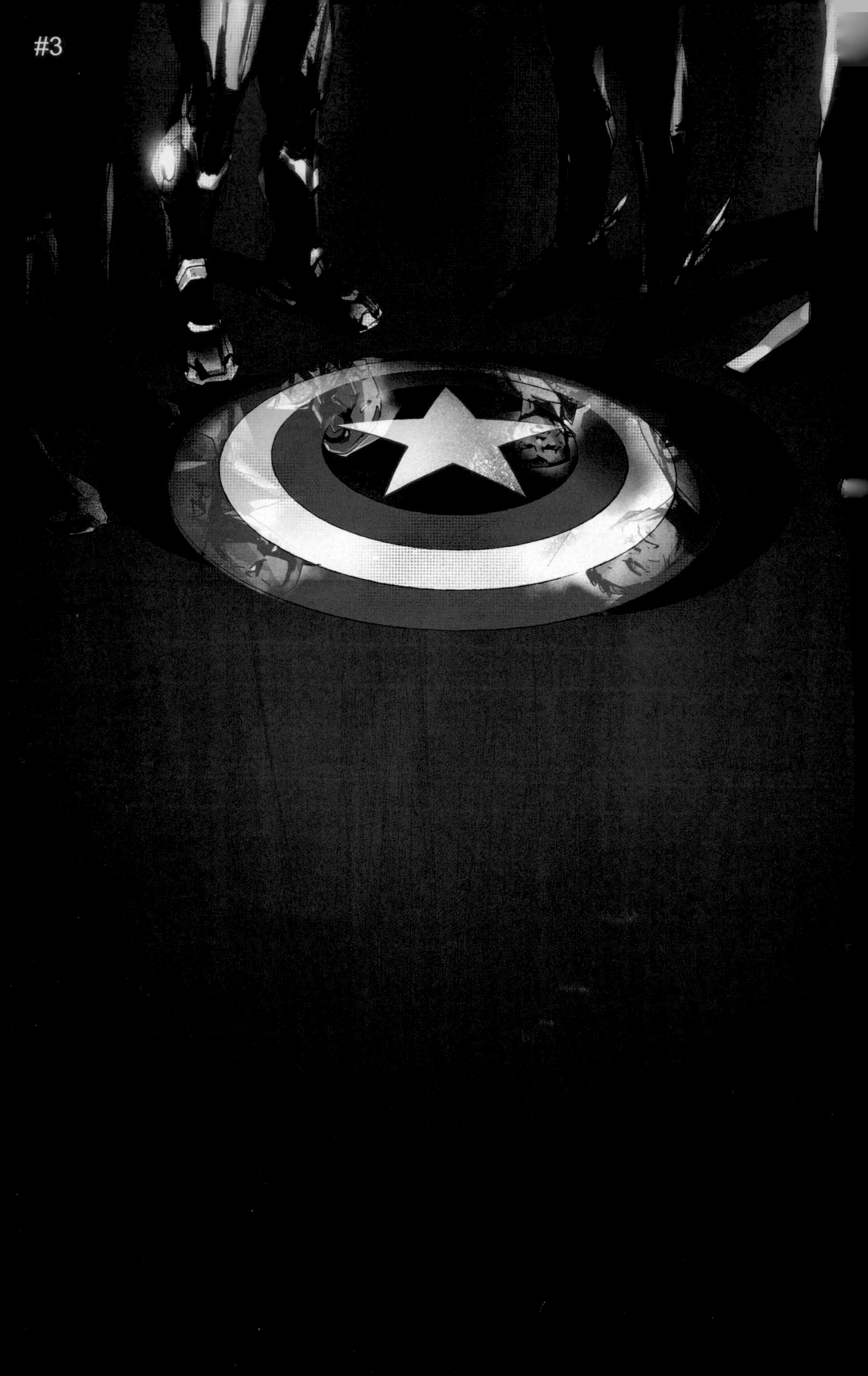

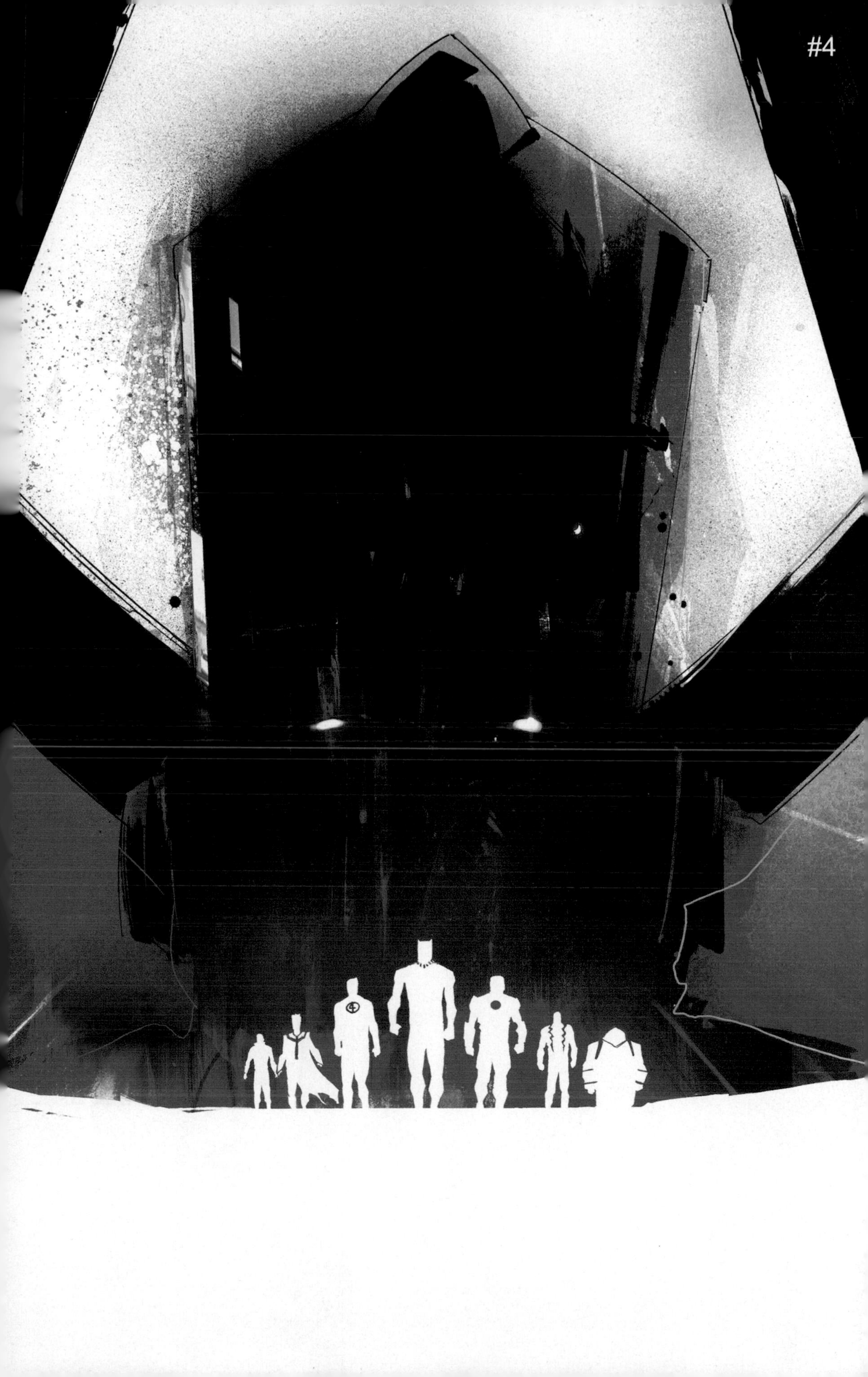
#4

#5

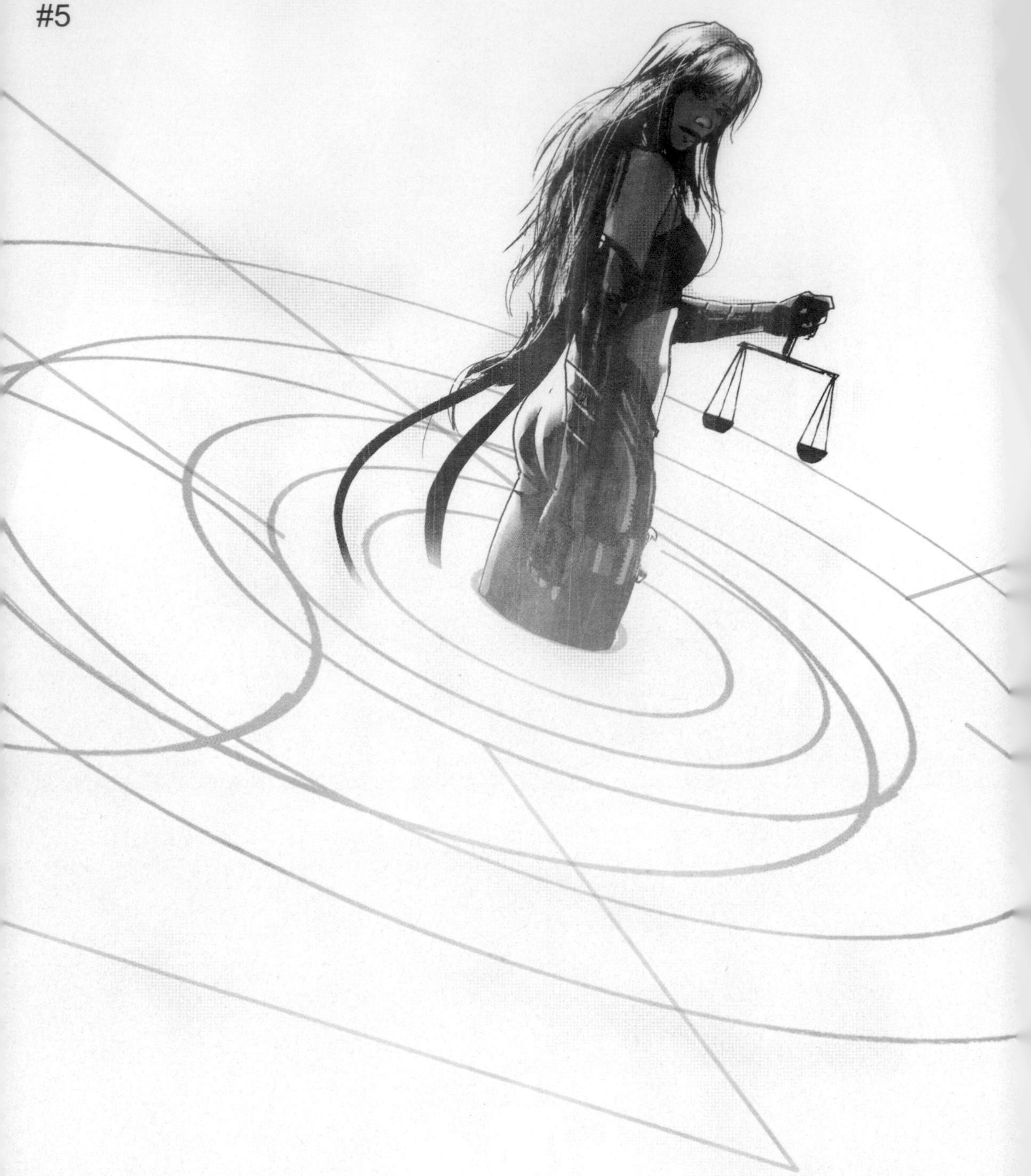

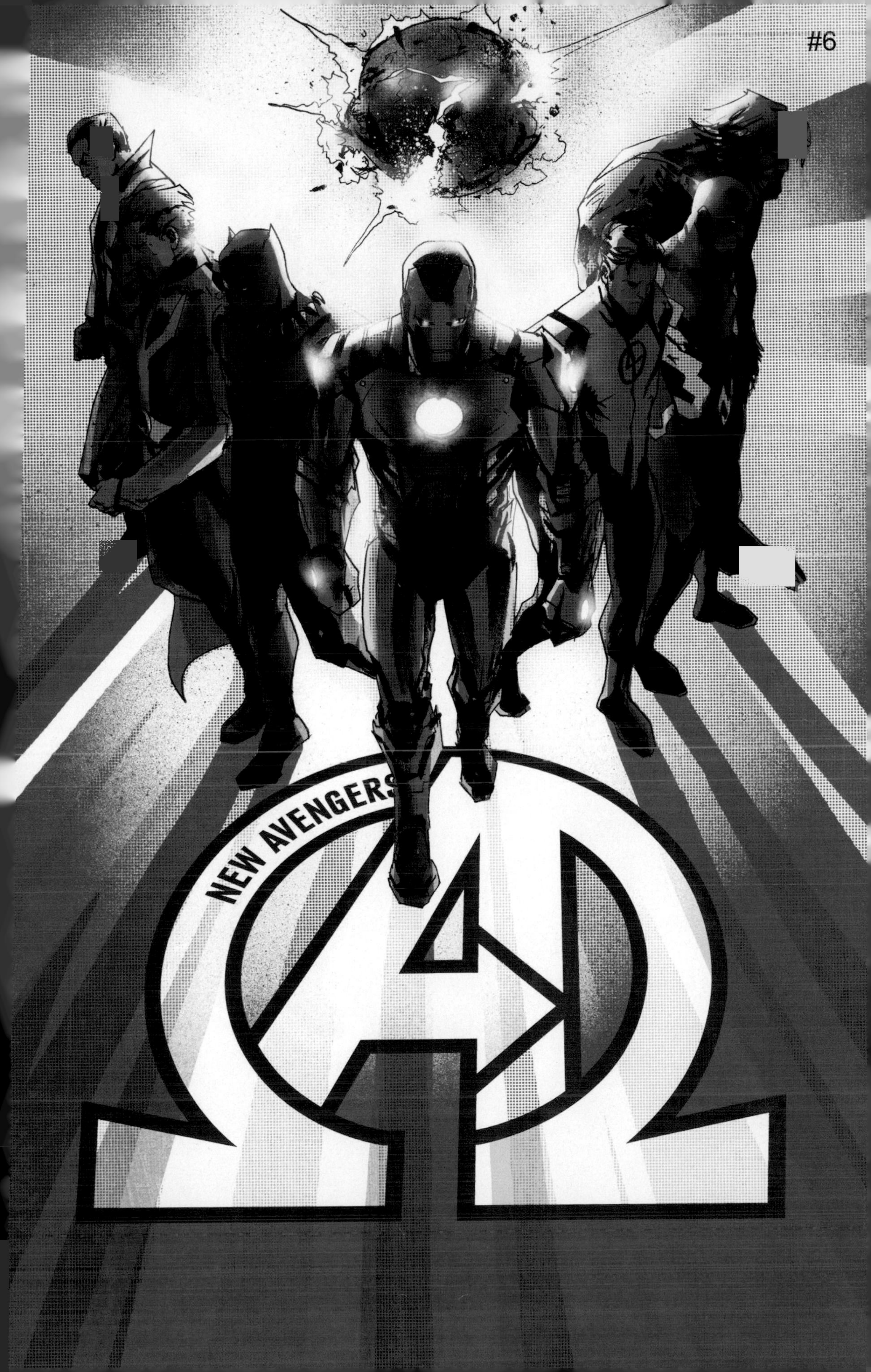
#6
NEW AVENGERS

#1 VARIANT BY **SKOTTIE YOUNG**

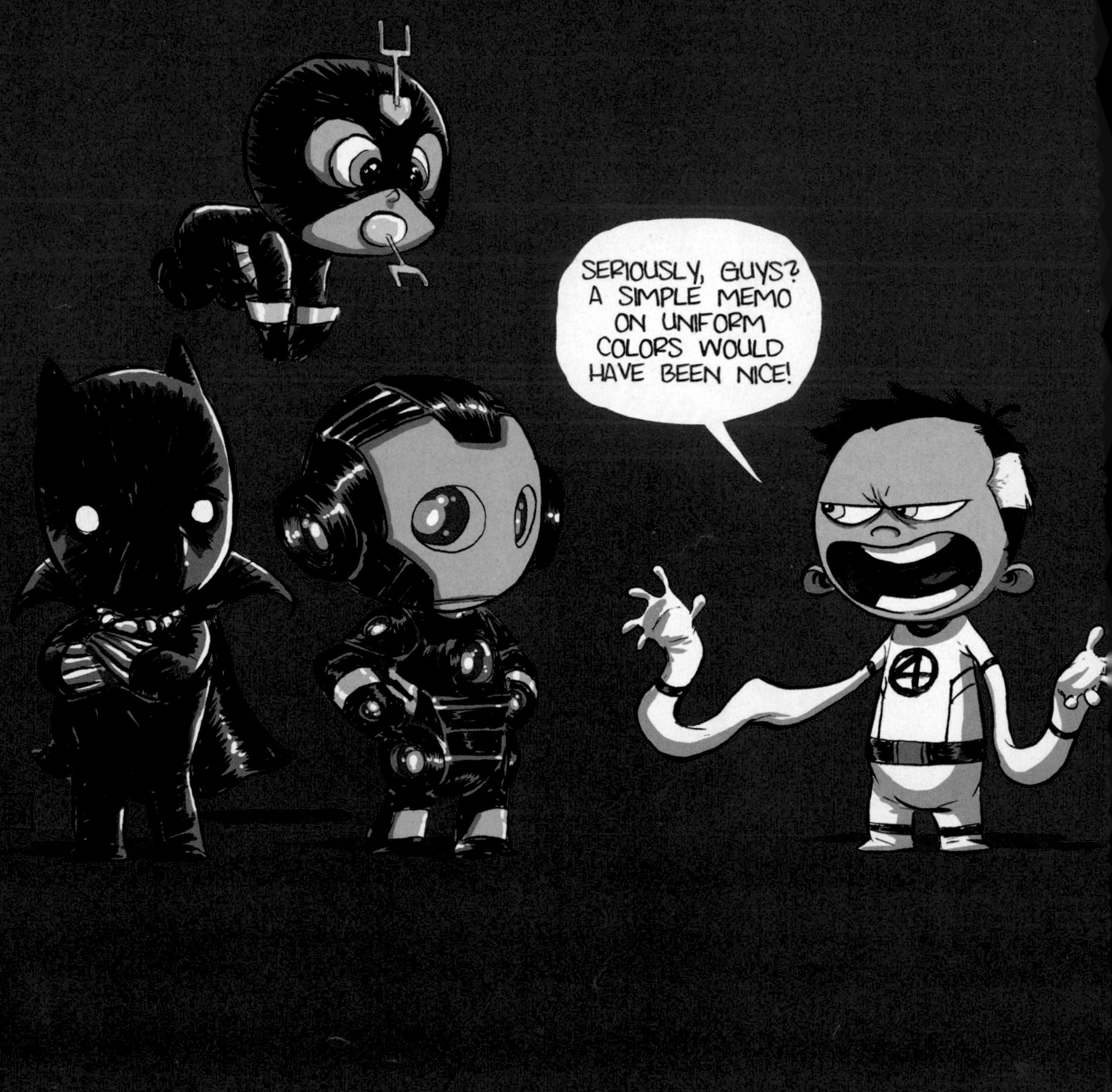
SERIOUSLY, GUYS? A SIMPLE MEMO ON UNIFORM COLORS WOULD HAVE BEEN NICE!

#1 VARIANT BY **STEVE EPTING**

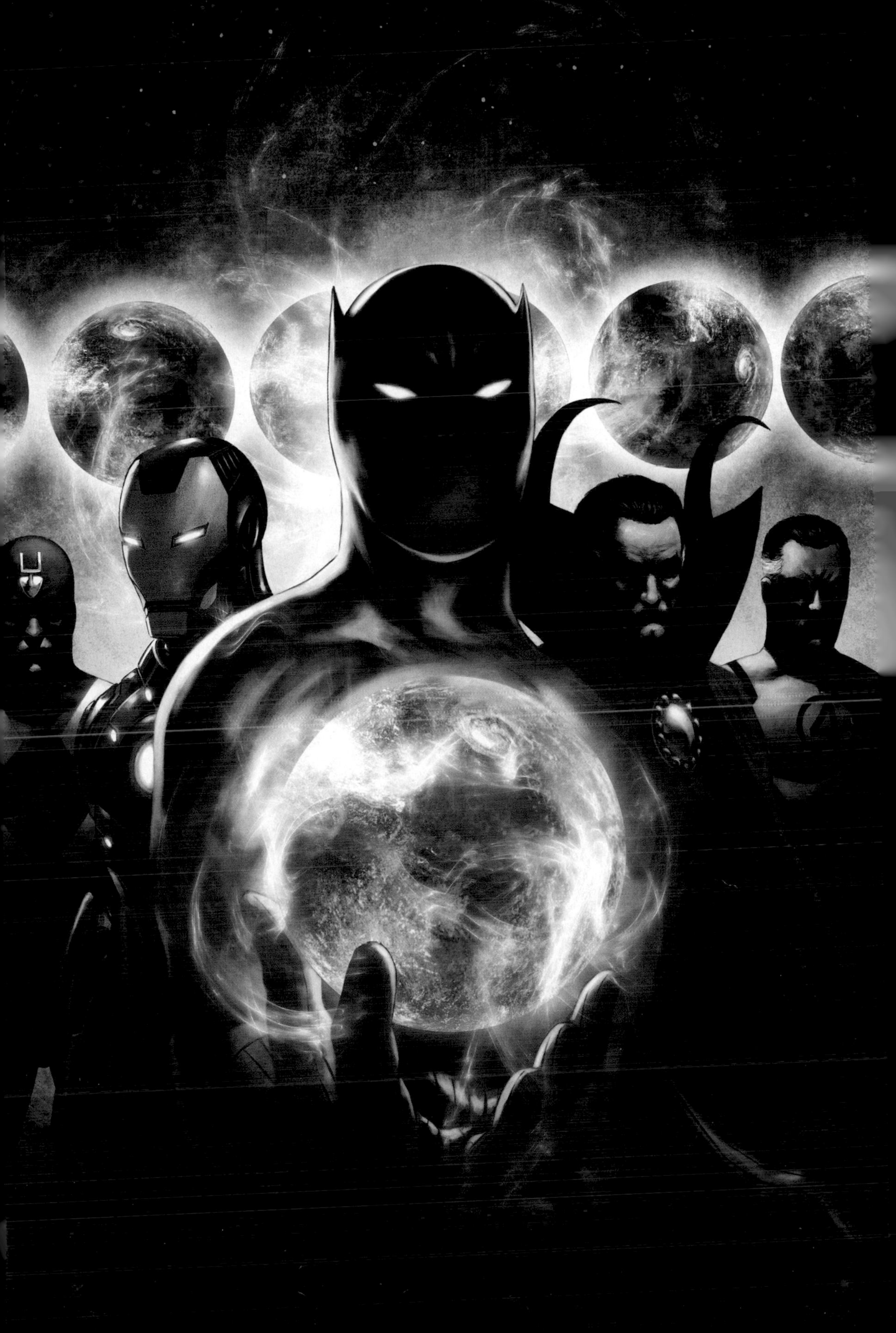

2 SKETCH VARIANT BY J. SCOTT CAMPBELL

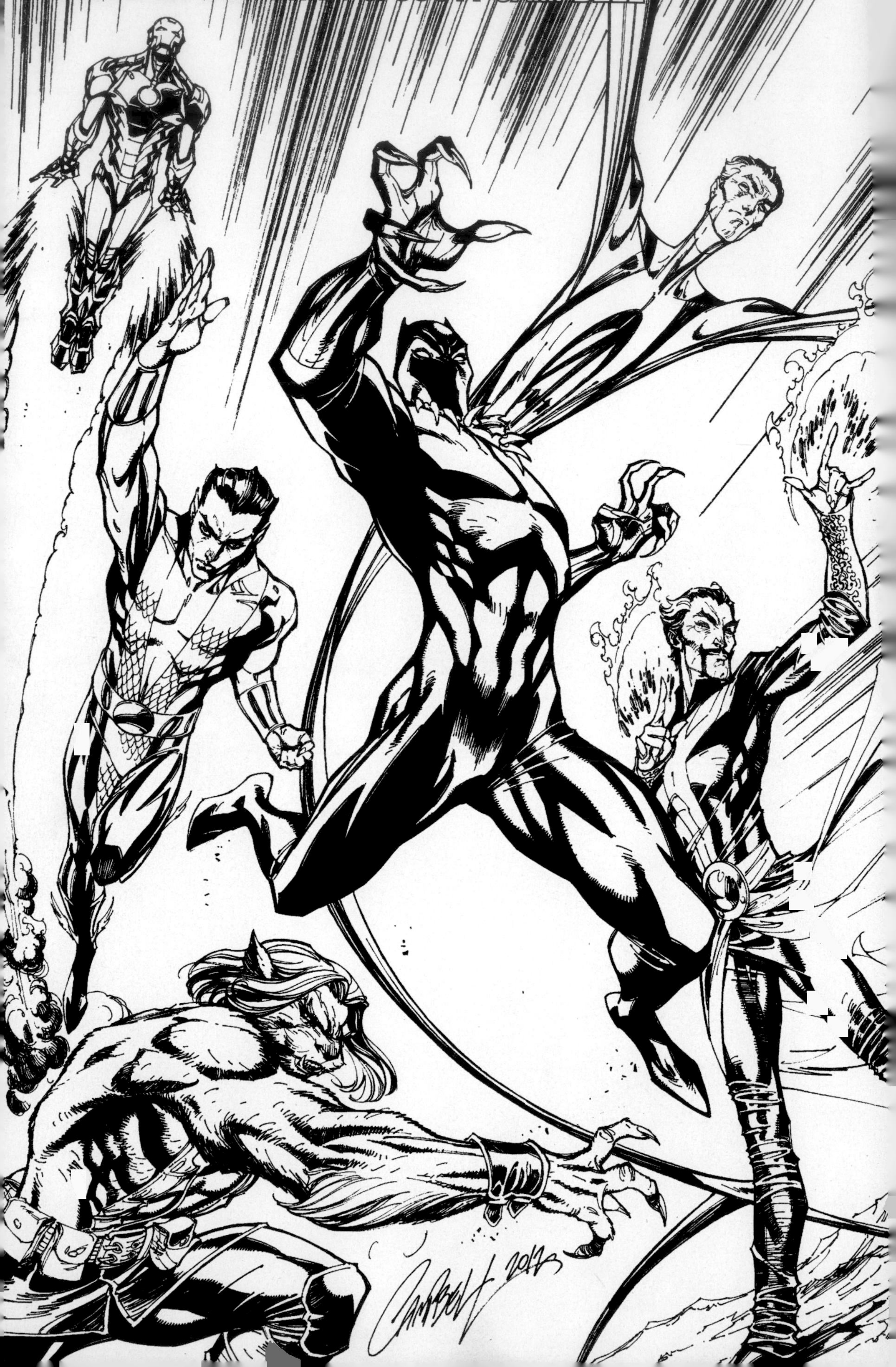

#2 VARIANT BY **J. SCOTT CAMPBELL & NEI RUFFINO**

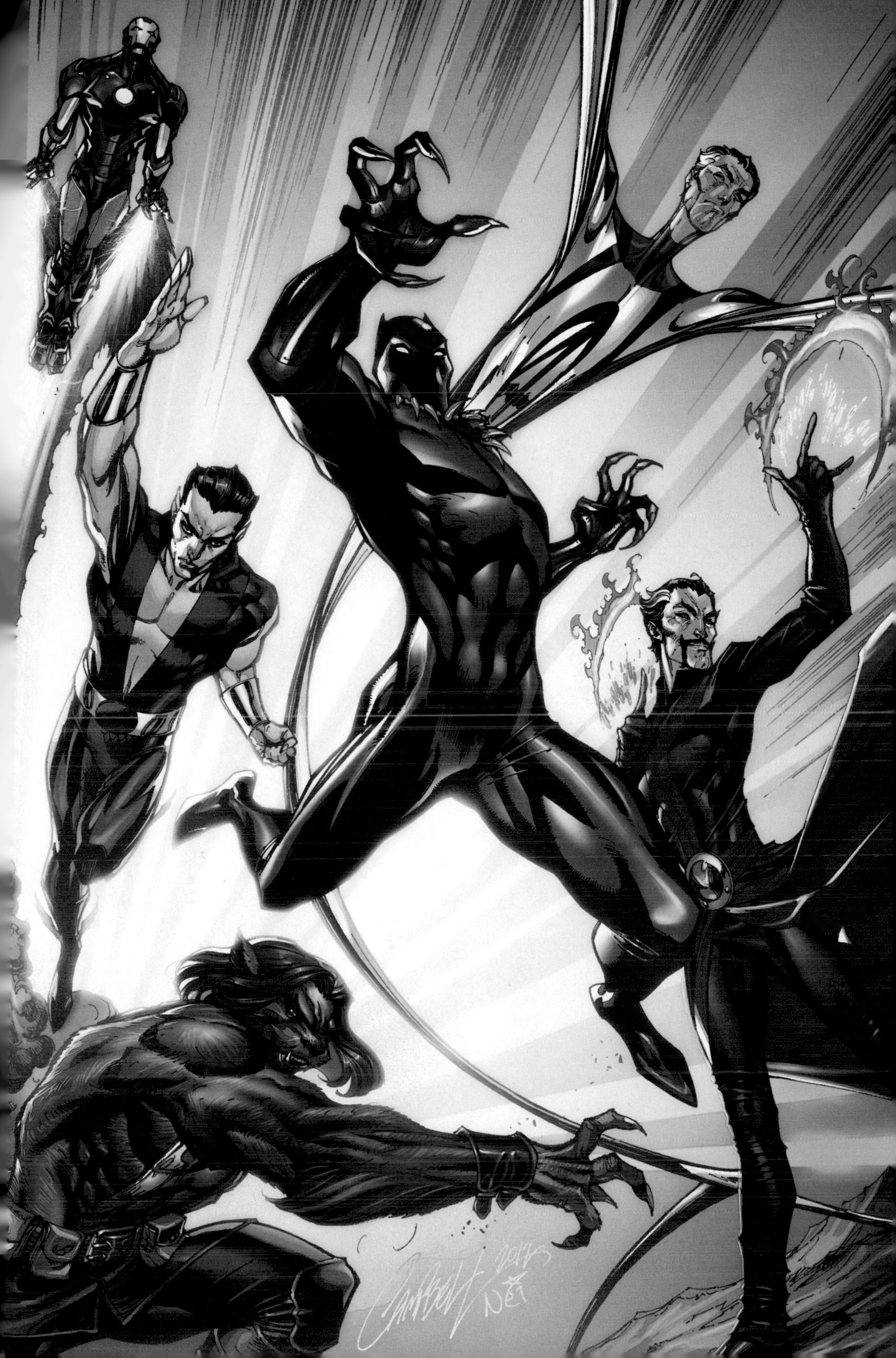

#2 VARIANT BY **SIMONE BIACHI & SIMONE PERUZZI**

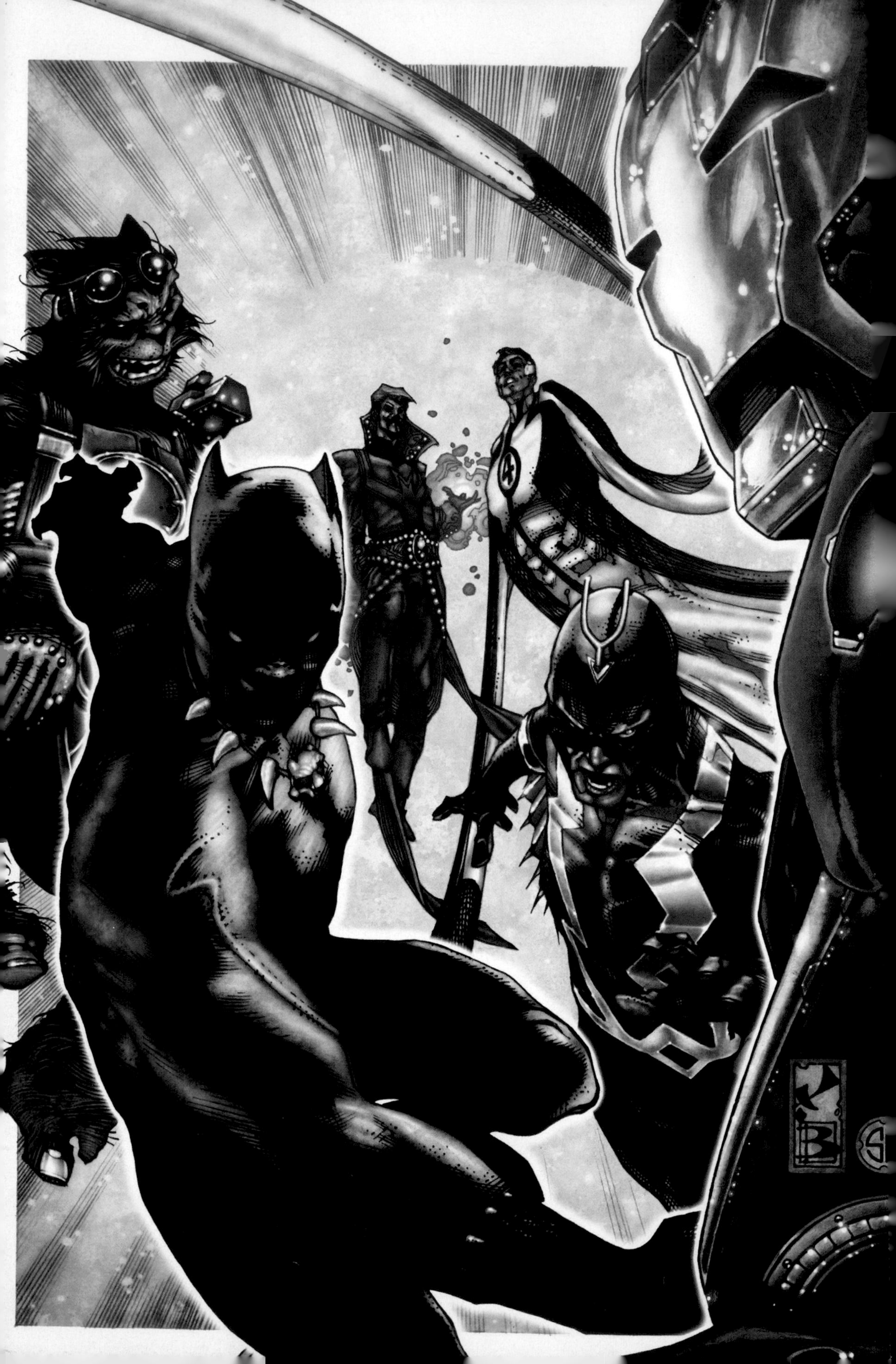

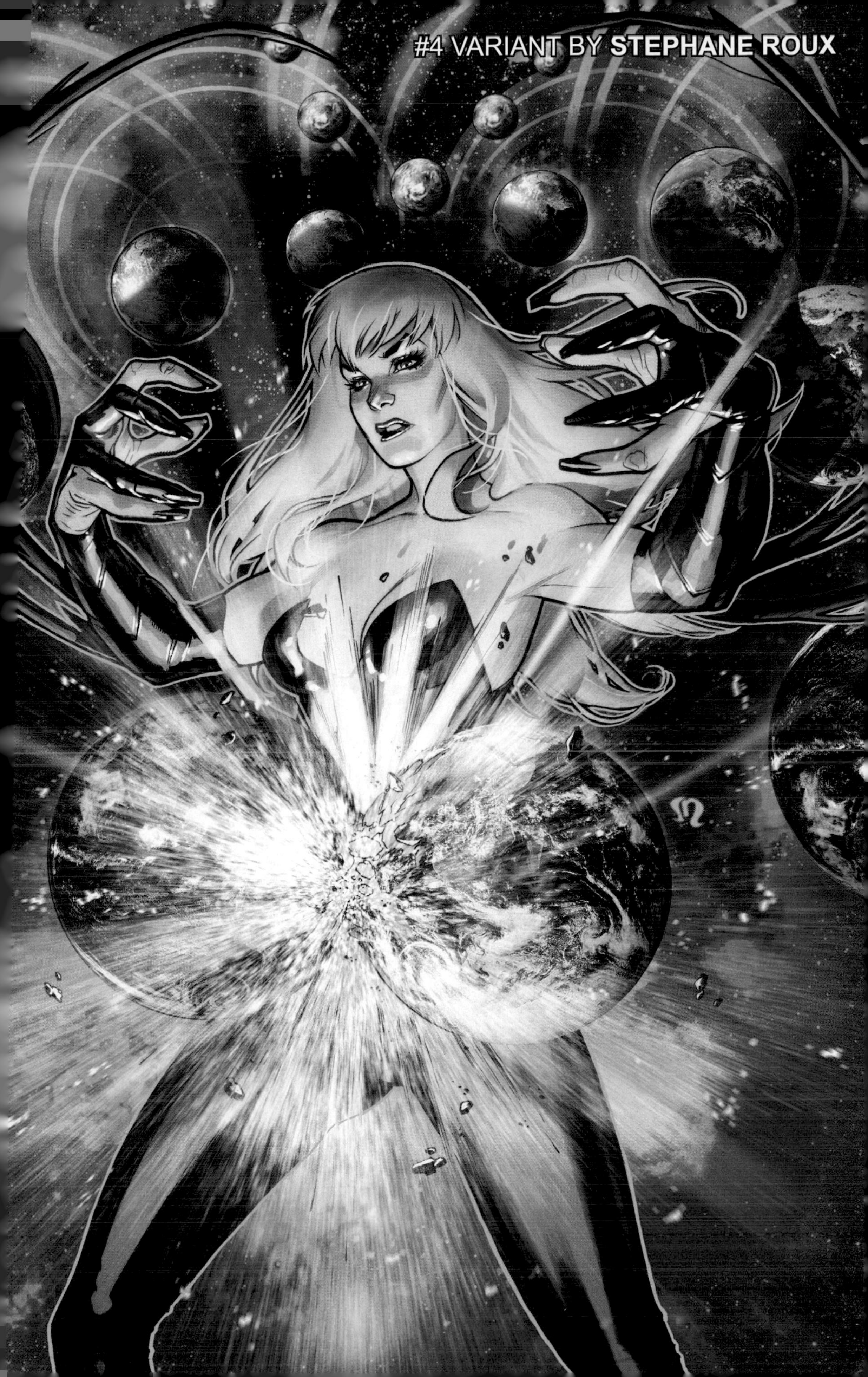
#4 VARIANT BY STEPHANE ROUX

#3 VARIANT PENCILS BY **DALE KEOWN**

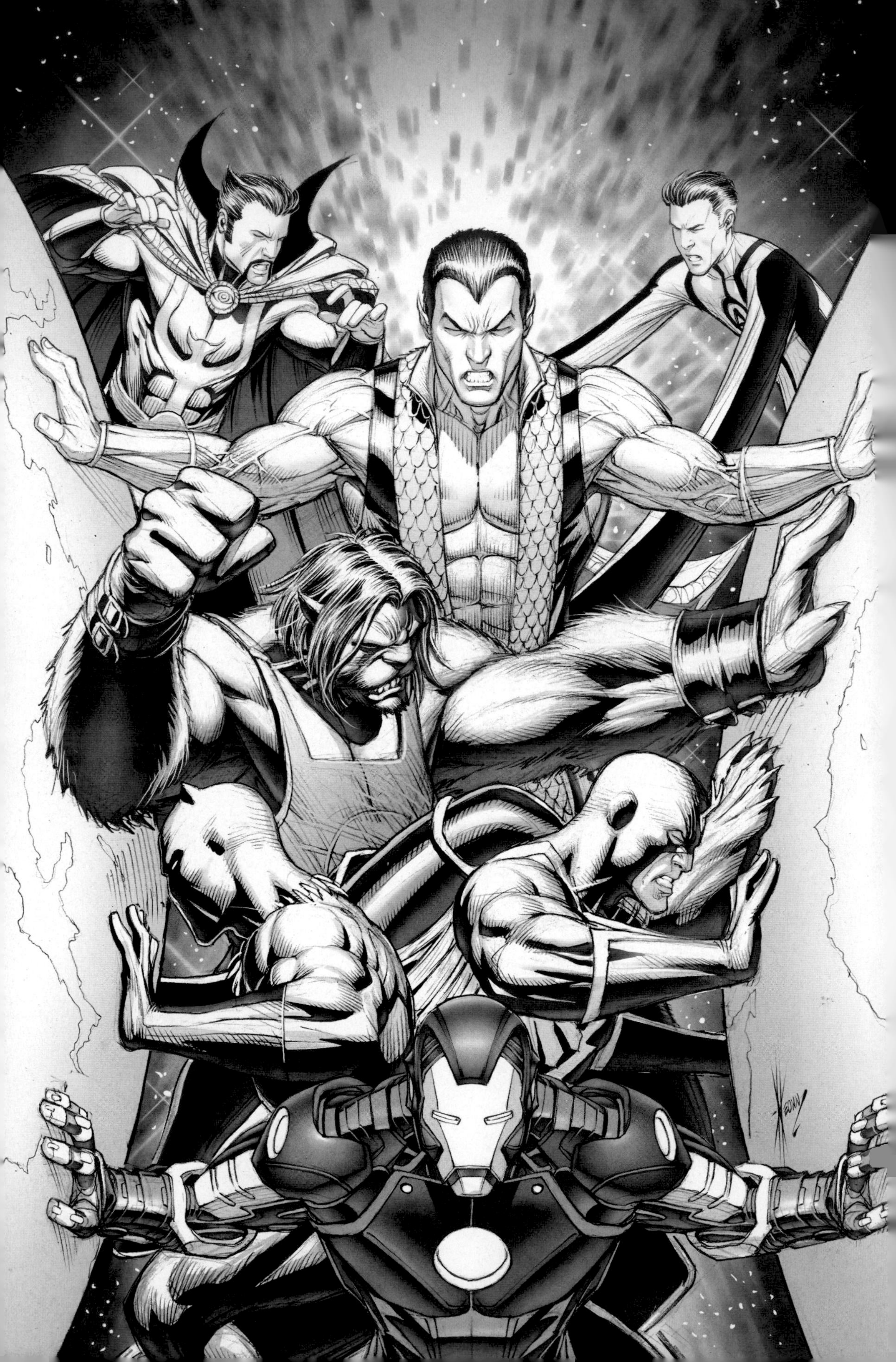

#3 VARIANT BY **DALE KEOWN & MORRY HOLLOWELL**

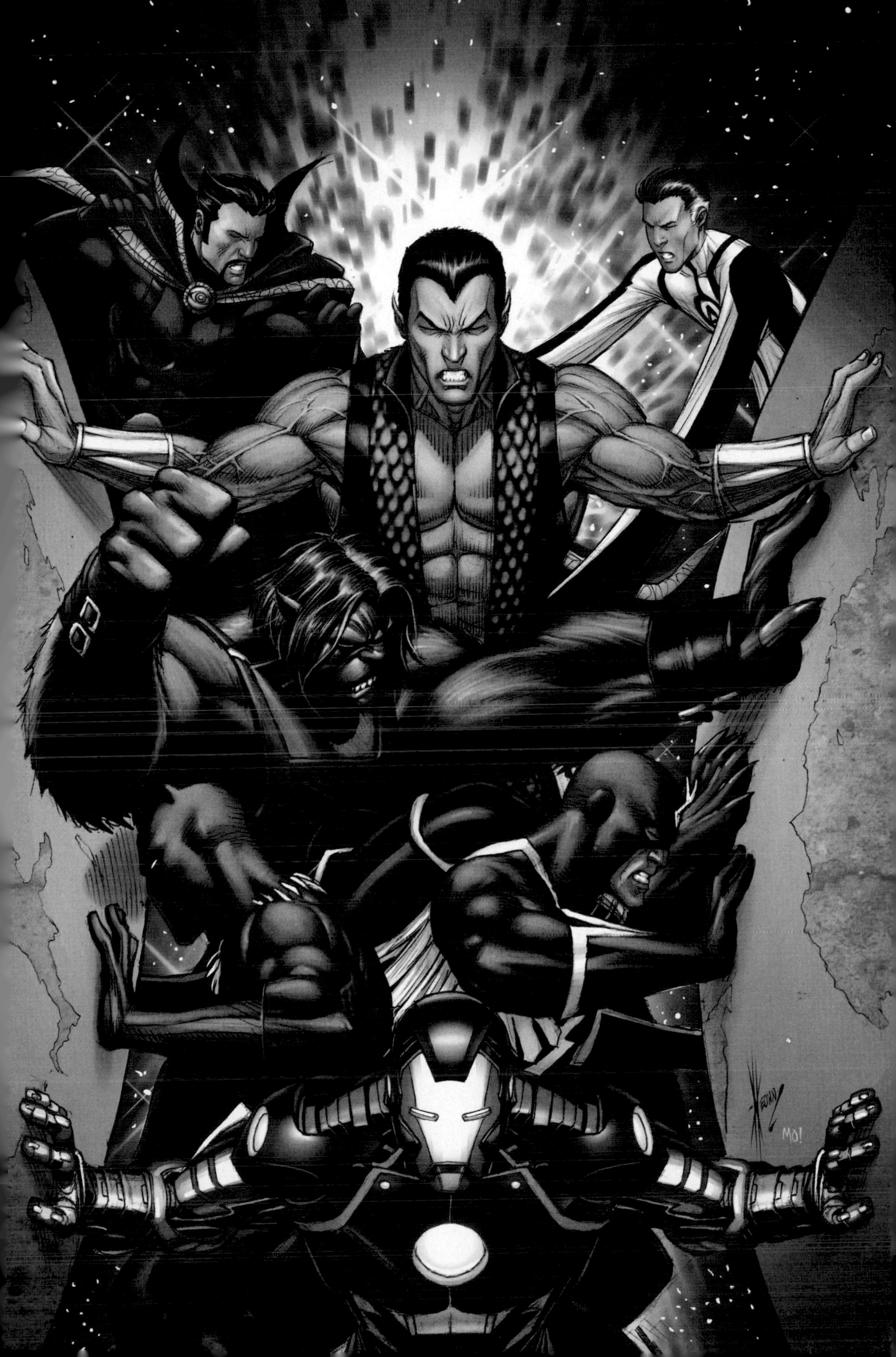

#6 VARIANT BY **JOE QUINONES & MATTHEW WILSON**

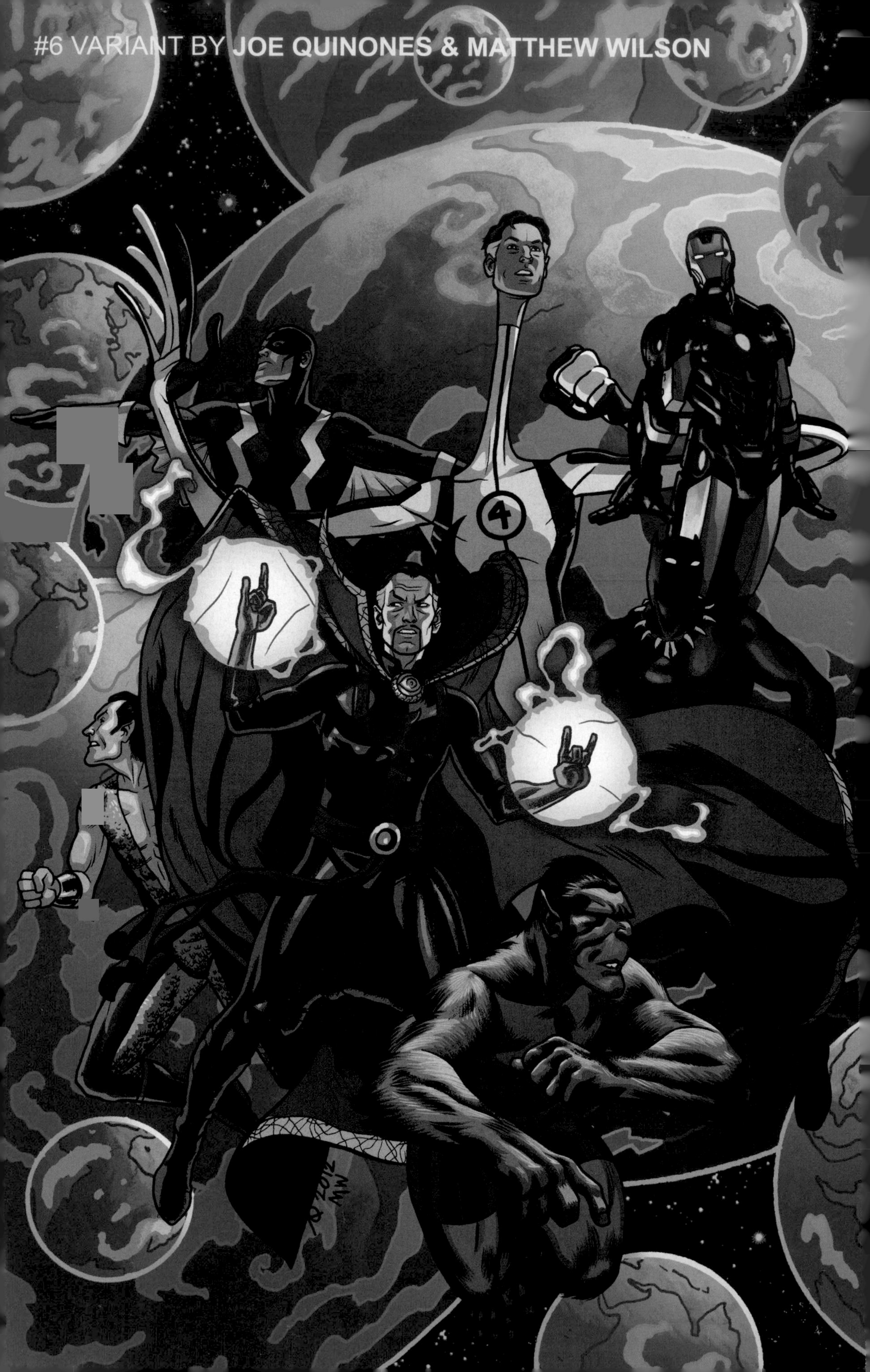

TO ACCESS THE FREE *MARVEL AUGMENTED REALITY APP* THAT ENHANCES AND CHANGES THE WAY YOU EXPERIENCE COMIC

1. Download the app for free via marvel.com/ARapp
2. Launch the app on your camera-enabled Apple iOS® or Android™ device*
3. Hold your mobile device's camera ove any cover or panel with the AR grap
4. Sit back and see the future of comics in action!

*Available on most camera-enabled Apple iOS® and Android™ devices. Content subject to change and availability.

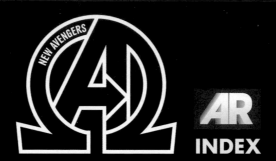

AR INDEX

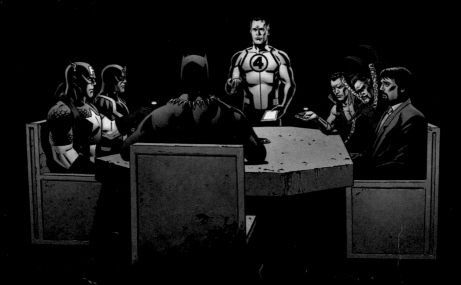